RECIPES and REMINISCENCES

OF

NEW ORLEANS

Published by

PARENTS CLUB OF URSULINE ACADEMY INC.

NEW ORLEANS, LOUISIANA

Copyright Nov. 1971

PARENTS CLUB OF URSULINE ACADEMY INC.

All rights reserved. No part of this book may be reproduced or utilized in any form, by any means, electronic or mechanical, including photocopying, without permission in writing from the publisher.

This book is dedicated to the Ursuline Nuns of New Orleans who have untiringly and unceasingly served this community since 1727. The nuns occupied the Old Ursuline Convent pictured on the cover from 1752 to 1825. It is the oldest building in the Mississippi Valley and the only one to survive from the French Colonial Period.

Copies may be obtained from

URSULINE CONVENT COOKBOOK

P.O. Box 7491

Metairie, Louisiana 70010

ISBN 0-9604718-0-4   8.95

Printed by
FRANKLIN PRINTING COMPANY, INC.
NEW ORLEANS

Original Committee

———

MRS. LOUIS SHERWOOD CREWS, *Chairman*
MRS. ROBERT J. ARMBRUSTER
MRS. EDMOND J. BENDERNAGEL, JR.
MRS. JOHN C. CLARK, JR.
MRS. EDWARD D. CONWAY, III
MRS. DONALD J. DeSAUTEL
MRS. JAMES S. HOTARD
SISTER ELIZABETH MARIE LANDRY, O.S.U.
MRS. LEON L. MARKS, JR.
MRS. JAMES F. O'NEIL, JR.
MRS. KENT SATTERLEE, JR.

Introductory Material and Commentaries
MRS. JOSEPH S. BARROIS

Cover and Other Illustrations
EMERY CLARK

Current Committee

———

MRS. LINDA SHEA, *Chairman*
MRS. LOUIS SHERWOOD CREWS, *Honorary Chairman*
MRS. ROBERT J. ARMBRUSTER, *Distribution & Sales Manager*
MRS. DIANE SAMPSON
MRS. JOHN R. BOLLING
MRS. GAYLE SPRABERRY

iii

First Printing November, 1971   10,000 copies
Second Printing February, 1972   20,000 copies
Third Printing November, 1973   20,000 copies
Fourth Printing November, 1974   20,000 copies
Fifth Printing May, 1976   30,000 copies
Sixth Printing July, 1978   30,000 copies
Seventh Printing November, 1980   30,000 copies
Eighth Printing September, 1987   10,000 copies

Acknowledgments

---

*The Committee expresses its deep appreciation
to the following*

Mr. Louis Sherwood Crews

Mr. John C. Clark, Jr., President of New Orleans
Import Co. Importers and Processors of Rex
Spices and Tokay Tea

Mr. Robert J. Armbruster, Business Manager

Mrs. Edward A. Lafaye

Mrs. Walter J. Crook, Jr.

Miss Linda Crook

Mrs. Ruth S. Nolan

Mrs. Stephen C. Harun

Mrs. G. W. Glezen, Jr.

Mrs. Thomas E. Johnson

Reverend Mother Mary Ann Luth, O.S.U.

Sister Carla Dolce, O.S.U.

Sister Madeline Kelly, O.S.U.

Sister Josephine Fabacher, O.S.U.

Sister Dolores Swanson, O.S.U.

Sister Loyola Weilbaecher, O.S.U.

Antoine's and Mr. Roy Alciatore

Brennan's and Mrs. Ella Brennan Martin

Delmonico's and Mrs. Angela L. Brown

Masson's and Mr. Ernest Masson, Sr.

T. Pittari's and Mr. Tom Pittari

Caribbean Room, Pontchartrain Hotel and
Mr. Lysle Aschaffenburg

Galatoire's

New Orleans Magazine

Family Circle Inc.

The Times-Picayune Cookbook

The Louisiana Folklore Miscellany

Ursulines In New Orleans

TABLE OF CONTENTS

—

The Old Staircase — Old Ursuline Convent
Chartres Street

DEDICATION

THE OLD STAIRCASE

Entering the Old Ursuline Convent from Chartres Street, one sees to the left the original old staircase of the building, curving gracefully to the floors above. It is time worn now and a bit dingy, but its handmade wooden pegs still hold the broad planks tightly in place and the iron balustrade is a strong support under the hand, as it was for all those generations who used it throughout 225 years. There are many exquisite stairways in New Orleans, some of them quite old and very grandly appointed with red carpeting for the stairs and carved rosewood for the hand rail. But there is more to the old Ursuline Convent stairway than a claim to beauty or a boast of strength. It has come rather to stand for a quality of humble and untiring service, a symbol of warm humanitarianism which men in all places and all times have need of — a service such as is afforded by the Ursuline Nuns of New Orleans.

Had it not been for M. Ignace Broutin, however, that stairway would not be there today — nor would the Ursuline Convent, perhaps not even the Ursuline Nuns. It was he, M. Broutin, the military engineer for the colony at New Orleans, who argued with the Ministry of France about the necessity for a new convent, since the first convent, built in 1734 (and poorly constructed), was hardly habitable any longer. It was he who in military fashion built it with walls several feet thick, and he who, to save money and please the Ministry, used the stairway out of the first convent building.

So the stairway is very old indeed. And what service it has seen! But one must turn to history for that.

First, perhaps it lent itself to the little female orphans, the survivors of the Indian massacres, whom the Nuns were caring for even before this convent was built. The old stairway knew them well, for the convent was their home all the years it took to help them make lives for themselves. The Nuns conducted an Academy, too, for the daughters of wealthy plantation owners, and special classes for Negro and Indian girls, who were taught reading, writing, the care of silkworms and the making of silk fabrics. Those were busy days for the old stairway, but pleasant heart-warming ones, full of love and simple goodness.

There was hospital work to be done also, for that was one of the principal reasons for the coming of the Ursulines to New Orleans. How wearily they must have climbed that stairway after a day of duty in the Royal Hospital just next door! After the Battle of New Orleans the hospital beds were all filled, and provision had to be made for more since the Nuns cared for the British wounded as well as the American. But who cares about fatigue when the letter comes all the way across the seas from the British Crown, thanking those gentle and compassionate women for their good offices and praising the generous spirit which had enabled them to see beyond the stupid façade

1

of war and national hatred to extend their care to the enemy.

But that isn't all. Andrew Jackson, standing near the stairway, conveyed his personal thanks to the Nuns for their prayers and their hospital work among his soldiers. The *"filles à la casette"* (the Casket Girls) were also there, special charges of the Ursulines. And didn't the Nuns welcome with kindness and solicitude the dispossessed and homeless Acadians? The annals of the convent are filled with acts of love.

The history of that stairway should leave one in wonder at its sturdiness. But perhaps it has survived through all these years not merely to offer extended service to a community, but to become for our generation the image of the unselfishness and dedication to humanity which the Ursuline work in New Orleans represents. This spirit, in its symbol and in its reality, is worth preserving.

The Porter's Lodge —
Old Ursuline Convent

3

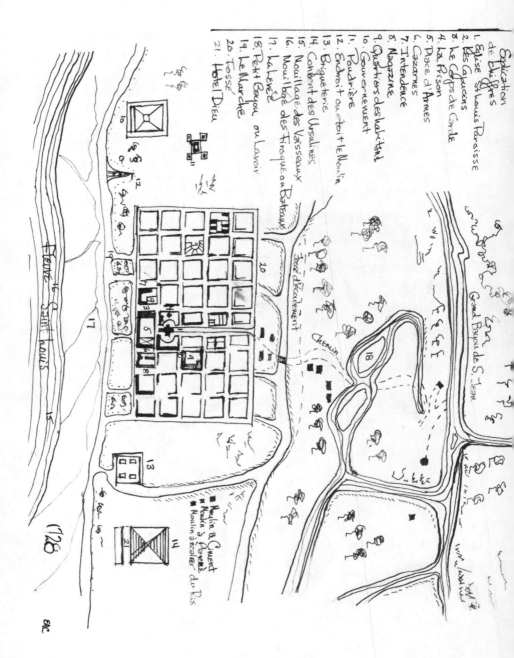

Map of New Orleans 1728

FOREWORD

History has a way of swirling and eddying, of bringing together people and places to produce the unexpected and the amazing. This is the case with the Ursulines of New Orleans. Who would imagine that this small group of teachers could exert so strong and so lasting an influence upon the cuisine of New Orleans! That they did so is attested to by many of the chroniclers of the city's early history. It was the Ursulines who educated the daughters of the plantation aristocracy and the French officials, and education in the 1700's meant cooking and the "wifely arts" before "reading, writing, and ciphering."

The nuns brought with them recipes from their homeland of France and adapted them to the native food resources. For instance, the praline was a favorite candy in the area of Orleans, France. It is said to have been first concocted by Jean Dulac, the chef of the Duc de Praslin, who was very fond of sweets, although there are several versions of the origin of this particular sweet. The French candy was made with almonds, but in New Orleans the nuns found none of these nuts but a plentiful supply of pecans. To the Ursulines, then, New Orleans owes its variant of the original recipe, called the pecan praline, which has remained a specialty of the city throughout the years.

Croquettes de Maïs is also another product of the resourcefulness of those early pioneering nuns. From the Indians they learned the use of cornmeal, which they combined with other ingredients to produce a deliciously seasoned fried meal cake. The recipe spread throughout the Deep South where, supposedly in Georgia, it received the name of "hush puppies" when a plateful was given to howling hunting dogs to keep them quiet.

The nuns maintained a good stock of wines from France and made many others of their own. They also kept a garden of traditionally used European spices, and became quite adept also in the use of local seasonings: bay leaf, thyme, shallot and filé. Combine this with the area's natural abundance of sea food and wild game, of rice and okra, of nuts and fruit, and one can foresee the birth of the New Orleans cuisine.

Creole cookery was devised by no man in no age, but evolved over the years out of the richness of the natural larder that is southern Louisiana. It has borrowed from other types, but is essentially itself, with perhaps a more marked tendency toward the French cuisine from which it took its early form.

That the old Ursuline convent nurtured Creole cookery in its incipient stages is a point fairly well established by historians. To gather recipes, both old and new, under its name, is a fitting tribute to the role which the convent and its valiant nuns played in giving New Orleans the distinctive character which makes it unique among American cities.

5

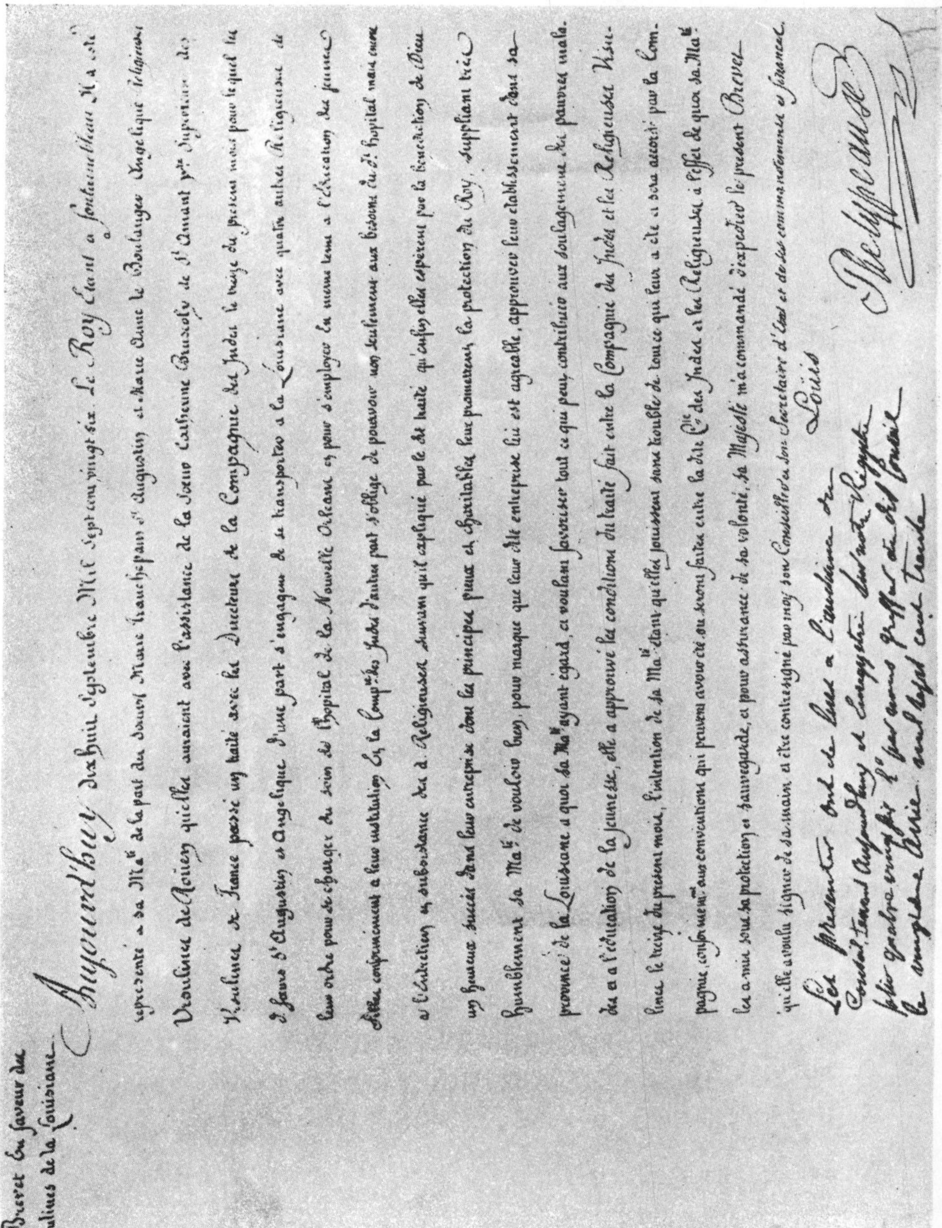

Brevet en faveur des Ursulines de la Louisiane

Aujourd'huy dix huit Septembre Mil sept cent vingt six. Le Roy Etant a Fontainebleau Il a été representé a sa Ma.té de la part des Soeurs Marie Tranchepain St Augustin et Marie Anne le Boulanger Angelique Religieuses Ursulines de Roüen qu'elles auraient avec l'assistance de la Soeur Catherine Bruscoly de St Amant p.re Superieure des Ursulines de France passé un traité avec les Directeurs de la Compagnie des Indes le treize du present mois pour lequel les d. Soeurs St Augustin et Angelique d'une part s'engagent de se transporter a la Louisiane avec quatre autres Religieuses de leur ordre pour se charger du soin de l'hopital de la Nouvelle Orleans et pour s'employer en meme temps a l'education des jeunes filles conformement a leur institution Et la Comp.ie des Indes d'autre part s'oblige de pourvoir non seulement aux besoins du d. hopital mais encore a l'entretien et subsistance des d. Religieuses suivant qu'il expliqué par le dit traité qu'enfin elles espérent par la benediction de Dieu un heureux succés dans leur entreprise dont les principes pieux et charitables leur promettent la protection du Roy, suppliant tres humblement sa Ma.té de vouloir bien, pour marque que leur d.te entreprise lui est agreable, approuver leur etablissement dans sa province de la Louisiane a quoi sa Ma.té ayant egard, et voulant favoriser tout ce qui peut contribuer aux soulagement des pauvres malades et a l'education de la jeunesse, elle a approuvé les conditions du traité fait entre la Compagnie des Indes et les Religieuses Ursulines le treize du present mois, l'intention de sa Ma.té etant qu'elles jouissent sans trouble de tout ce qui leur a été et sera accordé par la Compagnie, conformem.t aux conventions qui peuvent avoir été ou seront faites entre la dite C.ie des Indes et les Religieuses a l'effet de quoi sa Ma.té les a mis sous sa protection et sauvegarde, et pour assurance de sa volonté, sa Majesté m'a commandé d'expedier le present Brevet qu'elle a voulu signer de sa main et être contresigné par moy son Conseiller et son Secretaire d'Etat et de ses commandemens et finances.

Louis

Phelypeaux

Les presentes ont été lues a l'audience du Conseil tenant aujourd'huy et enregistrées sur notre Registre folio quatre vingt six ... par nous greffier du dit Conseil le vingtieme Avril mil sept cent trente

Facsimile of the Brevet of Louis XV

COMMISSION BY LOUIS XV OF FRANCE
TO THE URSULINES OF LOUISIANA

Today, the eighteenth of September, one thousand seven hundred twenty-six, the King being at Fontainebleau, it has been represented to his Majesty on the part of the Sisters Marie Tranchepain de St. Augustin and Marie-Anne Le Boullenger de Ste. Angelique, Ursuline Religious of Rouen, that they had with the assistance of Sister Catherine of Bruscoly, First Superior of the Ursulines of France, entered into a treaty with the Directors of the Company of the Indies on the thirteenth of the present month, by which the said Sisters of St. Augustine and Ste. Angelique, on the one side, engage themselves to go to Louisiana with four other religious of their order, to take charge of the Hospital of New Orleans and to employ themselves in the education of young girls, conformably to their Institute; and the Company of the Indies, on the other side, obliges itself to provide not only for the needs of the said hospital, but also for the sustenance of the said religious according as is explained in the said Treaty; that, in fine, they hope with God's blessing for a happy success in their enterprise, whose charitable and pious principles promise them the King's protection, very humbly begging His Majesty to be pleased, as a proof that their undertaking is agreeable to him, to approve of their establishment in the province of Louisiana; in consideration of which His Majesty, wishing to favor all that can contribute to the relief of the poor and the sick and to the education of youth, has approved the conditions of the treaty made between the Company of the Indies and the Ursuline Religious, on the thirteenth of the present month, the intention of His Majesty being that they enjoy without molestation all that will be granted them by the said Company conformably to the agreements that may have been made, or will be made between the said Company of the Indies and the said religious, for the purpose of which His Majesty places them under his protection and safeguard, and for assurance of his will his Majesty has commanded me to dispatch the present Brevet which he has been pleased to sign with his own hand, and to be countersigned by me, his Councillor, Secretary of State and of his commandments and finances.

LOUIS . . .

Phelypeaux

THE HERB GARDEN

In the 1740's the entrance to the old Ursuline Convent commanded a lovely unobstructed view down to the very banks of the Mississippi River, and that section of the convent property which today extends along Chartres Street was the rear yard. Here Sister Xavier had her herb garden. It had been specifically provided for in the treaty signed September 13, 1726, between the Company of the Indies and the Ursulines: "Sufficient ground, adjoining the house shall be granted . . . both to erect there the new buildings of which there may be need and to make a garden for the religious." The garden plot was found on Genichen's map of New Orleans dated 1731. It was planted by Sister Xavier, who compounded the medicines for the Royal Hospital and who became the first woman pharmacist in the New World. The teas, infusions and distillates which she brewed from the herbs represented the greater part of what was available in those days for the treatment of the sick. There was bay leaf for sprains, marjoram for convulsions and dropsy, oregano for rheumatism and dill to bring soothing sleep. The Royal Hospital commissioned by Louis XV stood next to the convent since nursing the sick was one of the primary reasons for the coming of the Ursulines to New Orleans in the first place.

The herb garden entered into every aspect of early life. Not only did it provide medicines, but also innumerable beverages: teas, such as mint, bay leaf and dandelion; liqueurs, such as anisette, citronelle, and absinthe; and beer, such as spruce beer and *bier douce*. Chervil was used to make vinegar and coriander seed as a pastry flavoring. Juniper flavored cabbage or venison, and caraway and celery seed were favorite pickling spices.

Not only were traditional spices used in the early Ursuline kitchen, but local specialties as well. The nuns soon learned the virtues of filé, made by the Chocktaw Indians from dried and powdered sassafras leaves. It entered into the preparation of stews and soups, the most famous of which today is gumbo filé. Herbs are used also in *courtbouillon*, bouillabaisse and jambalaya. In fact, few truly Creole dishes can be prepared without some variant of a herb bouquet to accentuate flavor and bring out the special delicacy of the central ingredient. Old Creole cooks always kept on hand a *bouquet garni*, made up of a sprig of parsley, one of thyme, a piece of celery and a bay leaf or two, with occasional variations, tied together with a length of fiber or cord.

The herbs that can be grown in the New Orleans climate successfully are thyme, sage, rosemary, mint, sweet marjoram, basil, lavender, anise, carraway, bene, sage, catnip, coriander, dill, fennel, horehound, pot marigold, dandelion, pennyroyal, rue, summer savory, tansy, tarragon and wormwood. In the early days of the city every household of any magnitude had its own herb garden and prepared its own supply for the winter. The herbs were gathered at the height of their growth, washed, and tied into bundles to dry. They were covered with netting to protect them from dust and insects, and hung, leaves down, in a warm place. When dry, the leaves, seeds or flowers were picked from the stems and put into dark bottles, tightly corked, for storage.

The use of herbs and spices is an art, and the success or failure of any dish depends to a great extent upon the skillful interpretation of the directive found at the end of most recipes: "Correct seasoning to taste." If you can do that well, you are a gourmet cook.

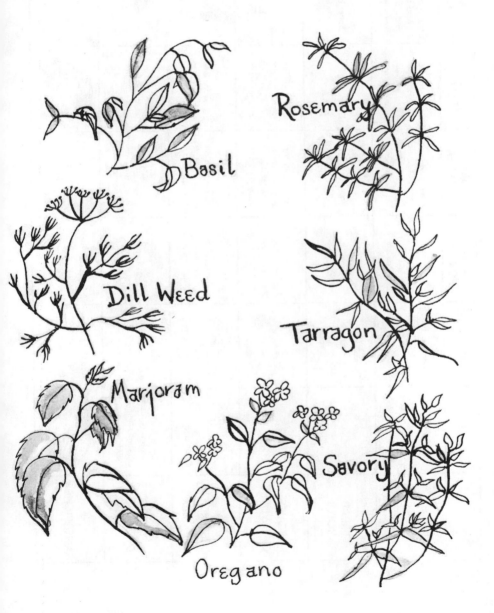

YOUR SPICE AND BLEND CHOICES	ALLSPICE	CARDAMOM	CHILI POWDER	CURRY POWDER	GINGER	ITALIAN SEASONING	PUMPKIN-PIE SPICE
	Like a blend of cloves, nutmeg, cinnamon. Comes whole or ground	Thin pods hide gingery black seeds to crush. Sold ground also	Blend of rich racy spices—the flavor spark to chili con carne	Deep gold-hued blend of exotic herbs and spices of the Far East	An aromatic, pungent root sold fresh or dried or ground	One of the newer herb blends and a good all-round seasoner	Easy alternate when you need cinnamon, cloves, nutmeg, ginger
When you make: BREAD ROLLS SWEET BUNS	Use sparingly in either yeast or baking-powder doughs	Flavor Old World coffeecakes, buns, and pastries with just a soupçon		Add ½ teaspoon to white bread dough for a subtle touch		Heat a bit in butter or margarine to brush on French bread	Add to flour in same amount as sum of all the other spices
SOUPS CHOWDERS			Zesty dress-up for thick bean chowder. Use dash in tomato soup	Use lightly for a teaser flavor, more for a good zippy curry bite	Borrow an Oriental seasoning tip and add a hint to chicken broth	Sprinkle a little into minestrone, garbanzo, and tomato soups	Season potato-onion chowder with a dash of this spicy mix
CASSEROLES	A pinch in beef, pork, veal, or lamb dishes adds a good zip	Use sparingly with meat balls and chicken dishes. It's spicy	Many Mexican recipes call for it. It's hot—so measure carefully	Use 2 teaspoons to season a 6-serving casserole mildly hot	Add to taste in gravies for beef, pork, veal, and vegetable combos	Gives a lift to meat and fish dishes. Crush it just a bit	Making biscuit topping? Stir ¼ teaspoon into 1 cup of mix
SALADS DRESSINGS	Just a touch in meat salads—especially ham—adds spiciness	It enhances most dressings. Try sparingly on fruits, too	A sprinkling gives zing to all kinds of picnic salads	Try a dash in chicken salad or its dressing for an exotic touch	Think of it for seasoning fruit salad lightly; dressing, too	Sprinkle over any green salad for a fragrant spunky seasoner	
SANDWICHES		Add with a very light touch to ham salad and cheese mixes	Baked-bean-sandwich enthusiasts say a dash makes the difference	Stir a little into chicken- or egg-salad, and cheese fillings		Hot tip: Top bread with slices of tomato, herb, and cheese; grill	

Category	1	2	3	4	5	6	7
DIPS SPREADS DUNKS	Mix a dash in deviled ham or liver pâté to spread on toast	Stir a speck into minced clams and sour-cream	Just the right seasoning for guacamole dip (mashed avocado)	Give sour cream or chili sauce a big dash for dunking shrimps	*[image]*	Make your own herb cheese with soft Cheddar. Add cautiously	Sprinkle buttered toast with sugar, then lightly with this mix
SAUCES GRAVIES	Just a bit does wonders to meat gravies such as beef, pork, veal	Add a dash to your favorite barbecue or basting sauce	Stir lightly into cocktail sauce or sauce for spaghetti	Curry-sauce tip: Cook long and lazily to bring out best flavor	Beat a little into sweetened whipped cream to top fruit	Use in spaghetti sauce; add a speck to gravy for roast pork	Stir some into lemon sauce; add, too, to sweet or sour cream
COOKIES	Try a soupcon in fruit bars and applesauce cookies. Good!	Gives an elusive "bite" to holiday sugar cookies	*(see TIPS block below)*		Recipes for big soft cookies and crisp snaps call for this spice	*[image: COOKIES jar]*	To substitute for other spices: Measure to nearest round figure
PIES	Add a dash or two to sugar when making summer fruit pies	Making a coffee or an orange chiffon pie? Use a dash	*(see TIPS block below)*		Stir 1/4 teaspoon into buttery cooky or crumb piecrusts	Pizza is "pie" in Italian, and here is the herb to sprinkle over	Named for its most favored use. Try, too, in apple pie
CAKES FROSTINGS	Add a spicy dash when making holiday fruitcake or its frosting	Stir lightly into vanilla, coffee, or orange butter frosting	*(see TIPS block below)*		Use, of course, in gingerbread. Try a whit, too, in applesauce cake	*[image]*	Blend it into sugar-and-water icing to drizzle over spicecake
PUDDINGS	Sprinkle a dash or two into hard sauce for Christmas plum pudding	Add a pinch to vanilla pudding mix for an enticing flavor	*(see TIPS block below)*		Stir a bit into eggs and milk when making rice or bread pudding	*[image]*	Sprinkle ever so lightly onto cup custards before baking
PICKLES PRESERVES	Use the whole spicy berry when making pickled tiny cucumbers	Goes well with homemade fancies like watermelon-rind preserves	Gives a "hot" touch to chopped tomato relish and piccalilli	Pickled carrot and green-bean sticks like curry. Use sparingly	An all-round spice for jams, jellies, pickled and spiced fruits	Use in any recipe that calls for zesty mint-like oregano	"Spice" fresh or canned peaches, pears, apples with this blend

TIPS FOR THE HERB AND SPICE COOK

- Cook with one herb or spice at a time until you learn its characteristics. And measure lightly, for flavor builds.
- Add herb for stews, soups, and sauces during the last hour of cooking.
- Give herb time to season in uncooked dishes like salad dressings, sauces, marinades.
- Want to know how strong or mild an herb is? Crush a bit in the palm of your hand, let it warm slightly, then sniff.
- Keep herb and spice containers tightly covered to save flavor.

11

YOUR HERB CHOICES	BASIL	DILL WEED	MARJORAM	OREGANO	ROSEMARY	SAVORY	TARRAGON
	Fresh and spicy and a never-fail seasoner for all tomato dishes	Its feathery green leaves add a delightfully mild bouquet	Fragrantly sweet herb of the mint family—a joy to all cooks	Mint herb, too, with a flavor that tastes a bit like thyme	"For remembrance." Valued for its subtle tang	A beginner's choice for a basic mild-flavor herb	Has a piquancy all its own. Use sparingly, for it's strong
When you fix: **BEEF**	Stew or goulash: Add 1/2 teaspoon to recipe for 4 to 6 servings		Roast: Rub onto meat or crumble a big pinch into roasting pan	Meat loaf: Stir 1/2 teaspoon into mixture for 2-pound loaf	Roast: Another good choice to sprinkle into roasting pan	Pot roast: Mix with flour to rub on meat before browning	Boiled beef: Making gravy? Season with a discreet dash
VEAL	Scaloppine: Crush a generous pinch and stir into tomato sauce	Cutlets in sour cream: Sprinkle into the rich so-good sauce	Roast: Mix with flour, salt, and paprika to season meat for cooking	Stew: Be miserly, for it's strong— 1/8 teaspoon for 4 servings		Braised chops: Crush a smidgen and add to pan when half cooked	Jellied loaf: Simmer a pinch in broth; strain for jellied base
PORK HAM		Spareribs: Bake with sauerkraut seasoned ever so generously	Roast and chops: Experts vote a soupcon or two about right	Braised pork shoulder: Add a big pinch to pan as meat browns	Ham patties or loaf: Crumble in a small pinch before shaping	Stuffed chops: Season 1 cup stuffing with 1/4 teaspoon	
LAMB	Barbecued shanks: Add to seasoned marinade for a mellow flavor	Stew: Sprinkle over stew or stir into it while it is cooking	Potpie: Stir 1/8 teaspoon into pastry or biscuit topping	Braised riblets: Sprinkle lightly on ribs or add to basting sauce	Roast: Perfect herb for all cuts. Just sprinkle into roasting pan	Scotch broth: Stir just a bit into soup before dishing it up	
CHICKEN TURKEY DUCK	Cookout chicken: Stir 1 teaspoon into 2 cups barbecue sauce	Chicken salad: Use lightly in the salad or as a pretty garnish	Oven chicken: Mix a pinch into melted butter for coating chicken	Roast duck: Sprinkle lightly inside duck or in baking pan	Chicken stew: Add to broth during cooking; strain for gravy	Hot turkey sandwich: Stir a bit into gravy while heating	Chicken cacciatore: Crumble a big pinch and add to sauce

FISH SEA FOOD	Sea-food cocktail: Crumble a speck into tomatoey sauce-dip		Fish chowder: Use sparingly; add just before dishing it up	Stuffed fish: Mix into dressing or sprinkle into pan for baking	Baked, broiled, or poached fish: It enhances all. Use as you like	Sea-food salad: Toss a smidgen with salad or add to dressing	Butter, cream, tartare sauces: Perfect seasoner for them all
POTATOES		Baked or boiled: Stir lightly into butter sauce or sour cream	Scalloped: Crush a touch and add to the seasoned flour mixture	Hash brown: Sprinkle a bit into drippings before browning		Salad: Mix with dressing; add to potatoes while still warm	German-fried: Crush and mix with other seasonings in pan
PEAS LIMAS GREEN BEANS	In herb butter: Heat with butter or margarine, then spoon over	In cream sauce: Stir 1/2 teaspoon into each 1 cup sauce	In salad dressing: Be miserly. Just a pinch does wonders		Simple seasoning: Add a few sprigs to cooking water in saucepan	With sour cream: Spoon the creamy topping over; add herb lightly	In sweet-sour sauce: Crush a generous pinch; add to sauce
TOMATOES	Broiled, stewed, fried: An always right, all-round seasoner	Sliced fresh: Use to taste along with salt and pepper	Scalloped: Mix with buttered bread cubes and sprinkle over	Juice appetizer: Add a bit to other seasonings and heat	Spaghetti sauce: Try just a touch for an elusive flavor	Soup: Sprinkle lightly over bouillon or cream soup	Salad bowl: Let a pinch mellow in the salad dressing
BROCCOLI CABBAGE CAULIFLOWER		Simple seasoner-garnish: Add to sauce or sprinkle over vegetable	Au gratin: Put a smidgen in cheese sauce or crumb topping		With corned beef and cabbage: Add a pinch to the cooking water	In salad dressing: Allow about 1/4 teaspoon for 1 cup dressing	In sweet-sour sauce: Use the same as with peas and beans
EGGS CHEESE	Welsh rabbit: Stir in just a bit for a pleasant zing	Scrambled eggs: Use amount to suit your own taste	Egg salad: Try just a pinch or two in the salad dressing	Pizza: A "must" to sprinkle on top of the cheese before baking		Cheese fondue: Stir a bit into egg-milk base before baking	Eggs Benedict: Crumble and add a dash to the sauce topper
RICE SPAGHETTI NOODLES	Spanish rice: Stir 1/2 teaspoon into prepared tomato sauce	Buttered noodles: Try just a sprinkle over hot noodles	Canned spaghetti in tomato sauce: Add 1/2 teaspoon to each can	Spaghetti with meat sauce: Let herb simmer in sauce	Minestrone: Add a very light sprinkle as the soup simmers	Noodles in sour cream: Use sparingly, tossing with cream	

Antoine's Restaurant
Established 1840

BEVERAGES

The inherited drinking tastes of the people of New Orleans go back to the earliest days when the Le Moyne brothers—the Sieur d'Iberville and the Sieur de Bienville—founded the colony of New Orleans and brought their wines and brandies with them. In the early days after its founding in 1718, the city was nothing more than a group of rude huts bordering on muddy streets, but there was about it even then a Parisian sophistication which allowed *les bonnes familles* to serve the best French wines. Even the ladies sipped imported spirits as they sat down to their games of *bourré* and *piquet* behind the shuttered doors of their *Vieux Carré* homes. There was an abundance of fine liquor, but claret was the universal daily table wine. As time went on and public restaurants began to appear, it was exceptional to see a person dining without a bottle of *vin ordinaire* and around the family table even the children were given a little claret diluted with water and sweetened. Often the water of the Mississippi became suspect or unpalatable and at such times Claret, economical and low in alcoholic content, took its place completely.

At social dinners in the city much wine was served. The guest was expected to drink a little light white wine with the raw oysters, and sherry or Madeira with the soup. With fish and entrées, a heavy white wine was served but claret with the *relevés* and *entremets*. About mid-meal a *Ponche Romaine* was poured as a spur to the appetite. Next came the Champagne with the roast, the Burgundy with the game, and with the dessert, *café noir* and liqueurs. The scheme of wine service tended to move from the lighter wines at the beginning of the meal to those that are sweeter and more full-bodied at the end so as to avoid anti-climax. Negro butlers were expertly trained in the service of wines and would never commit the grave fault of serving white wines insufficiently cooled (the sweeter the colder), or of serving the red at other than room temperature.

For a truly memorable crowning of a fine meal, the Creole host would serve a *grand* or a *petit brûle,* both of which were flamed as the lights were dimmed. The *petit brûle* was especially loved by the Creoles, the wonderful fragrance of the orange being refreshing to the diner at the end of these sumptuous banquets. *Petit brûle* was made by removing the fruit pulp from an orange and preserving the skin to serve as a cup into which brandies were poured over sugar cubes and spices, and then flamed.

In addition to maintaining cellars of imported liquors, the Creoles made their own wines, liqueurs and cordials, and guarded the recipes with serious jealousy. Among the favorites were anisette, absinthe, crème de menthe and cherry bounce. Many a family even today will concoct a favorite brew, feeling a nostalgic pride in possessing the recipe of a long-deceased ancestor, considering it a special legacy, a heritage from an aristocratic past of good taste and discernment.

At their *soirées* and gay carnival parties the Creoles served any number of delightful alcoholic concoctions: wine punches, champagne cups, brandy stews, sherry cobblers, juleps, sangarees, toddies and frappés, cordials, nectars, crèmes, meads and beers. And as the passing years brought changes in the city's entertaining and drinking patterns, there was to emerge out of the New Orleans scene a new name—the cocktail—born of the meeting of two of the city's cultures: the older French-speaking Creole and the more recent American. It is said that M. Peychaud, a druggist who came to the city in 1793, dispensed a "tonic" to the clients of his apothecary shop (now bearing municipal numbers 727-729 Toulouse Street). It was composed of cognac and a secret formula which came to be known as "bitters", and was mixed in a double-ended egg cup called in French a *coquetier*. This word most Americans found difficult to say. Eventually the pronunciation degenerated to give us the word "Cocktail", and the formula for Peychaud's drink became known in time as the world famous Sazerac cocktail. Other New Orleans drinks, such as the Ramos gin fizz and the absinthe frappé have joined the immortals also.

COFFEE

Creoles have always made a ritual of coffee drinking. To them, coffee, to be worth the drinking, should be

Noir comme le Diable
Fort comme la mort
Doux comme l'amour
Chaud comme l'enfer!

It is said that they preferred Mocha and Java coffees which the good wife bought green and parched herself. She ground the beans fresh each morning in the kitchen mill and always used the drip method of brewing. One recipe allows a cup of grounds to make four cups of good strong coffee, but such proportions varied depending on the strength of the brew preferred. To start off, about two tablespoons of boiling water were poured over the grounds, and then one waited until the puffing and bubbling ceased before pouring in more water. To pour in too much at the beginning of the process would result in a weaker coffee since the grounds would not yet be prepared to release their liquid. But once the grounds settled, the slow pouring process could proceed until the desired amount of coffee was brewed. *Café noir,* or black coffee, was the drink for early morning and after dinner. *Café au lait* (half boiled milk and half coffee) was the breakfast drink.

On a very special occasion *Café Brûlot* or *Café Royal* was served, and delicious and appropriate though both are in closing the meal, they represent more than a final beverage. Such a drink, rich in flavor, exciting in the making, adds the gourmet touch and demonstrates the principle which looms large behind all Creole entertaining. This is that fine foods, elegantly served, honor the guest and reflect the hospitality and graciousness of the host.

In New Orleans, coffee blended with chicory has been sold since Civil War days. Chicory is a cultivated leafy vegetable with a carrot-shaped root. During the Napoleonic wars when blockades cut off Europe from the coffee-growing regions of the world, chicory came into general use. It was found that the root, when dried, roasted and ground, made an excellent addition to coffee, and the supply of the then expensive and scarce coffee could be doubled by combining the two. People soon became accustomed to its unique flavor and continued to use it even after coffee became more readily available. Today in New Orleans there are as many drinkers of the chicory-blended coffees as of the pure.

ABSINTHE FRAPPÉ

1 teaspoon simple syrup   2 ounces Pernod

Shake well and pour over cracked ice. Top with a dash of club soda.

ANISETTE

6 ounces alcohol   Simple syrup sufficient quantity
6 drops oil of Anise   for 1 quart

URSULINE NUNS

CAFÉ BRÛLOT

1 cup brandy   2 pieces stick cinnamon (broken in
4 tablespoons sugar   half)
10 cloves   3   3-inch strips of lemon peel
                                           1 quart café noir

Combine all ingredients except coffee, in a brûlot bowl. Place bowl over warm water until brandy warms. (Do not let brandy get too hot or it will not burn.)

Ignite brandy and flame slowly adding brewed coffee. *Serves 8*

CHERRY BOUNCE

In a gallon jar or bottle put the cherries (about ¾ of the bottle). Fill the bottle or jar with brandy (brandy—½ alcohol and ½ distilled water). Let soak for a month or two or until all the juice of the cherries has been absorbed. Filter through filtering paper. Keep it unsweetened, if so desired, or prepare it with simple syrup.

Cherry Bounce   3 parts
Simple syrup   2 parts

URSULINE NUNS

CRÈME DE MENTHE

8 ounces alcohol   24 ounces simple syrup
24 drops oil of peppermint

If desired color with green.

URSULINE NUNS

DOUCE AMÈRE (BITTER SWEET)
OR
AMÈRE DE FAMILLES

1 ounce Spanish saffron
2 ounces calamus aromaticus
2 ounces gentian root
1 ounce zedoary root
1 ounce Roman chamomile
1 ounce coriander seeds
½ ounce orange peel

½ ounce cinnamon bark
2 drams macis or mace
1 dram cloves
½ ounce fennel
2½ gallons alcohol 95%
2½ gallons distilled water

Crush all ingredients in a marble mortar. Pour 2½ gallons of alcohol and 2½ gallons of distilled water in a demijohn. Add crushed ingredients. Allow to soak for 2 weeks. Shake well daily for 5 or 6 days. Allow to stand for 2 or more weeks. Filter through filtering paper and put in gallon bottles. Keep it unsweetened and prepare as needed, as follows:

Amère de familles	3 parts
Simple syrup	2 parts

URSULINE NUNS

EGG NOG

1 quart milk
4 eggs (separated)
½ cup sugar

nutmeg
whiskey

Scald milk. Beat egg yolks and sugar until creamy. Add small amount of scalded milk to egg mixture and stir. Combine egg mixture with remaining milk. Stir and cook on low heat until thoroughly blended. Beat egg whites until stiff and fold in. Add nutmeg and whiskey to taste. *Serves 4.*

CAROL M. VICKNAIR

HOLIDAY PUNCH

2 cups rose water
2 cups muscatel wine
¼ cup kummel
½ cup dry vermouth
1 piece of stick cinnamon

2 cloves
¼ lemon
½ cup sugar
Handful of raisins
3 cardamen seeds

Place all ingredients overnight in a china pitcher and let stand. Use the following day either cold or warm.

MYLDRED MASSON COSTA

NEW ORLEANS GIN FIZZ

1½ teaspoons lemon juice
1 teaspoon sugar
2 drops orange flower water

2 drops vanilla extract
1 jigger gin
1 jigger cream

Ice and shake. *Serves 1.*

CAFÉ AU LAIT

Simultaneously pour into a cup, boiling milk and hot, strong coffee brewed as in Café Noir. *Serves 1.*

CAFÉ NOIR

Using a drip coffeepot, put 2 tablespoons dark roast or coffee and chicory blend for each cup of water used. Add 2 tablespoons boiling water over grounds every few minutes until desired amount of coffee is brewed.

PEACH DAIQUIRI

3 ripe peaches	1 teaspoon sugar
1 can frozen pink lemonade or frozen limeade	½ cup white rum
	1 tray ice cubes

Blend in blender for 10 seconds. Serve in sherbet glasses with short straws.

FLORENCE LANDRY

SUMMER DAIQUIRI

1 can of 48 ounce pineapple juice	3 small 7 Ups
1 small can of frozen orange juice (made as directed)	2 cups rum
	1 package of pre-sweetened cherry Kool-Aid mix

Mix all together and freeze until solid. Cut up, place in blender until slushy. Re-freeze in quart containers. Let soften slightly before serving. Garnish with mint and cherry.

MARY ALICE McKAY

NECTAR SODA

Nectar syrup (see formula below)	Vanilla ice cream
	Club soda

Pour an inch of nectar syrup into a tall glass. Add a scoop of vanilla ice cream and club soda. Stir to mix. Serve with a scoop of ice cream on top or whipped cream and a cherry. Club soda may be substituted with any unsweetened carbonated drink or with carbonated water.

NECTAR SYRUP I

3 cups sugar	4 tablespoons vanilla extract
6 cups water	4 tablespoons almond essence
1 can sweetened condensed milk	2 teaspoons red food coloring

Over low heat dissolve sugar and water. Bring to boil. Cool. Add the condensed milk, vanilla extract, almond essence, and red coloring. Stir well. Store in the refrigerator. Makes about 1½ quart.

ELVÉ LOUISE IRELAND

NECTAR SYRUP II

3 cups granulated sugar	2 tablespoons almond extract
1½ cups water	½ teaspoon red food coloring
1 tablespoon of vanilla extract	

Bring sugar and water to a boil over medium heat. Let mixture cook about 8 to 10 seconds. Cool. Add vanilla, almond and coloring. Makes about 1 pint.

MARY ALICE McKAY

SAZERAC

1 teaspoon simple syrup	2 dashes bitters
1 teaspoon Pernod	2 ounces bourbon whiskey

Stir well and serve chilled or on the rocks.

SOUTHERN PUNCH–HOT

1 large bottle or can apple juice	2 sticks cinnamon
2-3 lemon slices	½ tablespoon cloves

Simmer 3 or 4 minutes. Serve hot with mint. *Serves 4.*

MARY ALICE TOSO McKAY

SUMMER SPECIAL

1 small can pineapple juice	1 jigger rum (light)
1½ jiggers crème de cacao	

Shake well with ice. Serve with slice of orange and piece of mint. *Serves 1.*

BOBBIE SANCHEZ DERBES

YELLOW BIRD

1 jigger crème de banana	1 dash pineapple juice
1 jigger rum	1 dash orange juice
1 dash lemon juice	

Put into a blender with crushed ice. Pour into a martini glass and top with a slice of lemon. *Serves 1.*

BOBBIE SANCHEZ DERBES

POUSSÉ CAFÉ

Grenadine
Maraschino
Green crème de menthe

Crème de Violette
Chartreuse
Brandy

In poussé café glass pour ⅙ of each in the listed order. *Serves 1.*

MINT JULEP

4 sprigs mint
3 ounces Bourbon

½ ounce simple syrup
crushed ice

Crush 3 sprigs mint in a tall glass. Add simple syrup and bourbon and crushed mint again. Fill glass with crushed ice. Garnish with sprig of mint. Serve when well frosted. *Serves 1.*

JOYCE LAFAYE CREWS

FROZEN ALEXANDER

1 ounce Brandy
1 ounce Crème de Cacao

2 scoops vanilla ice cream

Mix in blender. *Serves 1.*

BEVERLY LAFAYE CLARK

PETIT BRÛLE

1 orange
2 sugar cubes
2 cloves

1 inch stick cinnamon
2 ounces brandy

Remove pulp from orange. Place sugar and spices in hollow orange. Pour brandy over same and ignite. *Serves 1.*

GIN FIZZ

1 teaspoon sugar
1 teaspoon orange flower water
1 ounce cream
1 egg white

½ ounce lemon juice
½ ounce lime
2 ounces dry gin

Blend with ice in a shaker until smooth. *Yield 1.*

SIMPLE SYRUP

1 cup water
2 cups sugar

3 or 4 slices of lemon

Cook for five minutes.

AMERICA SOLOMON

Masson's Restaurant

HORS D'OEUVRES

The custom of serving a drink as an appetizer before dinner with an assortment of delectable dishes is said to have started in Scandinavia. The Russians picked up the custom from them, serving *zakuski* (little bits) with their vodka. During the 1800's France took over the custom, calling their appetizers *hors d'oeuvres à la Russe* (*hors d'oeuvres* meaning "outside the chef's principal work.").

In Creole days guests were invited to an evening at home, which they called a *Soirée,* or to dinner. Although appetizers and canapés were rarely served in the manner of today, many of our *hors d'oeuvres* are descendants of first-course appetizers served by the Creoles. These included *petits pâtés au jus* (small hot meat patties), *boudins noirs et blancs* (sausages, black and white) or *bouchées d'Huîtres* (little "mouthfuls" of oysters). But the universal favorite, that which was relished and appreciated, that which never failed to elicit the word of praise from the guest was that marvel of delicate flavor and smoothness: *foie gras.* This was made of the liver of the goose, served as a *pâté* with truffles, or *en matelote* or in the well-known jellied loaf, *pain de foie à la gelée.*

There is a special method of tending geese to produce the famous *foie gras* which is said to have originated with the Romans. This is the method of force feeding. It produces a liver of such delicate texture as to have warranted the classification of *foie gras* as a gourmet food down through many centuries. The French brought the process from Strasbourg to New Orleans where it was continued until just before the Civil War. A Creole woman is said to have operated such a farm on the site of the present Fair Grounds, and tradition has it that she grew rich catering to the discerning tastes of the city's *bon vivants.* Today, force feeding is illegal in the United States and the fat livers must be imported from France. Alsace is said to produce the best *foie gras* today. It is combined with truffles to produce a gastronomic masterpiece.

There is a region of southwestern France—Perigord—where the finest truffles grow. Truffles are wild fungi that grow in clusters among the roots of certain oak trees and are hunted out by *truffiers* who wander through the fields with a pig on a leash. The pig scents the truffle and the *truffier* uproots it with a digging spike. Truffles are very dark in color and about the size of a walnut. Their principal use is in combination with *foie gras,* although they are used to flavor other dishes and also as garnishes. Truffles have been highly prized as a delicacy throughout many centuries, but no one has ever succeeded in cultivating them successfully. Alexander Dumas wrote of them:

> The most learned men have been questioned as to the nature of this tuber, and after two thousand years of argument and discussion, this answer is the same as it was on the first day: we do not know. The truffles themselves have been interrogated, and have answered simply: "Eat us and praise the Lord."

ARTICHOKE BALLS

2 cloves garlic, pureed
2 tablespoons olive oil
2 8-ounce cans hearts of artichokes,
    drained and mashed

2 eggs, slightly beaten
½ cup grated Parmesan cheese
½ cup Italian bread crumbs

Saute garlic in oil. Add artichokes and eggs and cook over low heat about 5 minutes, stirring constantly. Remove from heat and add crumbs and cheese. Roll into individual balls, using about 1 tsp. mixture for each; roll in mixture of crumbs and cheese. Chill until firm. *Yield: 4 dozen.*

PATTI STERN HABANS

STUFFED CELERY

1 4-ounce cream cheese
2 teaspoons mayonnaise
½ cup finely chopped pecans

¼ teaspoon Worcestershire sauce
2 large stalks celery
Cayenne

Cream together the cream cheese, mayonnaise, Worcestershire and cayenne. Add pecans.

Clean and string celery before stuffing, using only inner, tender ribs. Will stuff 2 large stalks celery. Sprinkle with cayenne.

JULIA BERKERY LAFAYE

PARTY CHEESE BALL I

1 large block sharp cheese,
    grated coarsely
1 roll nippy cheese
1 large package cream cheese
1 small chive cheese

1 tablespoon Worcestershire sauce,
    or to taste
Garlic salt to taste
½ teaspoon dry mustard
Paprika
Chili powder

Soften cheeses and mix with Worcestershire, garlic salt and mustard. Shape into two balls and coat with a mixture of half paprika and half chili powder.

MRS. MARY ELLEN NICHOLAS

PARTY CHEESE BALL II

2 large packages cream cheese
1 jar roka bleu cheese spread

2 ounces bleu cheese
chopped pecans

Cream cheeses together when soft. Chill to harden. Then shape into a ball and roll in chopped pecans. Garnish with a stemmed cherry or parsley sprig. Serve with crackers.

JOYCE LAFAYE CREWS

CHEESE STRAWS

1 pound sharp cheddar cheese , grated
1 pound margarine
1 tablespoon salt

1 tablespoon Tabasco
1 tablespoon Worcestershire sauce
4¾ cups sifted all-purpose flour

Cream margarine until very soft; add cheese and mix thoroughly. Add salt, Tabasco and Worcestershire sauce. Add flour and mix well.

Fill cookie press to make straws about 2 inches long. Mixture may be rolled into bite-size balls. Bake in preheated oven at 375° for 6 to 8 minutes.

NINA NORMAN DeSAUTEL

CHICKEN PATTIES

100 cocktail patty shells
1 young hen cut in small pieces
1½ cooking spoons flour
2 medium onions, minced
1 No. 2 can strained tomatoes
2 toes garlic, finely chopped

3 slices green pepper, minced
1 sprig parsley (not chopped, and to
    be removed from gravy after
    cooking)
Salt and pepper to taste

Fry pieces of chicken (unfloured) to a light brown. Brown 1½ cooking spoons of flour in butter. Add onions until mellow. Add tomatoes, garlic, green pepper, parsley and salt and pepper to taste. Cook together about 10 minutes and add 1½ quarts of water. Put in chicken and cook until tender. Remove chicken from gravy. Strip meat from bones and mince. Add minced chicken and small can of chopped mushrooms to gravy and heat. Serve in heated patty shells.

JULIA B. LAFAYE

ICE BOX WAFERS

8 tablespoons butter or margarine
1 cup flour
½ teaspoon salt

¼ teaspoon red pepper
1 cup chopped pecans
2 cups grated cheese

Blend all ingredients. Make two rolls; wrap in foil. Refrigerate overnight. Slice in thin slices and bake at 375° for 10 minutes.

MRS. OWEN BRENNAN

CHICKEN LIVER PÂTÉ

12 tablespoons butter
½ cup chopped onion
¼ pound fresh mushrooms, sliced
¼ pound chicken livers
1½ teaspoons seasoned salt

1 teaspoon lemon juice
⅛ teaspoon black pepper
⅛ teaspoon cayenne pepper
2 hard-cooked eggs, quartered
¼ cup chopped pecans

In 8 Tbsp. of butter, saute onion—about 5 minutes. Add mushrooms and chicken livers, and cook just until liver is tender, about 5 minutes. Remove from heat, add remaining butter, seasoned salt, lemon juice, pepper and cayenne; stir until butter melts. Divide mixture into four parts. In electric blender, at high speed, blend the mixture one part at a time, adding 2 of the egg quarters to each part. Empty into a bowl as each part is blended. Stir nuts into entire mixture and refrigerate for about 30 minutes. Shape into ball on sheet of waxed paper or foil. Wrap well and refrigerate overnight. Serve with crackers. *Yield: 2½ cups, or enough for about 50 crackers.*

CRAB PUFFS

1 rib celery, minced
1 medium onion, minced
1 tablespoon cooking oil
2 cans or ½ pound crabmeat

½ cup thick white sauce
2 eggs, well beaten
½ teaspoon pepper
½ teaspoon seasoned salt
½ cup cracker crumbs

Saute onion and celery in oil. Drain on absorbent paper. Combine with crabmeat, white sauce, eggs, seasonings and cracker crumbs. Shape into bite size balls. Fry in deep hot shortening until golden brown. Drain and serve with tartar sauce. *Yield: 3 dozen puffs.*

CHEESE SPREAD

8 tablespoons butter
½ cup American cheese, sharp shredded

1 tablespoon minced parsley
½ teaspoon minced chives

On a very low fire, melt butter, add cheese, parsley and chives. Stir to melt cheese. Spread on hard rolls, rye or French bread and heat in 325° oven to warm bread.

PAULA PALMER

STUFFED MUSHROOMS I

24 large fresh mushroom caps
4 tablespoons butter, melted
6 green onions finely chopped

24 small oysters
Melted butter
Salt

Saute mushroom caps gently in melted butter for 3 minutes. Remove and place on greased cookie sheet, hollow side up. Saute onions in remaining butter; put about ¼ tsp. chopped onion inside each mushroom. Dip oyster in melted butter; place 1 inside each; sprinkle lightly with salt. Heat in broiler until oysters start to curl. Serve immediately.

LYNN BADEAUX BUNGAY

STUFFED MUSHROOMS II

12 fresh mushrooms
1 cup fresh lump crabmeat
1 tablespoon butter

½ cup hollandaise sauce
2 tablespoons whipping cream
2 teaspoons sour cream

Poach and dry mushrooms. Combine remaining ingredients. Heat and stir until fluffy. Spoon into mushrooms. Broil until lightly browned.

MAE O'NEIL

OYSTERS ODETTE

3 dozen oysters, drained
2 tablespoons butter
2 green onions, minced
2 tablespoons flour
2½ ounce can of mushrooms, stems
and pieces, drained

⅛ teaspoon nutmeg
Dash of cayenne
½ teaspoon salt
1 tablespoon Worcestershire sauce
½ teaspoon chopped parsley
1 egg yolk
Bread or cracker crumbs

Make brown roux with flour and butter. Saute onions in roux. Add oysters, mushrooms and all seasonings. Cook 10 minutes over medium heat or until liquid is reduced by half. Remove from heat and add egg yolk. Spoon mixture into six ramekins and cover with bread crumbs. Bake at 350° for 15 minutes. *Serves six as an appetizer.*

ANNE BADEAUX CONWAY

SALTED PECANS

1 pound pecan halves
¼ pound butter

Salt

Place butter in shallow baking pan in 400° oven. When melted, turn pecans in butter. To coat, turn pecans every two minutes. After 10 minutes, remove from oven, sprinkle evenly with salt and drain on absorbent paper.

JOYCE LAFAYE CREWS

DAUBE GLACÉE

¾ cup shredded meat (such as roast
   or soup meat)
20 stuffed olives, sliced
2 cans beef consommé

2 packages gelatin
1 bunch green onions, minced
6 tablespoons parsley flakes
2 tablespoons Worcestershire sauce

Place slice of olive in bottom of each mold and sprinkle meat over olive. Heat 1 can of consommé and dissolve gelatin in it. Add the other can of consommé, Worcestershire sauce, shallots and parsley. Stir and pour into molds. Made in individual molds; served on Ritz crackers. *Makes 4 dozen.*

MARY ALICE McKAY

ESCARGOTS BOURGUIGNONNE

12 snails (escargots)
8 tablespoons butter, room
   temperature
1 tablespoon fine dry bread crumbs

2 teaspoons finely chopped parsley
¼ clove garlic, minced
dash fresh ground black pepper
¼ cup Burgundy wine

Clean and dry shells; set aside. Cream butter; add bread crumbs, parsley, garlic and pepper. Gradually add wine. Put 1 tsp. butter mixture into each shell. Insert a snail into each. Cover with another tsp. butter mixture. Place snails in pans. Bake at 475° for about 10 minutes, or until crumbs are brown and snails heated through. Serve piping hot in pans with cocktail forks. *Makes 2 servings.*

HOGS HEAD CHEESE

4 pigs feet (raw)
4 calves feet (raw)
½ pound veal
½ pound pork
4 or 5 quarts water
4 onions
6 cloves garlic

3 stalks celery
8 green onions
5 sprigs parsley
1½ teaspoons paprika
Dash cayenne pepper
2 red peppers, chopped

Clean pigs feet and calves feet well. Cover meat with water; boil, then skim. When broth is clear, add onions, garlic, celery, 5 green onions and 1 sprig parsley. Boil until meat leaves bones. (3 hours).

Remove meat from broth and shred. Strain broth, and add to the strained broth the shredded meat, together with paprika, cayenne, red peppers, 4 sprigs parsley (finely chopped), and 3 green onions (minced). Place in small molds to set. When set, turn out of molds and garnish.

JULIA BERKERY LAFAYE

COCKTAIL PIZZAS

1 package hot roll mix
½ cup minced onion
1 tablespoon cooking oil
2 8-ounce cans tomato sauce

¼ teaspoon dried oregano
¼ teaspoon garlic salt
¼ pound Mozzarella cheese, grated
¼ pound sharp processed cheese, grated

Prepare roll mix according to package directions; let rise. Saute onion in oil, add tomato sauce and seasonings. Simmer 10 to 15 minutes. Punch down dough on lightly floured board and divide into 4 equal parts. Roll each part to ¼ inch thickness; cut into circles with floured 2 inch cookie cutter. Snip edge of each circle about every ¼ inch with scissors and pinch edge to make a rim. Brush center of each circle with additional oil, sprinkle with ½ tsp. Mozzarella cheese, then ½ tsp. tomato sauce mixture, then ½ processed cheese. Top some with sliced stuffed olives, some with green or ripe olives or halved cooked shrimp. Bake at 450° for 10 to 12 minutes. *Yield: 40 Pizzas.*

MARINATED MUSHROOMS

½ pound fresh or canned mushrooms
6 tablespoons olive oil
3 tablespoons wine vinegar
1 teaspoon dried tarragon
Dash celery salt

1 teaspoon grated onion
½ teaspoon salt
⅛ teaspoon freshly ground black pepper
1 clove garlic, crushed

Wash fresh mushrooms or drain canned mushrooms. Combine remaining ingredients. Pour over mushrooms. Stir to coat mushrooms with marinade. Cover, chill 6 to 8 hours, stirring gently several times. The mushrooms will darken. Serve on food picks.

ADELE SMITH

RUMAKI (POLYNESIAN APPETIZER)

2 tablespoons butter
2 tablespoons Soy sauce
1 can (8 ounces) water chestnuts, halved

⅓ pound chicken livers, halved
8 bacon slices, halved

Cook chicken livers in butter and soy sauce. Wrap chestnut half and piece of chicken liver with ½ slice bacon; secure with foodpick. Marinate 1 hour in soy sauce. Broil until bacon is crisp, about 15 minutes. Turn once.

BEVERLY LAFAYE CLARK

BACON FRIED SHRIMP

Bacon, sliced
Egg white, slightly beaten

Jumbo shrimp, peeled and deveined

Wrap half bacon slice around each shrimp. Dip in egg white. Use foodpick to seal bacon around shrimp. Fry in deep hot shortening until bacon is crisp.

SHRIMP DIP I

3 cans shrimp
1 medium onion, grated
3 8-ounce packages cream cheese
2 cloves garlic, minced
Juice of 1 lemon

2 tablespoons Worcestershire sauce
1 tablespoon chopped parsley
Red pepper and salt to taste
Juice of 1 can shrimp

Mix all ingredients, except shrimp, and beat until light and fluffy. Add the 3 cans of shrimp. Serve warm with Fritos.

MRS. OWEN BRENNAN

SHRIMP DIP II

10 large shrimp
¼ cup mayonnaise
Tabasco (3 shakes only)
1 teaspoon onion (grated or juice)

Salt
Pepper
Cream

Clean and cook shrimp. Mash to purée. Add remaining ingredients. Salt slightly; add cream to desired consistency.

BEVERLY KLUNDT

PICKLED SHRIMP

2½ pounds raw peeled shrimp
3 teaspoons salt
1 box crab boil (spices in bag)
2 cups thinly sliced onions
7 or 8 bay leaves

1¼ cups salad oil
¾ cups white vinegar
2½ tablespoons capers and juice
3 lemons thinly sliced and seeded
1½ teaspoons salt

Cover shrimp with boiling water. Add salt, crab boil bag. Cook 10 to 12 minutes. Combine remaining ingredients in large bowl. Add shrimp. Mix and cover well. Allow to marinate at least overnight.

CAROLINE E. COLES

SHRIMP RICHMOND

2 pounds shrimp, peeled and
    deveined (small to medium
    shrimp preferred)
1 large white onion, finely chopped
1 can stewed tomatoes
    (14-16 ounces), mash

2 medium carrots, grated
⅓ cup Chablis
Mild cheddar cheese
3 or 4 sprigs parsley
½ teaspoon sugar
4 tablespoons butter or margarine

Sauté onion in butter or margarine. Add raw shrimp and fry with onions until pink. Add stewed tomatoes. Cook until shrimp are done. Add grated carrots, Chablis, parsley and sugar. Mix thoroughly but do not cook. Spoon into individual ramekins and top with sliced Cheddar cheese. When ready to serve, heat through and allow cheese topping to melt and brown around the edges. Serve with hot French bread. *Serves 6 to 8 as an appetizer.*

MRS. JOSEPH S. BARROIS

SWEDISH MEAT BALLS

¾ pound ground beef
½ pound ground veal
¼ pound ground pork
1½ cups soft bread crumbs
1 cup light cream
½ cup chopped onion

3 tablespoons butter
1 egg
¼ cup minced parsley
1½ teaspoon salt
¼ teaspoon ginger
Dash pepper
Dash nutmeg

Soak bread crumbs in cream 5 minutes. Saute onions in 1 Tbsp. butter. Combine all ingredients and beat 5 minutes at medium speed in electric mixer plus 8 minutes by hand. Form in 1 inch balls. Brown in 2 Tbsp. butter; set aside. Make the following gravy:

2 tablespoons flour
1 can condensed beef broth

¼ cup water
½ teaspoon instant coffee

Stir 2 Tbsp. flour into fat in skillet, add ¾ can condensed beef broth, ¼ c. water, and ½ tsp. instant coffee. Stir until thickened over medium heat. Add meat balls, cover, cook slowly about 30 minutes, basting occasionally. Makes 5 dozen. Freezes beautifully.

MIRIAM THARPE

MOCK OYSTER DIP

1 package frozen chopped
   broccoli
1 large onion, minced
8 tablespoons butter or margarine

1 (6 ounce) roll of garlic cheese
1 can mushroom stems and pieces
Dash of hot sauce
1 can cream of mushroom soup

Cook broccoli in water (over done). Sauté onion in butter; add cream of mushroom soup, mushrooms and juice. Break up garlic cheese and add to mixture. Add hot sauce and broccoli. Mix well. Keep warm in chafing dish; eat with dipper potato chips. Can also be used in patty shells or over noodles as a casserole.

PATSY TALBOT HOTARD

Delmonico's Restaurant

ENTRÉES

Sister Marie Madeleine Hachard de St. Stanislaus of the New Orleans Community of Ursulines, wrote a number of letters to her father in Rouen, France, giving him what was to be a prophetic insight into the heart and personality of the City of New Orleans. She saw then, almost 250 years ago what any visitor to the city will tell you today—that it is a charming city, gay and pleasure loving, owing a lot of its *joie de vivre* to its French background.

Our city called New Orleans, capital of all Louisiana, is situated on the bank of the Mississippi River, which is at this place wider than the Seine at Rouen. (The city) is very beautiful, well constructed and regularly built . . . It suffices to tell you that there is a song sung here publicly in which it is said that this city has as fine an appearance as the City of Paris . . . There is here as much magnificence and refinement as in France. Gold and velvet goods are common, though three times dearer than at Rouen. The luxury that prevails in the city is the reason why it is difficult to distinguish the rich from the poor. All are of equal magnificence. The women here, as elsewhere, paint their faces with powder and rouge to hide the wrinkles of their faces, on which they also wear beauty spots.

But this propensity for gaiety and for enjoying the good things of life was not merely a matter of heritage! It rather became, little by little, second nature to a people living, as New Orleanians did then and still do today, in a paradise of plenty. Wild game was so unsurpassingly delicious and abundant that the greater part of the citizenry "lived in idleness" and applied themselves to scarcely anything except hunting and fishing. It is little wonder then, that out of the enormous bounty of this locale there evolved eventually a culture seriously devoted to the pleasures of the table and a cuisine so distinguished as to become known the world over.

Of the abundance of wild game and sea foods in these early times Madeleine's letters give proof:

Hunting, which commences in October, lasts all winter. (The hunting) is done at ten leagues from the city. Wild oxen are caught in large numbers . . . We pay three cents a pound for that meat and the same price for venison, which is better than the beef and mutton which you eat at Rouen . . . In fact, we live on wild beef, deer, geese and wild turkeys, hares, hens, ducks, teals, pheasants, partridges, quails and other fowl and game of different kinds. Wild ducks are very cheap (but) . . . we buy little of them for we do not wish to indulge in dainties. In a word, it is a delightful country all winter, and in summer, fish are common and very good . . . The fish are prodigious in size and are very delicious . . . There are none like them in France . . . We accustom ourselves wonderfully well to the wild foods of this country . . . and we are better off than we expected to be. Thank God, we have not yet wanted for anything.

Years later Thackeray was to pay a similar tribute to the city and its sumptuous foods. He referred to New Orleans as

... the old Franco-Spanish city on the banks of the Mississippi where of all the cities of the world, you can eat the most and suffer the least, where the claret is as good as at Bordeaux, and where a ragout and a bouillabaisse can be had the like of which was never eaten in Marseilles or Paris.

Many of the entrées for which the city prides itself draw their excellence from the quality of the superb local seafood; and the combination of the Spanish flair for seasoning with French delicacy in concocting recipes has made these dishes a heritage.

Bouillabaisse made in New Orleans has a distinct advantage over that made in other sea food capitals of the world in that the Creoles used slices of Redfish and Red Snapper in its preparation, both being of superior texture for this dish. An old tale recounts the manner in which the dish got its name. It is said that in Marseilles one Frenchman instructing another in the art of making a good Bouillabaisse mentioned that the most vital point in the preparation was to remove the dish from the fire when the ingredients begin to boil: "*Quand ça commence à bouillir, baisse!*" His tip became a byword in the preparation of the dish and in time gave it its name.

Pompano en Papillote deserves mention because it originated in New Orleans. Pompano is one of the most highly prized fish in southern waters and has been eaten variously prepared from the city's earliest days. However, *Pompano en Papillote* was created by one of the city's oldest restaurants to honor a famous balloonist-visitor to the city. It is cooked in a paper wrapper which, on the first occasion of its serving was intended to resemble an inflated balloon, although the main purpose was to retain flavor.

As Sister Marie Madeleine noted, game in great varieties and quantities has always been available to New Orleanians. The Canvasback Duck (*Canard Cheval*) is declared by gourmets to be the finest of the game birds. Since it takes on the flavor of the wild celery on which it feeds, it needs little seasoning and is cooked simply by roasting over a hot fire. But a *salmis* with olives and claret, or with turnips, will render any of the less prized game birds a dish beyond belief. A particular type of game preparation, *faisandé* curing, was said to have been introduced into New Orleans, and Louisiana in general, by the Acadians. This method of game handling is French, the term deriving from *faisan*, the French word for pheasant. In France the meat of the pheasant was often allowed to age somewhat before cooking, and as a result of this practice, any game so treated is said to be faisandé. Game birds were nailed by the feet, uncleaned and unplucked, to the side of the barn or hung by the neck from the fence until the bodies fell to the ground. If the meat cured, the game was cooked and eaten; if it deteriorated, it was thrown away. The process of faisandage was used for venison, rabbit and other game animals as well as for pork and sausage, and those who practiced it enjoyed the full ripened flavor of *la viande faisandée.* Of such meats it is said that the peak of perfection in their flavor is reached when they begin to decompose and that the birds should not be plucked too soon since feather loss interferes with the proper consummation of the aging process.

Of the beef and veal entrées, *grillades*, although a simple dish, is probably the one most often associated with New Orleans. The word actually means "fried" or "grilled" but the dish, in its most popular form, was prepared with sliced onions, garlic, tomatoes and green peppers, and the meat was allowed to simmer slowly and absorb the juices. *Grillades* were served with grits for breakfast, or with red beans and rice at luncheon or dinner. It was a favorite dish in Creole days, as it is today. *Daube Glacée* is made of a heavy cut of beef smothered in seasonings, cooked to perfect tenderness, and centered in a mold of jelled meat juices. These juices were coaxed to jell by the addition of pigs knuckles and veal joints to the stock. An early edition of the Times Picayune's Creole Cook Book says of it:

> *Daube Froide à la Créole* has only to be tried once to be repeated. It is a standing dish for luncheon in every Creole home during the winter, for it is never essayed in the summer, owing to the heated weather that would prevent the jellying of the beef. Even when put in an ice box, it is not the same as when made in the winter. It is a dish that may be served with little cost to the most fastidious.

One may not agree as to the "little cost" of the dish today, but there is no doubt that it is still a dainty dish to set before the fastidious, the gourmet, and perhaps even the king.

CHICKEN ALMONDINE

1 small can blanched	¼ cup sherry
chopped almonds	8 tablespoons margarine
1 small can mushrooms	8 boned chicken breasts
¼ cup breakfast cream	Salt and pepper

Salt, pepper and dust chicken with flour. Sauté chicken in melted margarine about 20 minutes. Add chopped almonds and saute 5 minutes more, stirring to brown evenly. Add mushrooms and their water and the sherry. Turn heat low and slowly add cream. Remove from heat as soon as cream is well mixed. Place in flat casserole and bake at 300° for 45 minutes. Can be frozen before baking. *Serves four.*

CHICKEN WITH ARTICHOKES

1 fryer chicken, cut up	1 cup heavy cream
2 tablespoons butter	Salt and pepper
2 tablespoons minced green onion	1 large can artihoke hearts,
¼ cup white wine or vermouth	halved and drained

Brown chicken pieces in butter; remove. Sauté onions in same butter until tender. Return chicken to pan and add white wine and cream. Season to taste with salt and pepper. Cover pan and simmer gently 20 minutes.* Just before serving add artichoke hearts and heat gently. Serve over rice. *Serves four.*

*Can be prepared up to this point, kept several hours and then reheated.

ANNE BADEAUX CONWAY

CHICKEN CLEMENCEAU

2 small chickens or 2 whole	2 large potatoes, cubed
chicken breasts, split	1 tablespoon chopped parsley
Salt and pepper	1 tablespoon Worcestershire sauce
8 tablespoons butter	Dash hot sauce
2 tablespoons flour	1 cup warm water
1 tablespoon grated onion	1 chicken bouillon cube
1 can (8 ounce) petits pois peas	½ cup dry wine (red or white)
1 can (4 ounce) whole mushrooms	

Season chicken; brown in butter and remove from skillet. Add flour and onion to drippings; brown over low heat. Add liquid from peas and mushrooms; stir thoroughly; add chicken. Cover and simmer until chicken is tender, about 30 minutes. Fry potatoes in deep hot shortening until brown. Drain. To cooked chicken, add potatoes, peas, mushrooms, parsley, salt and pepper, Worcestershire sauce and hot sauce. Dissolve bouillon cube in water and add to chicken mixture. Simmer 10 minutes longer. Add wine and serve immediately. *Serves four.*

CHICKEN A LA CREOLE

1   3 or 3½ pound spring chicken
3 tablespoons shortening
½ bell pepper, sliced
2 celery ribs, sliced
2 medium onions, sliced
½ lemon, sliced
½ teaspoon thyme
1 bay leaf

1 No. 303 can tomatoes
1   8 ounce can tomato sauce
2 chicken bouillon cubes
½ can water
2 tablespoons chopped parsley
3 toes garlic
½ teaspoon basil
Salt and pepper to taste

Cut, clean, salt and pepper chicken. Brown chicken in shortening in dutch oven or deep skillet. Remove chicken. Sauté sliced pepper, celery, and onions until tender. Add tomatoes, sauce and water. Add thyme, bay leaf, parsley, basil, lemon slices, and bouillon cubes. Press garlic and add to above. Salt and pepper to taste. Simmer about 15 minutes. Add chicken, cover, and cook over low heat for about 1 hour or until chicken is tender.

MRS. JACK EUMONT

CREOLE CHICKEN

1 large fryer or broiler
   (3-3½ pound), cut up
2 tablespoons flour
3 tablespoons margarine
1 large onion, chopped fine
2 or 3 green onions, chopped fine
3 sprigs parsley, chopped fine
1½ tablespoons fresh thyme or 1½
   tablespoons marjoram leaves

1 large can tomatoes, strained
1 small can tomato sauce
1 can cream of chicken soup
2 teaspoons sugar
Salt and pepper
Water
1 medium can of mushrooms

Wash and dry chicken. Heat 1 Tbsp. of margarine in large skillet and brown chicken on both sides. Salt and pepper lightly. When chicken is brown add 1 large can tomatoes. Some of the mashed pulp may be used if desired. Add tomato sauce and cream of chicken soup. Cook this mixture about 15 minutes over low heat. In another skillet blend 2 Tbsp. margarine and 2 Tbsp. flour until light brown. To this roux, add mixture of onion, pepper, green onions. Sauté until vegetables are limp. Add to the chicken in tomatoes. Add thyme or marjoram, sugar, and salt and pepper to taste. Cover and cook over low heat until chicken is tender. Stir and turn occasionally. It may be necessary to add a small amount of water. When chicken appears tender enough add parsley and mushrooms. Stir, turn off heat, and let stand about 5 minutes before serving. *Serves four.*

MRS. ALBERT J. WINTERS

CHICKEN FRICASSÉE

1 4 pound chicken, cut up	1 sprig thyme
Salt, pepper and flour	1 tablespoon minced parsley
1 tablespoon shortening	1 bay leaf
1 onion, chopped	3 cups boiling water

Season chicken with salt and pepper, coat with flour. Brown in shortening, add onion and sauté. Add seasonings and water. Bring to boil; cover and reduce heat. Simmer until tender, about 1 hour. *Serves six.*

CHICKEN AND DUMPLINGS
(A variation of Chicken Fricassée)

1 cup sifted flour	Sprig of parsley, minced
2 teaspoons baking powder	½ cup milk
½ teaspoon salt	

Mix all ingredients to thick batter and drop from spoon into boiling Chicken Fricassée, cover tightly and cook 20 minutes *without removing cover.*

SOUTHERN DUMPLINGS
(A variation of Chicken Fricassée)

⅓ cup shortening	2 teaspoons baking powder
2 cups sifted flour	½ cup milk
1 teaspoon salt	

Cut shortening into sifted dry ingredients. Add milk to make a stiff dough. Roll out to ⅛ inch thickness and cut into 1 to 1½ inch strips of diamonds. Sprinkle with flour and drop into boiling Chicken Fricassée. Cover and cook 30-40 minutes *without removing cover.*

GRANDMA'S CHICKEN AND GRAVY

1 4 to 5 pound hen, cut up	Salt and pepper to taste
2 tablespoons shortening	2 bay leaves
3 large onions, finely chopped	½ teaspoon thyme
½ bell pepper, finely chopped	½ teaspoon basil
1 rib celery, finely chopped	½ cup flour
5 toes of garlic	1 bottle (8 ounce) of olives
2 tablespoons chopped parsley	2 chicken bouillon cubes
8 cups water	Kitchen bouquet

Place shortening in dutch over. Salt and pepper chicken. Brown chicken in shortening; remove from pot. Add flour to shortening and stir continuously until golden brown. Add onions, pepper and celery; sauté until soft. Add bay leaves, thyme and basil. Slowly stir water into flour mixture so as not to lump flour. Add parsley and pressed garlic, olives and juice, bouillon cubes, kitchen bouquet (if necessary for color). Season to taste with salt and pepper. Put chicken back into pot; cover and simmer until tender and gravy thickens (about 1½ to 2 hours).

MRS. JACK EUMONT

CHICKEN JAMBALAYA

9 chicken thighs	Cayenne pepper
3 medium onions	Chili powder
4 ribs of celery	Parsley flakes
5 cloves of garlic	Worcestershire sauce
2 bell peppers	Tabasco
1 small can tomato paste	Salt and pepper
1 large can tomatoes	1 cup rice
1 pound smoked sausage	3 bay leaves

Boil chicken and sausage until tender. Reserve liquid. Sauté chopped onion, celery, pepper, garlic in light olive oil. Add cut up chicken and sausage, tomatoes and tomato paste. Add seasoning to taste, cook for 30-45 minutes on low heat. Add 2-2½ cups of reserved liquid and rice. Cook covered until rice is tender. *Serves about 8.*

ELSA G. NADLER

CHICKEN KIEV

8 large chicken breasts	Salt
8 tablespoons chopped green onion	Pepper
8 tablespoons parsley flakes	Egg
8 tablespoons butter	Seasoned bread crumbs

Skin and de-bone each chicken breast, leaving meat all in one piece. Place each piece between 2 pieces of plastic wrap and beat with a mallet until about ¼ inch thick. Remove plastic wrap and sprinkle each piece with salt, pepper, 1 Tbsp. green onion and 1 Tbsp. parsley flakes. Cut butter in half (cross wise), then cut each half into 4 "logs" (ending up with 8 "logs"). Place each butter log at the edge of each chicken piece and roll up like a jelly roll; seal ends. Dust with flour; dip in beaten egg and roll in bread crumbs. Chill at least 1 hour. Fry in deep hot fat until brown—about 5 minutes. *Serves four.*

SYLVIA GLEZEN

KING RANCH CASSEROLE

1 chicken, boiled, boned, cut into bite-sized pieces	2 onions, chopped
1 dozen tortillas, thawed and torn into pieces	2 cups grated American cheese
	½ bell pepper, chopped

Mix in blender or mixer:

1 can cream of chicken soup	½ soup can chicken broth
1 can mushroom soup	Salt and pepper
1 can Rotel tomatoes with green chilies	2 teaspoons chili powder

Butter a casserole, put in a layer of chicken and a layer of tortillas, then onions, bell pepper and cheese; cover with sauce; repeat with another layer of each, saving some cheese to sprinkle on the top. Bake one hour at 350° *Serves six.*

MRS. MARY ELLEN NICHOLAS

CHICKEN TETRAZZINI

¼ pound butter
1 cup flour
1 quart chicken stock
2 egg yolks
¼ cup pimento, chopped
¼ cup sliced mushrooms

Italian and American cheese
Salt and pepper
1 4-pound chicken (boiled,
   boned and cut into strips)
1 cup boiled ham (cut into strips)
½ pound spaghettini

Put butter in sauce pan and let melt, add flour and cook. Stir slowly until well blended, without lumps. Make sure flour is cooked. Add chicken stock, mix well, then add egg yolks and stir. Now add chicken, ham, mushrooms and pimentos, stirring to mix all ingredients. Fold in spaghettini that has been freshly boiled. Place in casserole dish, sprinkle with grated American and Italian cheese, also melted butter. Bake until cheese is melted golden brown. *Serves six.*

PITTARI'S

PAELLA

¼ cup olive oil
1 chicken (4 pound) cut up
¼ cup water
1 teaspoon oregano
1 clove garlic, minced
3 tablespoons butter
2 cups rice

½ cup chopped onion
⅛ teaspoon saffron
4 cups chicken broth or water
1 pound shrimp, cooked and shelled
12 thin slices Italian or Spanish
   sausage or 1 cup chopped ham
24 canned clams (optional)

Heat oil; add chicken and brown on all sides. Add water and oregano; cover and cook until chicken is tender (about 30 minutes). Remove chicken and set aside. Sauté onion and garlic in pan drippings. In another skillet melt butter; add rice and saffron; stir over low heat for 5 minutes. Add chicken broth; bring to a boil, cover and cook on low heat 17 minutes. Add onion and mix together. Arrange in layers in a 4 quart casserole the rice, chicken, clams, shrimp and sausage. Bake at 350° about 30 minutes; clams should be open. *Serves 8.*

CHICKEN ROCHAMBEAU

3 small chickens (halved)
6 bread rounds
6 slices of ham
8 tablespoons butter
3 tablespoons flour

10 ounces pineapple juice
1 tablespoon dark brown sugar
¼ cup vermouth, dry sherry or
   white wine
6 tablespoons bernaise sauce

Broil chicken and place on toasted bread rounds that have been topped with broiled ham slices. Pour Rochambeau Sauce over chicken and top with 1 tablespoon Bernaise Sauce. *Serves 6.*

Rochambeau Sauce: Melt butter; add flour and keep stirring until a dark brown roux is achieved. Add pineapple juice, brown sugar and cook until sauce thickens. Add vermouth, stirring until well blended.

JOYCE LAFAYE CREWS

SOUTHERN FRIED CHICKEN

2½ pounds chicken, cut up   Salt, pepper and flour

Season chicken; coat with flour. In heavy skillet, heat at least 2 inches shortening until very hot. Add chicken, largest pieces first, and brown on both sides, about 25 minutes. *Yield: 4 servings.*

Variation: Batter Fried
    1 egg   1 cup flour
    ¾ cup evaporated milk   Pepper
    1 teaspoon salt

Blend ingredients well. Dip chicken in batter and fry as above. *Serves 4.*

ROAST STUFFED CORNISH HEN

8 Cornish hens   Wild rice stuffing
    (14 ounces each)   8 tablespoons butter, melted

Place stuffing lightly into body cavities of hens. Skewer or sew openings. Truss. Brush with butter and place breast side up on rack in shallow pan. Roast, uncovered, in 350° oven about 1¼ hours. After 45 minutes, turn breast side down and roast until brown. Brush occasionally with butter. *Serves 8.*

WILD RICE STUFFING

1 cup uncooked wild rice   ¾ cup chopped celery
1 cup sliced mushrooms   1 clove garlic, minced
8 tablespoons butter, melted   ¼ cup minced parsley
1 bunch green onions, minced   Salt and pepper

Cook rice according to directions on package. Sauté mushrooms in butter 5 minutes. Remove mushrooms; add onions and celery; cook 8 minutes. Stir in garlic, parsley, cooked rice, salt, pepper and mushrooms. Mix thoroughly and stuff hens. *Serves 8.*

CRANBERRY STUFFING BALLS

In a bowl combine:
    9 cups fine dry bread crumbs   ½ teaspoon dried thyme
    2 eggs lightly beaten   ½ teaspoon summer savory
    1 cup coarsely chopped cranberries Salt and pepper to taste
    ¼ cup finely chopped parsley

Sauté in 12 Tbsp. of butter until limp, not brown:

    1 cup chopped onion   1 cup chopped celery

Stir the vegetables into the bread mixture thoroughly. Shape the stuffing into balls the size of a large walnut and put on baking sheet. Cover the stuffing balls with a sheet of foil and heat at 300° for about 10 minutes. *Serves six.*

MRS. OWEN BRENNAN, JR.

CORNBREAD STUFFING

6 cups cornbread crumbs
4 cups biscuit or white bread
   crumbs
¾ quart stock, milk or water
1½ chopped onion
1 cup chopped celery
6 tablespoons butter

4 eggs, well beaten
2 teaspoons salt
1 teaspoon pepper
1 teaspoon poultry seasoning
1¼ quart stock, milk or water,
   approximately

Soak cornbread and bread crumbs in stock. Sauté onion and celery in butter until golden brown. Combine crumbs and onion; mix with eggs and seasonings. Add approximately 1¼ quarts stock to thoroughly moisten. Mix well. Stuff turkey. If stuffing is baked in separate pan, bake at 325° for 1 hour. *Yield: stuffing for 12 pound turkey.*

OYSTER STUFFING I

5 tablespoons minced onion
1½ cups chopped celery
4 tablespoons butter
4 cups cooked rice or
   3 quarts bread
4 teaspoons chopped parsley

1 tablespoon poultry seasoning
Salt and pepper
2 dozen ground oysters and liquid
1 cup turkey stock and ground
   cooked giblets
2 eggs, slightly beaten

Sauté onion and celery in butter. Add rice or moistened bread, parsley, seasonings, oysters and stock with giblets. Mix and heat thoroughly; add beaten eggs and mix well. *Yield: stuffing for 10 pound turkey.*

OYSTER STUFFING II

Turkey liver and heart, minced
½ cup shortening, butter
   or margarine
2 large onions, minced
½ bunch green onions, minced
1 bay leaf
1 sprig thyme
½ cup celery, minced

3 cloves garlic, minced
4 teaspoons minced parsley
3 doz. small oysters, cut in half
1 loaf French bread
2 teaspoons salt
¼ teaspoon black pepper
2 eggs, slightly beaten

Brown liver and heart in hot shortening in a skillet over low heat (about 15 minutes). Add onions, bay leaf, thyme and celery; cook until tender over low heat (about 20 minutes). Add garlic, parsley and oysters; cook until almost all of the water leaves oysters (about 15 minutes). Remove bay leaf and thyme. Place bread under cold running water; press out excess moisture with hands. Break bread into small pieces and add to oyster mixture. Stir and cook until thoroughly heated (about 15 minutes). Remove from heat, add salt, pepper and eggs. Mix well. *Yield: Enough stuffing for a 10 pound turkey.*

HOT DIRTY RICE

4 pounds hot sausage
10 each chicken gizzards, necks,
    livers and hearts
8 tablespoons butter
2 large yellow onions, minced
1 bunch green onions, minced

1 large bell pepper, minced
4 ribs celery, minced
2 pounds cooked rice
1 cup chopped ham
2 tablespoons dry parsley

Boil gizzards, necks, livers and hearts in 2 quarts of water until done. Save water. Fry off hot sausage and render grease. Simmer onions, celery, pepper in 3 Tbsp. of sausage grease for 20 minutes. Add green onions and simmer 10 more minutes. Add chopped meat, ham and sausage to greens, with butter and parsley. Add some of the water you have saved to make mixture moist. Add salt to taste. Let simmer for 15 minutes more, then fold in rice. Put in double boiler to keep warm. *Serves 15.*

JUSTIN D. DOUGLASS

RICE DRESSING

2 pounds long grain rice
½ pound pork sausage
1 pound bacon
3 dozen oysters
½ cup chopped green onion

1 medium onion
5 or 6 sprigs parsley
Salt
Giblets
12 to 16 pound turkey

Cook rice according to directions on package 2 or 3 days before turkey is to be stuffed. Cool and place in refrigerator. The rice will become very dry; this is desirable and will keep the dressing from becoming mushy.

Boil in salted water until tender, the gizzard, neck, heart and liver. Remove from water, cool, and chop all coarsely except the liver which is mashed well with a fork. Set aside.

Broil bacon and drain on paper towel. Chop onions and green onions, including the green tops. Sauté in bacon drippings and drain well.

Cook pork sausage, drain all grease, discard drippings. Drain oysters well, do not wash. Chop. Place in skillet and cook only until the oysters begin to curl.

In a pot or bowl large enough to allow mixing, place the cold rice. With a wooden spoon or fork, separate each grain. Mix the prepared ingredients with the rice. Sprinkle the parsley in. Each grain of rice will be coated with one or more of the ingredients.

Salt well the cleaned and washed cavities of the fowl. Spoon in the stuffing and sew or skewer the openings. Bake according to directions recommended by the turkey shipper.

ALICE FOLSE BERTAUT

TURKEY GRAVY

Cover gizzard and neck in a saucepan with water. Bring to a boil over full heat. Reduce heat to medium and cook until gizzard is tender (about 1 hour). This stock can be used for gravy. Remove fat from pan in which turkey was roasted. Pour enough fat back into pan and add flour and stock to obtain thickness and amount of gravy desired. (See table below) Blend flour into fat in pan over low heat, stir until mixture browns. Then add liquid in which gizzard and neck were boiled and cook over medium heat, stirring until gravy is of desired consistency. Season with salt and pepper.

Thin gravy: 1 tablespoon fat; 1 tablespoon flour; 1 cup stock
Medium gravy: 2 tablespoons fat; 2 tablespoons flour; 1 cup stock
Thick gravy: 3 tablespoons fat; 3 tablespoons flour; 1 cup stock

TURKEY POULETTE

4 large slices turkey breast, cooked
4 slices toast
6 strips crisp bacon
Cheese sauce with mushrooms
¼ cup grated cheddar cheese
1 can (16-17 ounces) French fried
    onion rings

Place turkey slices on toast, top with bacon and pour cheese sauce over the entire surface. Sprinkle with cheese and onion rings. Broil until cheese melts and browns slightly. *Serves 2.*

CHEESE SAUCE WITH MUSHROOMS

2 tablespoons butter
3 tablespoons flour
1 cup milk
¼ teaspoon salt
1 can (4 ounces) mushroom pieces,
    drained
½ cup grated cheddar cheese

Melt butter; stir in flour until smooth. Add milk gradually. Cook over low heat until thick, stirring constantly. Remove from heat. Add salt, mushrooms and cheese. Stir until cheese melts.

TURKEY HASH

¾ cup minced onion
2 tablespoons chopped green
  pepper
2 tablespoons butter
2 cups finely chopped cooked
  turkey

2 cups diced boiled potatoes
½ cup turkey broth, or chicken
  bouillon
½ teaspoon salt
⅛ teaspoon pepper

Sauté onion and green pepper in butter. Add turkey, potatoes and broth. Season with salt and pepper. Cook over low heat, stirring occasionally until heated thoroughly. Increase heat the last 10 minutes to brown bottom. *Serves 4.*

CRANBERRY SAUCE

1 cup sugar
Grated rind of 1 orange
1 grapefruit shell

1 cup water
½ pound cranberries

Combine sugar, rind and water in a large saucepan. Bring to a boil over medium heat and boil for 5 minutes. Add cranberries, which have been thoroughly washed. Cook for 5 minutes or until cranberries burst. Place in bowl, cool and refrigerate until serving time. To serve, place in grapefruit shell.

BOILED CRABS, CRAYFISH OR SHRIMP

5 pounds shellfish or 1 dozen crabs	1 sprig thyme
1 pound salt	1 bay leaf
2 slices lemon	1 red pepper pod
2 whole allspice	¾ teaspoon celery seed
1 onion sliced	¼ teaspoon black pepper

Into a large container pour enough cold water to cover crabs or shellfish. To each quart of water add ¼ cup salt, 2 slices of lemon, 2 whole allspice, 1 onion sliced, 1 sprig thyme, 1 bay leaf, 1 red pepper pod, ¾ tsp. celery seed, ¼ black pepper. If commercial seasoning is available, use 2 tablespoons concentrated liquid or 1 bag (2 bags if more seasoning is desired) in place of seasoning listed above. Let salty seasoned water boil for 10 minutes, then add crabs or shellfish and boil for 15 or 20 minutes, or until the shells are a bright red. Turn off heat, allow crabs or shellfish to remain in water 10 minutes. Drain. Serve hot or cold. A large amount of salt added to water to make a brine is a must in boiling crabs or shellfish.

Crabs are always placed into the boiling salted water alive. Crabs and crayfish should be purged before boiling. To do so place crabs or crayfish in a tub of water and add ½ box of salt.

MARY ANN BENDERNAGEL

BROILED HARD SHELL CRABS

1 dozen live crabs	1 tablespoon salt
1 cup butter	1 teaspoon black pepper
3 teaspoons ground dill	2 cloves garlic
3 tablespoons olive oil	2 cups Sauterne wine

Put crabs in pan on back. Baste with 1 cup white wine, salt and pepper. Put under broiler until dead. Turn off. Leave in oven for 12 minutes. Remove shells, clean and break in half. Stand in deep bowl with meat exposed. Prepare sauce with remaining ingredients. Simmer for 15 minutes. Pour over crabs and serve.

PAT LAFAYE

BROILED SOFT-SHELLED CRABS

6 soft-shelled crabs	1 tablespoon sifted flour
1 cup milk	8 tablespoons butter, melted
Salt and pepper	Chopped parsley

Clean crabs; wash thoroughly in cold water, pat dry and season with salt and pepper. Season milk with salt and pepper; soak crabs for about 15 minutes. Sprinkle lightly with flour and brush with melted butter. Broil 3 to 4 inches from heat, top side down, for about 7 to 8 minutes. Turn, brush top side with butter, and broil for about 8 minutes or until golden brown. Garnish with chopped parsley and lemon wedges. *Serves 6.*

CRAB STEW

6 crabs
2 tablespoons flour
1 onion, minced
1 No. 2 can tomatoes
4 tablespoons butter

2 cloves garlic
2 sprigs parsley
2 green onions
1 sprig thyme
½ bell pepper, chopped

Brown flour in butter and add minced onion and pepper. When onion has melted, add tomatoes and seasoning, and salt and pepper to taste. Cook about 30 minutes on slow heat. Add crabs which have been cleaned and halved and cook in gravy for about 30 minutes. If gravy becomes too thickened add about ½ cup water. *Serves 4.*

JULIA BERKERY LAFAYE

STUFFED CRABS

1½ dozen crabs (wash & clean
12 shells)
Seasoning for boiling crabs—
    salt, pepper, bay leaf, onion,
    celery, parsley, hot pepper.
    "Crab Boil" may be used.

2 medium onions, minced
3 sprigs parsley, minced
3 green onions, minced
1 tablespoon sifted toast crumbs
3 tablespoons sweet cream
Lemon juice

Boil crabs for ½ hour in seasoned water. Pick crabs.

Simmer onions in butter. Add parsley and green onions. Add crab meat flakes, toast crumbs and stir until thoroughly mixed. Remove from fire (after cooking together above ingredients for about 10 minutes) and add cream. Blend thoroughly away from heat (do not cook after adding cream).

Stuff well cleaned crab shells with filling. Top with toast crumbs. Put about 10 drops lemon juice and small lump of butter on each crab. Brown in oven. *Serves twelve.*

JULIA BERKERY LAFAYE

CRAB MEAT CASSEROLE

5 tablespoons butter
3 tablespoons flour
2 cups milk
2 tablespoons minced onion
½ teaspoon celery salt
1 tablespoon minced parsley
1 tablespoon minced green pepper
1 pimento, minced

2 tablespoons sherry
1 egg, beaten
⅛ teaspoon hot sauce
1 teaspoon salt
⅛ teaspoon black pepper
1 pound crab meat
¼ cup bread crumbs
1 tablespoon butter

Make white sauce with butter, flour and milk; then add next six ingredients. Remove from heat. Add sherry. Add a small amount of hot mixture to egg; combine with remaining sauce. Add hot sauce, salt, pepper and crab meat. Place in 1¼ quart casserole; sprinkle top with bread crumbs mixed with 1 Tbsp. melted butter. Bake at 350° for 15-20 minutes. *Serves 6 to 8.*

CREAMED CRABMEAT

1 pound lump crabmeat	1 4 ounce cheddar cheese, grated
1 4 ounce cream cheese	¼ cup milk
	Bread crumbs

Mix crabmeat, cheddar cheese, milk and bits of cream cheese in casserole, adding more milk, a tablespoon at a time to make it creamy. Bake at 350° for 20 minutes. Remove from oven and place in individual ramekins or seashells. Dot with butter and sprinkle with bread crumbs. Reheat when ready to serve. *Serves 4 to 6.*

SUZANNE ARTIQUES CANGELOSI

CRABMEAT MORNAY

8 tablespoons butter	2 tablespoons dry white wine
2 tablespoons flour	1 pound lump crabmeat
1 bunch green onion, chopped	Salt, pepper and cayenne
1 pint breakfast cream	to taste
½ pound grated Swiss cheese	

Sauté green onions and parsley in stick of butter until soft. Add flour. Blend together and begin adding cream gradually until the sauce is smooth. Add cheese, wine and seasonings.

Fold in crabmeat very gently as not to break up the lumps.

HARRIET STERN

CRABMEAT RAVIGOTE

1 pound lump crabmeat	1 tablespoon chopped parsley
6 tablespoons butter	1 pimiento, chopped
3 ounces dry sherry	½ teaspoon garlic salt
1 5 ounce can mushrooms	½ teaspoon white pepper
(stems & pieces)	½ teaspoon celery seed
3 green onions, chopped	½ cup bread crumbs
½ small green pepper, chopped	

Sauté onions, green pepper, mushrooms lightly in butter. When they begin to soften, add pimiento, crabmeat, sherry and seasonings. Toss, but do not break up crabmeat lumps. Add ½ of bread crumbs and put into ramekins. Top with remaining bread crumbs. Run under broiler to heat thoroughly. Serve with toast points. *Serves six.*

BEVERLY LAFAYE CLARK

LES MERVEILLES DE LA MER EN CRÊPES

½ cup chopped shallots
½ cup sliced mushrooms
3 sticks butter
3 tablespoons flour
½ cup white wine
1 quart light cream
3 or 4 egg yolks

Salt and pepper
½ pound cooked lobster meat
½ pound cooked shrimp (pieces)
½ pound crabmeat
2 teaspoons cognac
8 crêpes

Sauté shallots and mushrooms in 2 sticks butter. Add flour and cook 2-3 minutes. Gradually add wine and cream and simmer 8-10 minutes. Remove from fire and stir in beaten egg yolks, adding enough to make a sauce of medium consistency. Season to taste. Saute seafood in 1 stick butter 4-5 minutes. Add cognac and ignite. After cognac burns out, add half of the sauce to the seafood mixture. Divide this onto crêpes and roll up. Cover crêpes with the remainder of the sauce. *Serves 4.*

MASSON'S

BOILED CRAYFISH

1 sack crayfish
  (approximately 40 pounds)
10 bags of crab boil
2   1½ ounce jars cayenne pepper
  or 2   1½ ounce jars red pepper

4 tablespoons creole granulated
  garlic
4 boxes (4 pounds) salt
12 lemons cut in half
8 onions cut in half
1 large bunch celery, separated

Add all of above ingredients (except crayfish) to 12 gallons of water in large stock pot. Bring to a boil. Place crayfish in boiling mixture and maintain maximum heat for 15 minutes. Cut heat off and let crayfish remain in water for 20 to 30 minutes to get maximum flavor.

CRAWFISH CARDINAL

1 pound cleaned crawfish tails
8 tablespoons butter
3 tablespoons flour
1 teaspoon garlic salt
1 medium onion, chopped

(Enough milk to make a medium
  cream sauce)
½ teaspoon white pepper
2 tablespoons chopped parsley
½ cup white wine
2 tablespoons tomato paste

Melt 4 Tbsp. butter, add flour and cream until it becomes a paste. Gradually add milk until you achieve the consistency of a medium cream sauce. Sauté onions and crawfish in the remaining 4 Tbsp. butter until onions are luminous looking. Add garlic salt, white pepper, and parsley. Combine this with the cream sauce. Add wine and tomato paste. The paste gives you the pink color.

EDWARD A. LAFAYE

CREOLE CRAYFISH

8 tablespoons butter   ½ cup flour

Make roux with the above ingredients.
Add:

Peel of ½ lemon (through blender)   ¼ teaspoon ground sage
1 whole bay leaf   ¼ teaspoon ground all spice
½ teaspoon cayenne   ½ bunch small celery, chopped
¼ teaspoon ground cloves   4 onions, chopped
¼ teaspoon ground thyme   4 cloves garlic, chopped
¼ teaspoon ground marjoram   1 bell pepper, chopped

Add to above and cook for 2 hours:
Crawfish fat   ½ gallon water
¼ can tomato paste   3 pounds peeled cooked crayfish
dash Worcestershire sauce   tails

Add right before serving:
½ bunch green onion tops   ½ bunch parsley, chopped

Serve over rice.

BEVERLY LAFAYE CLARK

CRAWFISH ÉTOUFFÉE

8 pounds fresh crawfish,   ½ cup water
  washed   ½ teaspoon corn starch
8 tablespoons butter   Salt, pepper and cayenne
6 medium onions, chopped   to taste
½ cup chopped celery   2 tablespoons chopped green
½ teaspoon tomato paste   onion tips
                                          2 tablespoons minced parsley

Place crawfish in large container of boiling water. Remove from heat and let stand 5 minutes. Drain. Remove heads, peel and devein.

In large saucepan, melt butter; add onions, celery and tomato paste. Cook until tender. Add crawfish tails. In a small bowl, combine water and corn starch. Add to onion mixture, stirring constantly. Add salt, pepper and cayenne. Bring to boil and cook 15 minutes. Add onion tops and parsley. Serve over rice. *Serves four.*

CRAYFISH NEWBURG

8 tablespoons butter   1 teaspoon M.S.G.
2 tablespoons flour   ½ teaspoon cayenne
1 teaspoon salt   2 tablespoons paprika

Cook above ingredients until proper consistency.
Add:

2 cups cream   2 tablespoons cognac
4 cups crayfish tails   4 tablespoons sherry
Cool and add:
4 beaten egg yolks

PAT LAFAYE

NOTE: SHRIMP may be substituted for crayfish resulting in Shrimp Newburg.

FROG LEGS SAUTÉ À LA CRÉOLE

6 frog legs	1 bay leaf
2 tablespoons butter	2 cloves garlic, chopped fine
3 large onions, sliced	6 sweet peppers, sliced fine
6 fresh tomatoes	1 cup consomme or boiling water
1 sprig thyme	Salt and pepper to taste

Brown washed frog legs in butter, being careful not to burn. After ten minutes take onion and brown with frog legs. Add tomatoes; cover and let brown. Cook very slowly, adding salt and pepper to taste, thyme, bay leaf and garlic. Smother mixture slowly 20-30 minutes, stirring frequently. Add sweet pepper and continue to smother until frog legs are tender. Add consommé or water and continue to cook slowly, covered, for ½ hour. Serve hot. *Serves four.*

MRS. SIDNEY BRADFORD'S RECIPE
SUBMITTED BY WALTER McILHENNY, AVERY ISLAND

BAKED OYSTERS

2 cups Italian bread crumbs	Dash nutmeg
16 tablespoons melted butter	2 tablespoons parsley—dehydrated
1 pint oysters	1 can cream of mushroom soup
½ teaspoon salt	½ cup sauterne wine
¼ teaspoon black pepper	

Combine bread crumbs and butter. Cover bottom of a 9-inch pie plate with crumb mixture, reserving enough to sprinkle on top. Lay oysters on top of crumb mixture in pie plate. Combine seasonings and sprinkle over oysters. Mix soup and wine and pour over oysters. Top with reserved crumb mixture. Bake at 350° for about 50 minutes. Place under broiler to brown. *Serves six.*

MRS. ROBERT E. FORTIER

OYSTERS BIENVILLE

1 bunch green onions and tops, minced	⅓ cup white wine
2 tablespoons butter	1 teaspoon salt
2 tablespoons flour	Dash cayenne pepper
⅔ cup chicken broth	2 dozen oysters on half shell, drained
⅓ cup mushroom pieces	½ cup French bread crumbs
1 egg yolk	1 tablespoon Parmesan cheese

Sauté green onions and tops in butter in a skillet over low heat. Add flour and cook until brown. Stir in chicken broth and mushrooms. Beat egg yolk with wine and slowly add to sauce, beating rapidly. Season with salt and pepper. Cook for 10 to 15 minutes over low heat, stirring constantly. Place a pan of ice cream salt in a 400° oven for 30 minutes. Leaving oysters on half shell, place shells in hot ice cream salt and return to oven for 5 minutes. Pour sauce over each oyster; cover with combined bread crumbs and cheese. Place in 400° oven until lightly browned. *Serves 4.*

OYSTERS BEACH HOUSE

¼ cup chopped shallots	¾ cup flour
¼ cup sliced mushrooms	2 cup milk
1 teaspoon dry mustard	½ cup dry sherry
Pinch cayenne	2 egg yolks
1 stick butter	2 dozen raw oysters

Sauté shallots, mushrooms, mustard, and cayenne in butter. Add flour and cook 3-4 minutes. Add warm milk gradually, and cook 8-10 minutes. Add sherry. Remove from fire and stir in beaten egg yolks. Place room-temperature raw oysters in cleaned oyster shells and cover with sauce. Bake 10-12 minutes at 350°. *Serves 4.*

MASSON'S

OYSTERS BROCHETTE

10 bacon slices	⅓ cup olive oil
36 shucked raw oysters	12 toast triangles
Seasoned flour	1 teaspoon chopped parsley
⅔ cup butter	1 teaspoon lemon juice

Cut bacon in one-inch pieces; sauté until partially cooked, turning to cook both sides, and draining off fat as it accumulates in skillet. On each of 6 skewers, string 6 pieces of bacon, alternating with 6 oysters (sticking skewer through eye of oyster). Roll in flour. Heat butter and olive oil; add skewered food; sauté, turning to cook all sides. Lay each skewer on two toast triangles. Add parsley and lemon juice to butter in skillet; pour a little over each portion. *Yield: 6 portions.*

ANTOINE'S RESTAURANT

OYSTERS CASINO

12 strips of bacon	3 tablespoons chopped parsley
½ large green pepper,	6 tablespoons butter
chopped fine	3 dozen oysters in deep bottom
8 tablespoons butter	halves of shells
3 tablespoons chopped chives	Juice of 3 lemons

In a skillet cook bacon until it is translucent and still limp. Cut the bacon strips into thirds and reserve it. Discard the fat. In the same skillet, cook green pepper in 2 Tablespoons butter for several minutes. Combine chives and parsley and blend in 6 Tablespoons butter.

Place oysters in deep bottom halves of the shells and place on a layer of rock salt in shallow baking pans. Put a little of the green butter mixture on top of each oyster, sprinkle with a few drops of lemon juice, and cover each oyster with a piece of the reserved bacon. Bake at 450° for 8 to 10 minutes, or until the bacon is crisp and the oysters are heated through.

BARBARA CONNICK

MERE'S OYSTER PATTY

12 tablespoons butter
½ tablespoon leaf thyme
2 tablespoons all purpose flour
3 cups milk

1½ bunches green onion, chopped
  fine
1½ tablespoons chopped parsley
Red pepper to taste
3 dozen oysters

Sauté green onions in 8 Tablespoons of butter in a deep skillet. Add the thyme and flour and cook over low heat. Stir constantly; do not brown the flour. Cook 3 to 5 minutes. Remove skillet from heat; add milk gradually, stirring briskly to prevent lumping. Return pan to heat until sauce thickens, stir constantly. Add oysters to the sauce and cook over low heat until oysters curl. The sauce will now be thinner, if too thin stir some of the sauce into about 2 tablespoons flour to make a smooth, light paste. Add more sauce to this and then while stirring, pour this thickening agent slowly into sauce skillet. Cook a few minutes longer. If sauce is too thick after cooking, add some of the oyster water. Lastly add 4 Tablespoons butter and parsley. Recipe will be enough for at least 1 dozen patty shells.

LOU BERTAUT DOUGLASS

OYSTER PIE

1 onion, minced
½ cup minced celery
¼ cup minced green pepper
8 tablespoons butter
1½ tablespoons flour
4½ dozen oysters, drained;
  reserve liquid

¼ cup minced parsley
1½ teaspoon Worcestershire sauce
Dash hot sauce
½ teaspoon salt
1 recipe plain pastry

Saute onion, celery and pepper in 2 Tablespoons butter until soft. Brown flour in remaining 2 Tablespoons butter; stir in sautéed mixture. Add oysters and simmer 5 minutes. If mixture is too dry, add small amount oyster liquid. Add parsley, sauces and salt to taste. Pour into unbaked 9 inch pastry shell. Cover with top pastry and make several slits in top. Bake at 425° for 20 minutes. *Serves 4-6.*

OYSTER-ARTICHOKE CASSEROLE

8 large artichokes
2 teaspoons salt
3 tablespoons flour
12 tablespoons butter
3 tablespoons minced green
  onions

2½ dozen oysters, cut in
  half, and liquid
1 can (7 ounce) mushroom pieces
  and liquid
Salt and pepper
Bread crumbs
2 tablespoons butter

Cook artichokes, covered, in 1 inch boiling water; sprinkled with salt, until tender, about 45 minutes. Drain; cool slightly. Scrape meat from leaves and cut hearts in half. Stir flour in heated skillet over low heat until lightly browned; set aside. Melt butter, add onion and sauté about 5 minutes. Add flour to butter mixture and stir until smooth. Mix in remaining ingredients, except artichoke hearts, bread crumbs and butter. Simmer 10 minutes. Place hearts in casserole, add oyster mixture; top with crumbs and dot with butter. Bake at 350° for 15 minutes. *Serves 6 to 8.*

OYSTERS ROCKEFELLER

½ package frozen chopped
  spinach
6 green onions
2 ribs green celery
⅓ bunch parsley
⅓ head lettuce
8 tablespoons butter
¾ cup bread crumbs

1 tablespoon Worcestershire sauce
1 teaspoon anchovy paste
Dash hot sauce
1½ tablespoons absinthe
¼ teaspoon salt
3 dozen oysters
¼ cup grated Parmesan cheese

Place spinach, onions, celery, parsley and lettuce in blender jar and mince finely. Mix together softened butter and ¼ cup of bread crumbs in a large mixing bowl. Add blended greens and stir to mix. Add remaining ingredients with the exception of oysters, cheese and remaining bread crumbs. Mix thoroughly. Drain oysters from shell. Place oysters back on half shells, set on pan of ice cream salt which has been heated for 20 minutes in 450° oven. Spread 2 Tablespoons sauce over each oyster. Combine Parmesan cheese and remaining bread crumbs and top each oyster with 1 teaspoon of the mixture. Bake at 450° for about 25 minutes or until lightly browned. *Serves six.*

OYSTER STEW

1 pint oysters, with liquid
8 tablespoons butter, melted
1 cup light cream, scalded
3 cups milk, scalded

½ teaspoon paprika
½ teaspoon salt
Pepper

Simmer oysters in butter and oyster liquid until edges curl. Add cream and milk. Heat to boiling, season with paprika, salt and pepper. Serve at once. *Serves four.*

SPINACH-ARTICHOKE-OYSTER CASSEROLE

4 packages frozen chopped
    spinach
2 packages frozen artichoke
    hearts
2 pint jars fresh oysters
8 tablespoons butter
1 large package cream cheese

1 onion
1 bunch green onions
Parsley
1 green pepper
1 or 2 lemons
Italian bread crumbs

Cook artichokes and spinach according to directions. Cook oysters until edges curl and remove from liquid. Fry onion, green onions (chopped) and green pepper in butter until golden and limp. Add spinach and juice of lemon. Add cream cheese and stir until smooth. Add parsley and bread crumbs —enough to absorb butter. Add salt and pepper to taste. Arrange artichoke hearts on bottom of greased casserole, top with oysters, and then the spinach mixture. Dot with butter, bread crumbs and more lemon juice. Warm in oven. May be made in advance, refrigerated, and heated at 350° for about 30 minutes when ready to serve. *Serves 7.*

SHRIMP AU GRATIN

1½ cups shrimp, cooked
1 cup thin white sauce
⅔ cup grated American cheese

1 tablespoon finely chopped
    parsley
½ cup buttered bread crumbs

Alternate layers of cleaned cooked shrimp, white sauce and ½ cup cheese in greased baking dish. Sprinkle with parsley and remaining cheese, then with buttered crumbs. Bake at 400° for 20 minutes or until crumbs are brown. *Serves 4.*

SHRIMP AND CRABMEAT AU GRATIN

8 tablespoons butter
1 pound lump crabmeat
2 pounds peeled, deveined shrimp
1 center rib of celery
2 onions
2 green onions

2 tablespoons parsley
1 can cream of mushroom soup
1 can mushroom stems and pieces
1 cup grated American cheese
½ cup vermouth or white wine

Sauté onions, green onion and celery in butter until soft. Add shrimp; cook until pink. Add crabmeat, soup and mushrooms. When well blended, add parsley, cheese and vermouth or wine. *Serves 6.*

JOYCE LAFAYE CREWS

BAR-B-Q SHRIMP

8 pounds large shrimp, unpeeled
½ pound butter
1 cup olive oil
8 ounce chili sauce
3 tablespoons Worcestershire
  sauce
2 lemons, sliced
4 cloves garlic, chopped

3 tablespoons lemon juice
1 tablespoon parsley, chopped
2 teaspoons paprika
2 teaspoons oregano
2 teaspoons red pepper
1 teaspoon Tabasco sauce
3 tablespoons liquid smoke
Salt and pepper to taste

Wash shrimp. Spread out in shallow pans. Combine ingredients in sauce pan over low heat and pour over shrimp. Refrigerate. Baste and turn shrimp every 30 minutes while refrigerated for several hours. Bake at 300° for 30 minutes, turning shrimp at 10 minute intervals. Serve in soup bowl with French bread to dip in sauce.

JOYCE LAFAYE CREWS

SHRIMP CREOLE

2½ pounds cleaned and deveined
  shrimp
4 tablespoons fat
⅓ cup flour
1 (14 ounce) can of tomato
  sauce with tidbits of tomato
¾ cup chopped onion
½ cup chopped bell pepper

½ cup chopped celery
1 clove minced garlic
½ teaspoon thyme
1 bay leaf
2 tablespoons chopped parsley
2 teaspoons sugar
1¾ cups hot water
Salt and pepper to taste

Sauté shrimp in fat in a large skillet for five minutes or until pink. Remove from pan, add flour and brown lightly; add chopped seasoning and sauté. Add tomato sauce, water, thyme, bay leaf, sugar, garlic, salt and pepper. Stir well and simmer in covered pan for 20 minutes, stirring occasionally. Add shrimp and cook until tender, add parsley just before serving. This may be made several hours early and reheated until piping hot at serving time. Serve over hot rice. *Serves six.*

AMANDA MARTIN

SHRIMP CURRY

5 pounds shrimp, cleaned and boiled 5 minutes in shrimp boil, salt and garlic. Let cool in water; save water.

12 tablespoons margarine	Rice
1 whole rib celery	Chutney
2 onions	Crumbled bacon
1 cup flour	Angel coconut
1 pint scalded milk	Chopped peanuts
1½ teaspoons curry powder	Sweet relish

Sauté celery and onions in 4 tablespoons of margarine. Melt 8 tablespoons margarine; add flour, let bubble, add 1½ pint hot juice from shrimp, stirring constantly until thickened. Add shrimp, scalded milk, and sautéed mixture. Cook slowly 30 minutes to 1 hour. Serve on rice.

May be served with chutney, crumbled bacon, angel coconut, chopped peanuts, or sweet relish.

MRS. LAWRENCE R. SMITH
TEXAS CITY, TEXAS

SHRIMP ÉTOUFFÉE

8 tablespoons margarine	Salt
1 onion	Pepper
1 sweet pepper	Cayenne
3 pounds fresh shrimp, shelled	4 tablespoons flour
and deveined	Parsley

Saute onions and sweet pepper in margarine until wilted. Add shrimp and cook until bubbly. Sprinkle flour over mixture. Cover tightly and let simmer about 1 hour. Serve over hot rice. Crayfish may be substituted for shrimp.

BARBARA SANCHEZ DERBES

FRIED FAN TAIL SHRIMP

2 pounds raw shrimp, cleaned

Batter:

1 cup sifted enriched flour	2 eggs
½ cup yellow corn meal	1 cup ice water
1 teaspoon baking powder	2 tablespoons oil
1 teaspoon salt	

Mix all dry ingredients together. Beat together liquid ingredients; add to dry mixture. Wash, peel and dry shrimp; dip in batter; fry in hot oil. Drain on paper toweling. If used as an hors d'oeuvres shrimp may be dipped in a sweet and sour sauce.

MARY ANN VALENTINO

SHRIMP JAMBALAYA

2 pounds fresh jumbo shrimp,
   peeled and deveined
2 tablespoons vegetable oil
½ pound of diced seasoned
   sausage
½ cup chopped green onions
2 cloves garlic, chopped
¼ cup chopped fresh parsley

1 cup chopped green pepper
1½ cups canned tomatoes
1 bay leaf
1 teaspoon crushed thyme
⅛ teaspoon cayenne pepper
½ teaspoon salt
1 cup long grain rice (uncooked)
1½ cups water

Prepare shrimp. Sauté sausage in oil about 3 minutes. Add garlic, onion and pepper. Cook to tender stage. Add parsley, tomatoes, seasonings, rice and water. Stir in thoroughly. Add shrimp. Bring to a boil. Reduce heat and cover closely. (Best to use heavy cooking vessel). Cook without stirring over a low temperature for 25-30 minutes. Rice should be fluffy. The sausage gives this popular New Orleans recipe a special "zip". Serves six.

MRS. JACK (MARY S.) PARKMAN
MONTICELLO, MISSISSIPPI

SHRIMP MUSHROOM CASSEROLE

2 teaspoons creole onion flakes
2 teaspoons sweet pepper flakes
3 tablespoons butter, melted
4 tablespoons flour
1½ cups breakfast cream
½ teaspoon creole celery salt
½ teaspoon white pepper

½ teaspoon paprika
½ teaspoon salt
1 cup grated cheese
2 cans (6 ounce each) mushrooms
2 pounds shrimp, cooked, peeled
   and deveined
Buttered bread crumbs

Sauté onions and green pepper in melted butter until tender, but not brown. Add flour and blend. Add remaining ingredients, except bread crumbs, and pour into a buttered casserole dish. Top with bread crumbs and bake at 350° for 20 minutes. *Serves eight.*

SHRIMP ORLEANS

1 medium onion, chopped
¼ cup parsley
¼ cup celery
1 clove garlic
1 can of peas
2 pounds shrimp, peeled
   and deveined

½ cup of sour cream
1 tablespoon Worcestershire sauce
Salt and pepper
6 pattie shells or a loaf of
   New Orleans French bread

Sauté onions until tender in a small amount of cooking oil. Add parsley, celery and garlic. Cook for 3 minutes. Add shrimp and cook until pink and tender. Stir in sour cream and Worcestershire sauce. Cook until mixture comes to a slow boil. Season to taste, and simmer for 5 minutes. Add peas, simmer for 2 more minutes. Serve in pattie shells or in French bread with ¼ of middle of bread removed (to resemble a canoe).

MARY MARKS

BAKED STUFFED SHRIMP I

3 dozen large shrimp
1 egg
¼ cup milk
½ cup seasoned bread crumbs
1 teaspoon paprika
1 pound crab meat
1 teaspoon Worcestershire
Salt and pepper
Tabasco

2 tablespoons mayonnaise
1 teaspoon yellow mustard
1 teaspoon celery seed (do not omit)
¾ cup bread crumbs
1 bunch green onion, chopped
2 tablespoons butter
8 tablespoons butter
½ green pepper, chopped

Peel shrimp and split backs; dip into mixture of egg and milk, then roll in mixture of bread crumbs and paprika.

In a separate bowl, mix together the crab meat, Worcestershire sauce, salt, pepper, Tabasco, mayonnaise, mustard, celery seed and bread crumbs.

Sauté the green onions and green pepper in 2 tablespoons butter until wilted. Add to crab mixture.

Stuff shrimp firmly and place on greased, shallow pan. Drizzle with 8 tablespoons melted butter. Bake at 400° for 20-30 minutes.

SYLVIA GLEZEN

BAKED STUFFED SHRIMP II

2 pounds large shrimp
  (about 24 shrimp)
1 large onion, chopped fine
½ medium bell pepper, chopped
  fine
2 green onions, chopped fine
2 sprigs parsley, chopped
  fine
1 tender rib celery and
  leaves, chopped fine

1 egg, well beaten
1¾ cups stale bread
Juice of 1 lemon
Paprika
½ to 1 cup bread crumbs
1 teaspoon sugar
6 tablespoons margarine
Salt and pepper

Peel shrimp except for tails, slit backs, devein, and open out as much as possible. Place shrimp with juice of ½ lemon and 1 tablespoon margarine and a little salt and pepper in a sauce pan over a very low flame. Simmer until shrimp are all pink (a few minutes). Put aside to cool.

In a skillet, heat 2 tablespoons margarine and add onion, bell pepper, green onions, celery. Simmer until vegetables are limp. Add stale bread alternately with a well beaten egg. Add sugar, parsley and salt and pepper to taste. Let cool.

After stuffing has cooled, add to it the liquid which remained from the original sautéing of the shrimp. Mix. Pack some of this mixture around each shrimp except the tail, dipping entire shrimp in dish of 1½ cups of bread crumbs. Place shrimp in a well greased pan and dot each with margarine. Sprinkle with paprika. Bake at 325° for about 15 minutes, turning each shrimp over with a spatula. Bake another 15 minutes or until shrimp are brown. Sprinkle with juice of ½ lemon and serve.

MRS. ALBERT J. WINTERS, SR.

SHRIMP TONTI

2 pounds medium size boiled
   shrimp, peeled and deveined
Into a blender container place the following:
   1½ cups dry sherry
   ¾ cups real butter, softened
   3 cloves garlic
   1 teaspoon dry tarragon
   2 teaspoons fresh parsley leaves

2 cups French bread crumbs

1 cup chopped green onions
3 tablespoons chopped white onion
¼ teaspoon salt
Fresh ground black pepper,
   to taste

Blend slowly adding French bread crumbs—enough to make a thick paste (about two cups).

Arrange shrimp on a baking dish and top with sauce. Bake at 400° until golden and bubbling.

This may be served as an individual hot appetizer or luncheon entrée. Add white wine, green salad and hot rolls for a late supper. May be prepared ahead and refrigerated or frozen until needed. (If you freeze, add extra tarragon.) *Serves four.*

SANDRA FRANZ MARTIN

SEAFOOD PATTIES

8 purchased pattie shells
4 tablespoons butter
2 tablespoons corn starch
1⅛ teaspoons salt
2 cups milk
⅛ teaspoon dry mustard

1 pound cooked shrimp
1 cup fresh crab meat
¼ teaspoon pepper
1 tablespoon Worcestershire
   sauce

Melt butter. Blend in corn starch, salt, pepper and dry mustard. Remove from heat. Gradually add milk and Worcestershire sauce until smooth. Add shrimp and crab meat. Cook over medium heat, stirring constantly, until mixture thickens. Bring to boil and boil one minute. Spoon into heated pattie shells. *Serves eight.*

MRS. JACK EUMONT

SHRIMP ROCKEFELLER

2 packages frozen chopped
   spinach
6 slices bacon
1 cup minced onion
3 tablespoons minced parsley

2 bay leaves
½ teaspoon celery salt
8 tablespoons butter
1 cup seasoned bread crumbs
2 pounds cooked shrimp

Cook spinach with bay leaves. Remove leaves. Mix parsley, bacon and celery salt; add to drained spinach. Sauté onions in butter until soft. Add spinach mixture and simmer 1 minute. Stir in bread crumbs. Place shrimp in shallow, greased casserole. Arrange spinach on top. Bake at 350° for 10 minutes.

MRS. LAWRENCE BENSON

SHRIMP SAKI

30 jumbo shrimp saki
3 lemons
½ pound butter

1 tablespoon paprika
Salt and pepper

Split the shrimp from the back and wash thoroughly under running water. After shrimp are washed thoroughly place them in a pan completely opened. Season with salt and pepper and sprinkle paprika on each shrimp. Pour the melted butter on each shrimp then put them in a hot oven for about 8 minutes. Remove from oven and put under broiler for 5 minutes. Strain juice from three lemons in the melted butter and serve with each portion of shrimp. *Makes 6 portions.*

CARIBBEAN ROOM
PONTCHARTRAIN HOTEL

SHRIMP SALAD

2 cups cooked shrimp
1 cup celery (coarsely chopped)
2 hard-cooked eggs
   (coarsely chopped)
2 tablespoons dill pickles, minced

Mayonnaise
1 tablespoon ketchup
½ teaspoon Worcestershire sauce
Salt and pepper

If shrimp are large, cut into halves or quarters. Mix shrimp, celery, eggs and pickles together lightly with mayonnaise to which has been added the ketchup, Worcestershire sauce, salt and pepper. Serve on lettuce leaves and garnish with sliced tomatoes. *Serves four.*

STEAMED SHRIMP IN JACKETS

5 pounds headless shrimp*
1 cup cooking oil
1 cup chopped green onions
1 cup chopped celery

1 cup chopped bell pepper
2 cups chopped onion
Salt, black pepper and red
   pepper to taste

Wash and drain shrimp. (When using fresh shrimp drain more thoroughly.) Season with salt, pepper and red pepper. Place vegetables in hot cooking oil about 20 minutes (Medium heat). Add shrimp and stir until it turns red. Cover and lower heat, stirring occasionally. Cook about 15 minutes. Add additional seasoning if necessary. Cook about 15 more minutes. Serve hot with garlic bread. Do not overcook as shrimp will be too hard to peel. Proper seasoning is absolutely necessary.
*8 pounds of fresh shrimp, with heads, will yield 5 pounds of headless shrimp.

MRS. ALBERT A. ROBBERT, JR.

BAKED RED SNAPPER WITH SHRIMP STUFFING

1   4 to 6 pound red snapper,
   cleaned
Salt and pepper
8 tablespoons butter
3 tablespoons minced onion
1 tablespoon flour
½ teaspoon crumbled dried
   basil

1 tablespoon minced parsley
½ cup milk
½ pound shrimp, cooked and
   chopped (about 1 cup)
1 cup cooked rice
3 tablespoons lemon juice
Lemon slices and parsley for
   garnish

Wipe the fish with damp paper towels. Sprinkle inside generously wtih salt and pepper.

Melt ¼ cup of the butter in a skillet. Add the onion and cook until transparent. Stir in flour, basil and parsley. Season with salt and pepper. Gradually add milk, stirring to form a thick sauce. Add shrimp, rice and lemon juice. Stir until blended. Remove from heat.

Place fish in foil-lined pan. Place skewers through both edges of body cavity and fill with stuffing. Lace closed with string. Cover tail with foil to prevent burning.

Melt remaining butter and pour over fish. Bake at 400° for 50 to 70 minutes, or until fish flakes easily when tested with a fork. Baste occasionally. Serve garnished with lemon slices and parsley. *Serves six to eight.*

WILFRID MIRE BEAUFORD

SALMON CROQUETTES

8 tablespoons margarine
1 to 2 tablespoons flour
1 onion, chopped
1 cup milk

Juice of 1 lemon
1 large can salmon, save liquid
Cracker crumbs
1 egg, beaten

Brown onions in margarine until clear. Add enough flour to thicken. Stir in all of the salmon juice and milk to the onion mixture. When this thickens, add mashed salmon and lemon juice. Mix well. Chill in the refrigerator 3 to 5 hours.

When thoroughly chilled, shape into croquettes. Dip in beaten egg and roll in cracker crumbs. Fry in hot oil until tender. *Serves four.*

MRS. V. CLYDE MADDOX

TROUT AMANDINE

4   6-8 ounce trout fillets
½ cup flour
⅓ cup cooking oil
½ cup butter

½ cup slivered almonds
Salt and pepper to taste
1 lemon, thinly sliced
1 teaspoon parsley

Season cleaned trout with salt and pepper. Coat lightly with flour and sauté in hot oil until trout is golden on both sides. Drain oil from pan. Add butter and brown almonds slightly. Pour over trout. Garnish with parsley and lemon slices. *Serves 4.*

MARY ANN BENDERNAGEL

BAKED STUFFED FLOUNDER

½ cup chopped celery
½ cup chopped green onions,
   tops included
1 clove garlic, minced
8 tablespoons butter
1 cup bread crumbs
4 tablespoons lemon juice

½ pound boiled shrimp, chopped
½ pound lump crab meat
2 tablespoons chopped parsley
1 egg, slightly beaten
Salt, black pepper and cayenne
4 flounders, medium size

Sauté celery, onion and garlic in melted butter over low heat. Add bread, shrimp, crab meat, parsley and egg; mix well. Season with salt, black pepper and cayenne. Split thick side of flounder, lengthwise and crosswise, loosen meat from bone of fish to form a pocket for stuffing. Brush well with melted butter and lemon juice; salt and pepper, and stuff pocket. Place in pan with enough water to cover bottom of pan. Broil 3 inches from heat until fish flakes very easily with a fork. Baste every few minutes with liquid in pan. Serves four.

JOYCE LAFAYE CREWS

POMPANO EN PAPILLOTE

3 green onion and tops, chopped
3 ounces mushrooms, chopped
1 tablespoon butter
2 tablespoons flour
2 cups stock
Salt and pepper to taste
⅓ cup white wine

2 pounds pompano fillets
1 cup crabmeat
4 tablespoons butter
1 tablespoon white wine
½ teaspoon salt
1 egg yolk
1 lemon sliced

Brown mushrooms and onions lightly in butter; mix in flour; add stock; season and boil five minutes. Add wine (¼ cup). Sauté fillets and crabmeat separately in butter for five minutes. Add wine, salt and slightly beaten egg yolk to crabmeat and cook until thickened, stirring constantly.

Place some of the crab meat mixture on half of each fillet; fold other half on top; cover with sauce; fold well in parchment cooking paper, or place in paper bag and bake at 425° for about ten minutes. Arrange on platter garnished with lemon. Serves six.

FAVORITE RECIPE OF THE LATE MRS. EDWARD J. EBLE,
SUBMITTED BY CAROLYN EBLE LEVY

SCALLOPS ST. JACQUES

1 pound scallops
2 cups water
Juice of 1 lemon
3 tablespoons butter
½ teaspoon Tabasco sauce
1 teaspoon minced onion
1 bay leaf

2 tablespoons flour
1 teaspoon salt
2 egg yolks
½ cup grated cheese
2 tablespoons dry white wine
Paprika
1 cup light cream

Wash and dry scallops. If large, cut into pieces. In saucepan, simmer water, lemon juice, 1 tablespoon butter, ¼ teaspoon Tabasco, onion and bay leaf for 5 minutes. Drain. Melt remaining 2 tablespoons butter and stir in remaining Tabasco, flour and salt. Gradually stir in cream. Cook over low heat, stirring constantly, until mixture thickens and comes to a boil. Add small amount to egg yolks, stirring constantly. Return to saucepan; add cheese, wine and scallops. Pour into buttered shells; sprinkle with paprika. Bake at 350° for 10 to 15 minutes until golden brown. *Serves four.*

PHYLLIS DEBLANC ROBERT

COURTBOUILLON OF RED FISH

1 6 pound red fish
½ cup salad oil
¼ cup flour
2 large onions, sliced
1 can (No. 2½) tomatoes
2 bay leaves, chopped
¼ teaspoon allspice
1 teaspoon salt

4 green peppers, chopped
4 green onions and tops,
   chopped
1 clove garlic, minced
1 cup water
2 thin slices lemon
1 teaspoon minced parsley
1 cup claret wine

Slice red fish across the backbone in 3 inch wide slices. Make a roux with salad oil and flour; add onions and brown. Add tomatoes; cook for 5 minutes. Add remaining ingredients with the exception of the wine and fish; cook for 30 minutes at simmering temperature. Add fish and continue to simmer for 20 minutes. Add wine, bring to boil and serve. *Serves eight.*

LOBSTER THERMIDOR

3 live lobsters (1½ pounds each)
2 tablespoons olive oil
2 tablespoons butter
3 shallots, chopped
½ cup dry white wine

1 teaspoon English mustard
1 teaspoon parsley, chopped
2 cups Mornay sauce
1 tablespoon whipped cream
Parmesan cheese

Remove and crack claws. Split lengthwise, clean, dot with butter, salt and pepper. Put olive oil in flat pan, place lobsters and claws on it and bake in hot oven 20 minutes. Melt butter in saucepan, add shallots and wine. Cook until reduced ½ of original quantity. Add mustard, parsley and Mornay sauce. Cook to combine ingredients. Remove lobster meat and mix with ⅔ of sauce. Put a little sauce in each shell and fill them with lobster mixture, spread tops with remaining sauce mixed with whipped cream. Sprinkle with Parmesan cheese and brown under broiler flame.

TROUT MARGUERY

4 fillets of trout	½ cup cooked crab meat
Salt and pepper to taste	½ cup mushrooms, sliced
3 tablespoons olive oil	1 tablespoon flour
2 egg yolks, beaten	¼ cup dry white wine
16 tablespoons butter, melted	Paprika
1 tablespoon lemon juice	Salt
1 cup cooked shrimp, chopped	Pepper

Season fillets; place in baking pan and add olive oil. Bake at 375° for about 25 minutes. As fish bakes, prepare sauce. Place egg yolks in top of double boiler over hot, not boiling, water and gradually add melted butter, stirring constantly until mixture thickens. Add lemon juice, shrimp, crab meat, mushrooms, flour, wine and seasonings to taste. Stir and cook for 15 minutes longer to heat thoroughly. Place baked fish on platter or on individual dishes, cover with sauce and place in broiler to brown lightly. *Serves four.*

TROUT VERONIQUE

1 filet of trout from 1½ pound trout	½ cup very rich Hollandaise sauce
½ pint Vermouth	8 seedless grapes or deseeded grapes

Poach trout in Vermouth in pan that will cover trout, about seven minutes. Remove from poaching liquor and place on plate well drained. Then reduce liquid over fast fire to two cooking spoons of liquid. (Do not let fish bubble) Add Hollandaise sauce and stir briskly. Place grapes on trout, then sauce and glaze quickly in the broiler.

Hollandaise Sauce

½ cup butter	¼ teaspoon salt
3 egg yolks	Pinch of cayenne
2 tablespoons tarragon vinegar	

Heat the butter to bubbling in a small saucepan. Place the egg yolks, tarragon vinegar, salt and cayenne in the container of an electric blender. Cover and turn motor on low speed. Immediately remove the cover and pour in the butter in a steady stream. When all the butter is added, turn off the motor. *Serves 4.*

CARIBBEAN ROOM
PONTCHARTRAIN HOTEL

NEW ORLEANS BOUILLABAISSE

8 tablespoons butter
1 cup white onion, chopped
½ cup green onion, chopped
½ cup celery, chopped
1 teaspoon minced garlic
1 teaspoon parsley, chopped
1 tablespoon flour
2 cups whole tomatoes
3 cups fish stock
2 cups water
1 pound whole, raw shrimp,
    peeled, cleaned and deveined
2 dozen raw oysters
1 pound lump crabmeat
1 pound crayfish tails, peeled
3 gumbo crabs, cooked lightly
    in 2 tablespoons oil
1 teaspoon salt
1 teaspoon cayenne pepper
1 teaspoon thyme
1 teaspoon ground allspice
3 bay leaves
3 pounds trout or red snapper,
    filleted and cut in 3 inch
    slices
½ cup white wine
Saffron

Rub fillets in salt, pepper, thyme and allspice and garlic salt mixture.

In a large pot, melt butter and saute onion, green onions and garlic. Stir in flour and cook five minutes. Add tomatoes, salt, pepper, fish stock and water and spices. Cook 20 minutes. Add shrimp, oysters, crayfish, crabs, crabmeat and cook 5 minutes. Add wine. Bake seasoned fish at 350° for 15 minutes. Place fish in pot containing other ingredients; heat and serve in soup bowls; garnish with lemon slice. *Serves six.*

JOYCE LAFAYE CREWS

VENISON STEW MONTANA STYLE

2½ pounds cubed venison
2 stems of celery
1 medium bell pepper
½ pound carrots
1 large onion
1 bunch of shallots
3 tablespoons flour
Thyme
Bay leaf
Salt and pepper to taste

Sauté venison cubes in pot till brown, add celery, pepper, carrots, onions, shallots. Then take some of the drippings and make roux with flour. Add this to pot then add water and mix thoroughly. Cook till tender about 3 hours.

PITTARI'S

BAKED QUAIL IN SHERRY SAUCE

8 quail whole or breasts (soak
    overnight in 3 cups milk)
Salt and pepper to taste
1 cup flour
1 cube butter
1 chopped onion
1 chopped green sweet pepper
1 can cream of chicken soup
¼ cup white sherry wine
½ cup milk

Salt and pepper quail. Roll in flour. Brown in butter, (just brown, do not over cook). Place in baking dish. Pour off ½ drippings. Sauté onion and green pepper in same skillet. Add soup, wine, and milk. Mix well. Pour over quail. Cover and bake in 300° over 45 minutes.

PITTARI'S

DUCK WITH TURNIPS

3 teal ducks, cleaned and
    halved; or
2 French ducks, cleaned and
    quartered
1½ tablespoons flour
1 onion, chopped

1½ tablespoons butter
1 sprig parsley, not chopped
1 green onion, not chopped
4 1 inch squares of celery
5 medium turnips, parboiled
    separately

Fry duck lightly on both sides.

Make gravy as follows: Brown flour in butter. Add chopped onion and let mellow. Add parsley, green onion and celery with 3 cups of water. Let all simmer for about 10 minutes. Add duck to gravy and cook until it begins to tenderize. Add parboiled turnips and cook until duck is tender. *Serves four to six.*

JULIA BERKERY LAFAYE

SALMIS OF DUCK

3 teal ducks, cleaned and
    halved; or
2 French ducks, cleaned and
    quartered
1½ tablespoons flour
1½ tablespoons butter

1 onion, chopped
1 green onion, not chopped
1 sprig parsley, not chopped
4 1 inch squares of celery
2 dozen minced green olives
½ cup claret or Dubonnet

Fry duck lightly on both sides.

Make gravy as follows: Brown flour in butter. Add chopped onion and cook until mellow. Add parsley, green onion, celery and 2 cups water. Simmer 10 minutes. Add duck and cook until tender. Add olives and wine to gravy and simmer a few minutes. Serve on toast or minced in patty shells. *Serves four.*

JULIA BERKERY LAFAYE

SALMIS OF RABBIT

1 rabbit, cut up
Claret wine, enough to
    cover rabbit
2-3 cloves of garlic
3-4 dashes allspice

1 tablespoon flour, heaping
1 tablespoon butter
1 onion, chopped fine
Salt and pepper to taste
Tabasco sauce

Cover rabbit with wine. Add garlic and allspice. Refrigerate several hours. Drain rabbit. Dredge rabbit with flour; fry to a light brown. Make a roux with flour and butter. Add onion, salt and pepper. Add ½ pint cold water and stir. Add browned rabbit. Cover tightly and cook until tender. Serve with thin pieces of toast on top. Season with Tabasco sauce. *Serves four.*

MRS. SIDNEY BRADFORD'S RECIPE
Submitted by Walter McIlhenny, Avery Island

STEWED KIDNEYS I

1 onion
1 toe garlic
Thyme
Bay leaf
2 green onions

1 teaspoon flour
3 veal kidneys
Vinegar
Red wine

Fry a good sized onion, garlic, thyme, bay leaf and green onions until done. Add a scant teaspoon of flour and brown. Add kidney which has been cut in small pieces and freed of all fat and soaked overnight in a bath of vinegar and wine. After a few minutes, add more wine. Do not cook more than 15 minutes as kidney will harden. *Serves 4.*

MYLDRED MASSON COSTA

STEWED KIDNEYS II

4 medium size veal kidneys
1 large onion, chopped
2 small green peppers, chopped
2 cans tomatoes

1 can tomato sauce
1 tablespoon lard
Pinch salt and pepper

Clean kidneys. Cut in small blocks and rinse in water. Put all ingredients in cold water, cover and cook on medium fire for about 60 minutes. *Serves 4.*

INEZ ROSSI

TRIPE A LA CREOLE

2 pounds tripe
1 tablespoon salt
1 tablespoon vinegar
2 onions (sliced)
2 tablespoons butter
2 cloves garlic, chopped

3 tablespoons chopped ham
½ teaspoon thyme
2 bay leaf
1 can tomatoes
1 green pepper, sliced
Salt, pepper, cayenne

Wash tripe thoroughly in cold water. Cover tripe with water in saucepan. Add salt and vinegar. Boil 3 hours or until tender. Cut tripe in 2 inch x ½ inch strips. Sauté onions in butter until soft. Add garlic, ham, thyme, bay leaf and cook 2 or 3 minutes. Add tomatoes, green pepper, salt, pepper and cayenne. Boil 10 minutes and add tripe. Cover and boil 30 minutes longer. Serve with rice. *Serves 6.*

CALF'S BRAINS VINAIGRETTE

3 calf's brains
2 tablespoons vinegar
1 teaspoon salt
5 peppercorns
½ onion

1 carrot
4 sprigs parsley
1 bay leaf
¼ teaspoon thyme
Vinaigrette sauce

Wash brains in cold water. Remove membranes and soak in cold water for 1 hour. Place brains in a saucepan with enough cold water to cover. Add vinegar, salt, peppercorns, sliced onion, sliced carrot, parsley, bay leaf and thyme. Bring to boil, cover and simmer for 25 minutes.

May be served hot or cold with vinaigrette sauce. *Serves 6.*

CORNED BEEF

¼ teaspoon saltpeter dissolved
     in ¼ cup warm water
2 tablespoons sugar
2 cloves garlic (sliced)
1 tablespoon mixed pickling spices
4 bay leaves

2 teaspoons paprika
1 cup salt dissolved in 2 quarts
     water
5-6 pounds brisket beef
1 teaspoon cloves
1 medium sliced onion

Pour mixture over a 5 to 6 pound brisket of beef in a stone jar and cover with a weighted-down plate. Refrigerate—let this stand 3 weeks, turning the meat occasionally. Cover the meat with cold water, bring to a boil and simmer 1 hour. Drain, cover with fresh cold water, add 4 bay leaves, 1 teaspoon cloves and 1 medium sliced onion. Bring this gradually to a boil and simmer gently until meat is tender.

ENCHILADAS

1 pound ground beef
1 clove garlic, minced
1 teaspoon chili powder
1 medium onion, minced

6 tortillas
1 recipe enchilada sauce°
½ pound sharp cheese, grated

Brown beef, garlic and chili powder on controlled surface heat set at 325°. Dip tortillas in hot enchilada sauce and fill with cheese, onions and ground beef mixture. Roll and place with folded edges down in baking dish. Pour hot sauce over, sprinkle with remaining cheese and bake in 350° oven for 15 minutes or until cheese melts. *Serves 2-3.*

*ENCHILADA SAUCE

¼ cup oil
1 medium onion, minced
1 clove garlic, minced
1 can (10 ounces) tomato paste
2 cups water
2 teaspoons chili powder

1 teaspoon vinegar
1 teaspoon sugar
½ teaspoon oregano
½ teaspoon salt
⅛ teaspoon cayenne pepper

Combine oil, onion, garlic and tomato paste and simmer for 3 minutes. Add remaining ingredients and bring to boil. Reduce heat and simmer 15 minutes.

TACOS

1 pound ground beef
1 clove garlic, minced
½ medium onion, grated
½ teaspoon Worcestershire sauce
2 teaspoons salt

1 teaspoon chili powder
Pepper
½ cup cooking oil
8 tortillas, uncooked
Lettuce and tomatoes, chopped

Mix beef, garlic, onion, Worcestershire, salt, chili powder and pepper. Heat 2 teaspoons oil in skillet, add meat mixture; cook until brown. Keep hot. Heat remaining oil in separate skillet and fry one tortilla at a time. As tortilla is frying, fold it over in half (pocket book fashion) before it becomes brittle; fry until brown and drain. Fill pocket with small amount of beef mixture, top with lettuce and tomatoes. Serve at once. *Serves 4.*

SOUR CREAM TACOS

12 Tortillas
1 large onion, chopped

2 cloves garlic, chopped
2 tablespoons bacon fat

Cook onion and garlic in fat until soft, but not browned.

Add:

1 pint sour cream
1 can tomatoes
½ green pepper, chopped
½ pound American cheese, grated

4 hot peppers, chopped (for a milder flavor use 1 small can taco sauce)
Salt and pepper

Fry each of the tortillas in shortening or salad oil for just a few seconds to soften; drain and place six in a baking dish. Pour over these ½ of the above mixture. Place six more of the tortillas in the dish and pour remaining mixture. Bake at 350° for 30 minutes. *Serves six.*

MRS. ELLEN NICHOLAS

GRILLADES
(pronounced "gree-yads")

1 beef round, ½ inch thick	1 tablespoon chopped parsley
2 tablespoons shortening	1 clove garlic, minced
1½ tablespoons flour	1 cup hot water
1 large onion, sliced	1½ teaspoon salt
1 can #2 tomatoes	¼ teaspoon pepper
1 green pepper, minced	

Cut beef into individual servings. Brown meat in shortening; remove and set aside. Brown the flour in same shortening, add onion and cook until soft. Add remaining ingredients and place meat back in pan. Simmer for 1½ to 2 hours or until meat is tender. *Serves 4.*

ALINE RAULT KEHLOR

BARBECUE BEEF

5 pound roast	1 bottle barbecue sauce
1 can beer	

Salt and pepper roast and cook in oven as usual. When meat is done, slice and put into large pot. Add meat drippings, one can of beer, one bottle barbecue sauce. Simmer for at least one hour. The longer it simmers, the better the flavor. Any left over meat can be added; or freeze leftover meat during week, just add barbecue sauce and beer and simmer.

BARBARA CARL

BEEF STROGANOFF

2 large onions, chopped	3 bay leaves
1 stick butter	Dash Tabasco
1 large can sliced mushrooms	Salt, pepper, paprika
2 pounds round steak (sliced thin)	Garlic salt
12 ounces tomato juice	1 pint sour cream
2 tablespoons Worcestershire sauce	½ cup Vermouth

Sauté onions in large skillet until soft. Add mushrooms and brown meat. Add tomato juice, Worcestershire sauce and spices. Cook until meat is tender. Add Vermouth. When ready to serve, add sour cream. Serve over noodles. (Left over steak is a marvelous meat substitute.) *Serves 6.*

JOYCE LAFAYE CREWS

QUICK AND EASY POT ROAST

4-6 pound boneless roast
¼ cup chopped green pepper
1 large onion, chopped
2 toes garlic, minced
½ teaspoon salt
¼ teaspoon pepper

3 bay leaves
1 tablespoon parsley flakes
½ teaspoon onion powder
⅛ teaspoon garlic powder
⅛ teaspoon powdered thyme
1 cup water

Salt and pepper roast. Rub onion and garlic powder on meat. Place on a very large sheet of heavy duty foil. If meat has been stored in the freezer, it is not necessary to thaw it. Add remaining ingredients, except water, around roast. Roll foil to seal top and sides. Add water before sealing last side. Bake at 250° for 6-7 hours. When done, thicken gravy with flour and water. By cooking at such low temperature and having foil tightly closed, there will be less shrinkage of the meat.

Because of the low cooking temperature for this roast, it can be left unattended while you are out. You can also run it in the oven at bedtime and have a delicious Sunday noon meal ready with no effort.

MRS. ROBERT J. ARMBRUSTER

STUFFED BREAST OF VEAL

Have pocket cut in breast of veal from large end. Season inside and out with salt and pepper. Fill pocket with Sausage Stuffing. Fasten edges together with skewers or sew with string. Place on rack in shallow roasting pan and roast, uncovered, in 325° oven until done, allowing 30 minutes per pound

SAUSAGE STUFFING

¼ pound bulk pork sausage
⅔ cup fine dry bread crumbs
¼ cup water
⅓ cup grated onion
⅓ teaspoon salt

⅛ teaspoon pepper
⅛ teaspoon nutmeg
1 egg
2 tablespoons butter

Combine all ingredients.

BAKED BREADED MEAT

2 veal rounds (cut in
    3 inch squares)
3 cups bread crumbs
¼ cup chopped onions
½ teaspoon oregano

2 tablespoon chopped parsley
1 cup canned tomatoes
1 teaspoon salt
1 teaspoon black pepper
1 cup lard

Wipe meat with damp cloth. Mix bread crumbs, chopped onions, oregano, salt, pepper and tomatoes until it forms a soft ball in hand.

Spread lard on one side of meat; put it in the mix and spread lard on other side; put in mix.

Put in baking pan at 400° oven for 45 minutes or until brown.

MRS. JOHN SEGRETO

GREEN CHILI STEW

6 pounds pork loin
Large chopped onion
6 cloves garlic—minced

2 cans mild jalapeno peppers
1 jar hot jalapeno peppers
1 can tomatoes

Cut pork loin into cubes and brown in a little fat. Add onion and garlic and wilt. Rinse all the peppers in cold water, dice them, and add to stew. Mash the tomatoes and add them too. Add salt and pepper. Simmer uncovered until meat is tender.

This is good over rice and excellent in patty shells as a Hors d'oeuvre.

SYLVIA GLEZEN

SHORT RIBS, BAYOU STYLE

2 tablespoons shortening
3 pounds short ribs, cut
    in pieces
Flour
2 bay leaves
8 whole cloves
1 clove garlic, minced

½ green pepper, chopped
¼ cup chopped celery leaves
1 tablespoon salt
¼ teaspoon pepper
1 can (8 ounces) tomato sauce
1 cup water
½ lemon, sliced

Heat shortening in electric skillet set at 300°. Coat meat lightly with flour. Brown in skillet 5 to 8 minutes. Add remaining ingredients and turn temperature to 200°. Cover and cook 2 to 3 hours or until meat is very tender. Add more water, if necessary. *Serves 6.*

CHINESE SWEET AND SOUR PORK

Cube: 1 pound pork shoulder, set aside.

Make batter: 1 beaten egg; ½ cup flour; ½ teaspoon salt; 4 tablespoons water.

Salt and pepper pork and coat each cube with batter. Fry in deep oil until brown, drain, reserve. Mix following ingredients and heat to boiling:

1 cup drained pineapple chunks	¼ cup brown sugar
1 green pepper cut diagonally in 1 inch strips	¾ cup water
	1 tablespoon molasses
½ cup vinegar	½ carrot, raw, thinly sliced

Mix 2 tablespoons corn starch and ¼ cup water. Add to boiling mixture, lower heat and stir gently until thickened. Add reserved fried pork, mix well, serve at once with rice or fried noodles. *Serves 4.*

BEVERLY LAFAYE CLARK

PORK STUFFED CABBAGE ROLLS

2 pounds sauerkraut	2 lightly beaten eggs
2 heads green cabbage	2 tablespoons Hungarian Paprika
2 tablespoons bacon fat	⅛ teaspoon marjoram
1 cup chopped onions	1 teaspoon salt
2 cloves chopped garlic	Freshly ground pepper
1 pound ground lean pork	1 cup water mixed with 1 cup
¾ cup cooked rice	tomato purée

Place sauerkraut in bottom of large casserole. Boil head of cabbage until leaves are tender enough to roll up. Brown onions and garlic. Mix onions, garlic, pork, rice, eggs and spices together. Place a small amount of stuffing in each cabbage leaf. Roll up into small tight bundle. Place these on top of sauerkraut. Pour tomato purée over this. Close lid. Bake at 350° for 1 hour 45 minutes. Serve with sour cream sauce.

MRS. CHARLOTTE KELLY

VEAL PAPRIKA

3 tablespoons butter	⅛ teaspoon pepper
¼ cup thinly sliced onions	1½ cups chicken stock
4 veal cutlets, ¼ inch thick	¾ cup commercial sour cream
¼ cup flour	1 teaspoon paprika
1 teaspoon salt	

Melt butter in electric skillet set at 250°. Add onions and sauté until soft and golden brown. Remove onions and add cutlets that have been rolled in seasoned flour. Add stock and onions. Cover and turn to 200° Cook for 1 hour. Add sour cream and paprika and cook slowly until well blended. Serve with buttered noodles or rice. *Serves 4.*

SCALOPPINE À LA MARSALA

1 pound leg of veal, lean, sliced
    and beaten as thin as
    possible
1 wine glass (about 2 jiggers)
    Marsala wine or sherry

3 ounces butter
¼ cup flour
1 teaspoon salt

Mix flour and salt and dip veal slices in mixture.

Melt butter in frying pan and brown veal on one side for about 3 minutes. Turn and brown the other side about 3 minutes. Add the Marsala and cook for another minute or two.

Serve very hot, placing scaloppine on warmed serving dish. Cover with sauce from the pan.

NOTE: for good results meat must be very thin and cooking time very short.

CARIBBEAN ROOM
PONTCHARTRAIN HOTEL

VEAL CHASSEUR

2 pounds veal cutlet,
    ¼ inch thick
¼ cup butter
2 green onions, minced
1 small garlic clove, minced
1 pound mushrooms, sliced

½ cup dry white wine
2 tablespoons chopped parsley
1 teaspoon salt
Freshly ground black pepper
°Brown sauce

Trim fat from veal cut into 1 inch pieces. Saute in butter 10 minutes or until golden brown. Remove from skillet and keep hot. Saute shallots and mushrooms in butter, remaining in skillet for 5 minutes. Add wine and simmer 15 minutes or until liquid is reduced one half. Stir in brown sauce, parsley, salt and pepper. Add meat and simmer 5 minutes. *Serves 6.*

*BROWN SAUCE FOR VEAL CHASSEUR

1 onion, chopped
¼ cup diced celery
1 large carrot, chopped
½ cup butter
1 clove garlic, chopped
3 tablespoons corn starch

3 cups beef bouillon
2 tablespoons dry Madeira wine
½ teaspoon ground thyme
1 large bay leaf
½ teaspoon salt
6 peppercorns

Sauté onion, celery, carrot and garlic in butter, 10 minutes. Add corn starch to ½ cup cold bouillon. Stir into onion mixture. Add remaining bouillon, wine, thyme, bay leaf, salt and pepper. Bring to boil, reduce heat, cover and simmer 30 minutes stirring occasionally. Strain. *Makes 2 cups.*

ADELE SMITH

LASAGNE

1 onion, minced
1 clove garlic, minced
1 pound ground beef
2 tablespoons shortening
1 can whole tomatoes
1 can (6 ounce) tomato sauce
1 teaspoon oregano

1⅓ tablespoons salt
¼ teaspoon pepper
½ pound lasagne noodles
2½ quarts boiling water
1 cup ricotta cheese
½ pound sliced Mozzarella cheese
¼ cup grated Parmesan cheese

Sauté onion, garlic and meat in shortening, over medium heat, until redness disappears, about 20 minutes. Add tomatoes, tomato sauce, oregano, 1 teaspoon salt and pepper. Simmer, stirring occasionally, about 45 minutes. In another saucepan, cook lasagne in water with remaining 1 tablespoon salt 15 to 20 minutes. Drain. Pour ⅓ hot tomato-meat sauce in baking dish; add layer lasagne, ½ the ricotta cheese; ⅓ the Mozzarella slices and ½ the Parmesan cheese. Repeat layers as above, ending with remaining tomato-meat sauce and Mozzarella cheese. Bake at 350° 20 Minutes or until bubbly. *Serves 6.*

STUFFED TUFOLI

1 box Tufoli #82
3 onions
9 green onions
8 tablespoons margarine
½ cup parsley
2 pieces chopped celery
2 cans tomato sauce

1 can tomato paste
½ teaspoon sugar
3 pounds ground meat
10 toes garlic
½ cup Parmesan cheese
4 slices Mozzarella cheese

Preboil ½ box Tufoli at a time with one tablespoon lard. When slightly tender pour out in colander, pour cold water over them, and place immediately on wax paper.

Tomato Gravy (cook separately)—Chop two medium onions, four green onions, five pieces garlic; add these to one stick margarine and brown slightly. Add two pieces chopped celery, two large cans tomato sauce, 1 can tomato paste, juice from 2 cans stewed tomatoes, ½ teaspoon sugar (or less) and salt and pepper to taste. This gravy should be thick. Cook over very slow fire for about 2 hours.

Ground Meat Stuffing—3 pounds all beef ground meat, 5 green onions, finely chopped, ½ cup chopped parsley, 1 large onion—chopped, 5 pieces garlic—chopped. Let this cook some and then stuff the tufoli.

Put stuffed tufoli in long baking pan. Sprinkle ½ cup grated Italian cheese over tufoli, also spread strips of Mozzarella cheese over tufoli. Pour tomato gravy all over. Cover with foil and bake in oven at 350° approximately ½ hour—or until the tufoli are fully cooked.

INEZ ROSSI

CREOLE BEANS AND RICE

1½ cups dry red or kidney beans
1 large onion, diced
1 green pepper, chopped
1 can (2 cups) tomatoes
1 8 ounce can (1 cup)
    tomato sauce
1 bay leaf

Parsley to taste
1 clove garlic, minced
1 teaspoon chili powder
1½ teaspoon salt
Dash of cayenne and paprika
1 pound ground round steak
2 tablespoons bacon grease

Rinse beans; add to 1½ quarts cold water in heavy cooking vessel. (Iron pot is best!) Bring to rolling boil; simmer 2 minutes; remove from heat; cover, set aside and let stand for 1 hour. (You may prefer to let beans set overnight.)

After soaking period is completed, add 1 teaspoon salt to beans and return to stove. Cook with cover for 1 hour on very low heat.

Brown onion, green pepper and meat in hot fat. Add to beans. Stir in other ingredients. Cover and simmer 1½ hours; serve on fluffy cooked long grain rice. *Serves 6.*

Note: Before serving time, remove a cup of the beans and mash into a pulp. Return this paste to beans. This thickens the good bean liquid and gives a bean gravy appearance.

MRS. JACK (MARY S.) PARKMAN, MONTICELLO, MISS.

SWEET PEPPER CASSEROLE

6 bell peppers, chopped
3 medium onions (finely chopped)
4 tablespoons shortening
4 cloves garlic
2 eggs
3 slices stale bread

2 pounds ground beef
2 bay leaves
½ teaspoon thyme
2 tablespoons chopped parsley
1 cup seasoned bread crumbs
Salt and pepper to taste

Place oil in dutch oven over medium heat. Brown meat and remove from pot. Sauté peppers and onions in oil stirring frequently until soft. Return meat to pot and mix with peppers and onions. Put garlic through press and add to mixture. Soak stale bread in water. Squeeze water from bread. Add bread to mixture and blend. Stir in seasoned bread crumbs. Remove from heat. Let stand a few minutes. Beat eggs slightly and blend well into mixture. Salt and pepper to taste. Place mixture into 2 quart casserole. Sprinkle lightly with bread crumbs. Heat in oven preheated to 350° for 15 to 20 minutes or until thoroughly heated.

MRS. JACK EUMONT

GRANDMA MAE'S MEATLOAF

3 pounds ground beef, pork and
   veal combination amount
   to suit your family
⅓ cup chopped peppers (green)
¼ cup chopped onions
1 cup grated bread crumbs

2 beaten eggs
½ teaspoon black pepper
1 tablespoon salt
2 slices of bread (grated
   to roll meat in)

Mix meat, then add pepper, salt. Add chopped pepper and onions and mix well. Add beaten eggs and the cup of bread crumbs. Form meat into a roll and carefully roll the meat loaf in the 2 slices of grated bread crumbs.

Place meatloaf into a greased pan, dot meat with butter and sprinkle paprika on top.

Add 1½ cans of stewed tomatoes (chop tomatoes before adding them to the pan) by pouring them around the meat.

Bake in 350° oven for 45 minutes or until done. Occasionally check during the cooking period to see if more tomatoes should be added. Do not allow the stewed tomatoes to dry up. Add a little water if this begins to happen. *Serves 4-6.*

MRS. H. JESSUP

ROAST LEG OF LAMB

5-6 pound leg of lamb
1 teaspoon salt
¼ teaspoon pepper

1 teaspoon rosemary
1 cup orange juice
Mint

Place lamb on rack in shallow roasting pan. Sprinkle with salt, pepper and rosemary. Roast in 325° oven 2½ hours. Pour orange juice over lamb. Roast 45 to 60 minutes longer basting frequently. Garnish with orange slices and mint. *Serves 10 to 12.*

LIVER BROCHETTES

3 pounds calves liver
½ pound bacon

Pick over calves liver, eliminating gristle; cut liver in small pieces, approximately 2" square. Salt and lightly pepper the liver. Now, with scissors, cut sliced bacon in squares of about the same size; (bacon slices won't be "square" of course). Don't salt and pepper bacon. With skewers, put on first a piece of liver, then one of bacon, now another piece of liver, and of bacon. Continue until you have a serving—about as big as a good-sized chicken's drumstick. Allow ½ pound of liver for each person. When liver and bacon have been threaded on skewers—bacon piece on top of each— put in a lightly greased baking dish. Prop skewers partially erect, rather than laying them flat. Bake for 30 minutes in average oven. Delicious and inexpensive! *Serves 4-6.*

MRS. REGINALD C. WATSON

LIVER AND ONIONS

1 pound veal, lamb or calves
    liver, sliced
¼ cup flour
2 tablespoons shortening

½ teaspoon salt
¼ teaspoon pepper
2 onions, sliced

Coat liver slices with flour. Melt shortening in electric skillet set at 300°. Brown meat and season. Turn heat to 225° and cook 10 to 15 minutes. Set liver to one side of skillet. Add onions and brown in small amount of shortening. Turn to cook and brown evenly. Season onions and serve with liver. *Serves 4.*

STUFFED LAMB CHOPS

4 lamb chops (2 inches
    thick)
1 cup sliced mushrooms
4 chicken livers, chopped

½ stick butter
Salt and pepper
Garlic salt
¼ cup olive oil

Split chops in half, cutting to the bone. Sauté mushrooms and chicken livers in butter until done, but not brown. Season with salt and pepper; stuff into chops. Sprinkle with garlic salt and brush with olive oil. Broil on both sides until brown, about 10 to 12 minutes on each side. *Serves 4.*

BACON, APPLES AND SWEETS CASSEROLE

4 medium sized sweet potatoes
1 pound sliced bacon

2 apples

Wash potatoes and boil in salted water until soft, 20 to 30 minutes. Peel and arrange in greased casserole or baking dish. Core, pare, slice apples and place between potatoes. Arrange strips of bacon on top. Bake at 375° about 25 minutes until bacon is crisp. Baste occasionally with bacon fat.

MRS. GEORGE T. GUEDRY

BROILED HAM STEAK WITH PINEAPPLE SAUCE

1 cup brown sugar
1 teaspoon prepared mustard
2 tablespoons pineapple juice

⅛ teaspoon ground cloves (optional)
1 ready-to-eat ham slice,
    ¾ inch thick

Combine first four ingredients to make sauce. Slash fat edge of ham steak. Brush with sauce and broil 3 inches from heat about 10 minutes. Turn with tongs, brush with sauce and broil until brown. Pineapple rings may be placed on ham during the last few minutes of cooking time. *Serves 4.*

BAKED HAM

Temperature: 325°   Time: 15 to 18 minutes per pound

Ham   ½ teaspoon cinnamon
2 teaspoons dry mustard   2 tablespoons vinegar
½ cup sugar   Cloves

Place ham in shallow pan, fat side down and bake. Remove ham from oven and skin. Then score and insert whole cloves. Spread mixture of mustard, sugar, cinnamon and vinegar over ham.

Replace in oven and set control to 400° and bake 15 minutes more.

MRS. RUBY ARMBRUSTER

HAM LOAF

2 cups leftover ham, minced   Dash pepper
24 saltines, crushed   ½ cup brown sugar
½ onion (medium), minced   3 teaspoons vinegar
2 eggs, slightly beaten   2 teaspoons dry mustard
½ cup milk   1 8½ ounce can crushed pineapple

Blend ham, saltines and onions. Mix well. Add eggs, milk and pepper to mixture to form loaf in 5"x9" loaf pan or small casserole. Combine brown sugar, vinegar, dry mustard and pineapple. Pour over loaf. Bake in 350° oven for 30 minutes. *Serves 6.*

MRS. OWEN BRENNAN, JR.

SAUSAGE—HAM JAMBALAYA

1 pound hot sausage cut in   3 green onions
½ inch cubes   2 bay leaves
1 thick slice ham, diced   Pinch of thyme
thickly   2 cups uncooked rice
1 large onion, chopped   3 cans tomatoes
3 celery sticks, chopped   Salt to taste
½ green pepper, chopped   Chopped parsley

Use a heavy iron pot or aluminum. Brown sausage, add ham. After browning, add all ingredients until tender then drain off fat residue. Add tomatoes, cook a few minutes, add uncooked rice, salt, thyme, bay leaves.

Cook uncovered ½ hour. Turn occasionally with fork. Cover and simmer 1 hour, stirring with fork so as not to stick. If needed, add a little water. Should cook dry, grain for grain.

Above may be cooked with shrimp also. Delicious. *Serves 8 to 10.*

MRS THEODORE DEYNOODT HALLER

*Garden of the Second Ursuline Convent
Destroyed by the River in 1912*

Soups and Sauces

SOUPS

Soup is probably more truly characteristic of the French Cuisine than any other dish, and in this respect, New Orleans has retained her French heritage throughout the years. In France, the morning cup of bouillon was served in the most exclusive homes, and a plate of good soup with a cup of claret was the unvarying breakfast collation of the peasantry. Because of New Orleans fondness for Café a la creole, the serving of soups became relegated to later meals, but the rule was still "a daily plate of soup," with the varieties increasing with the years.

Soupe-en-famille, a beef vegetable soup, might be called the daily soup of the Creoles. In any well regulated household the big soup kettle, with its *"bouilli"* or meaty soup bone, was put on to boil on the back of the stove before breakfast, where it simmered for six or seven hours before the vegetables were added, and then for another hour afterwards. A large bowl of such a soup, a thick slice of *bouilli,* a salad, a loaf of hot French bread, with, of course, claret to wash it down—who could ask for more?

Gumbo is New Orleans own concoction, not French and not Spanish, but rather an original dish developed out of the specialties of the area. One type is made of okra combined with shrimp, crabs, ham, chicken or sausage. Okra came to the New World from Africa, and the Angolan word for it—*kingombo*—is claimed by some to have given the dish its name. Another variant is made with filé, called *kombo ashish* by the American Indians, and others see here the derivation of the word. The Choctaws dried sassafras leaves and pounded them in a mortar to a fine powder. This they used as a thickener for soups and stews, a practice soon adopted by the early settlers, and gumbo filé is as popular today as when the Indian first gave it to the white man. *Gumbo Z'Herbes,* a corruption of the original French *Gumbo aux Herbes* was made of seven greens and was especially cooked on Holy Thursday for good luck. Always on that day the vendors in the French Market would invite housewives to "buy your seven greens for good luck." *Gumbo Choux,* or Cabbage Gumbo, was the soup of the poor, but as soul foods go, it was none the less a feast when a ham hock simmered gently in the fragrant "pot likker."

The *potages maîgres* were fast-day soups prepared during Lent in Catholic New Orleans. They included the soups made of beans, peas and lentils, the various purées and cream soups, and the specialties developed in the city such as corn soup, winter okra soup, rice soup (Riz au Maîgre) sorrel soup (the famous Potage à la Bonne Femme), and summer fast day soup (Potage Maîgre d'Eté). When these were served with buttered croutons or hot crusty rolls, the Lenten fast lost its penitential nature.

New Orleans bisque is a rich soup very complicated in preparation.

Any of the Louisiana seafoods may be the basis of a bisque, but without doubt the most popular was (and is) crawfish bisque. The base is made with—among other things—a *roux brun,* conventional seasonings, and the powdered shells of the crawfish. The well cleaned and scrubbed heads are stuffed with a hot and spicy filling of the meat and are placed in the center of the bowl of bisque to be eaten as best one can. But delicacy is no question here so long as one has the bisque to eat.

Let us reverence the Creole of passing memory who scoured the swamps for crawfish and turtle; who stirred the herbs of his one-time enemy, the Indian, into his stews; who sowed the okra seeds brought to the city in the ears of African slaves. Venturesome indeed, and much to be praised, for he it was who gave us—our menu of delectable soups.

GUMBO Z' HERBES

1 bunch each in any combination,
    but use at least five: spinach,
    collard, mustard and turnip
    greens, watercress, chicory,
    beet tops, carrot tops, pepper
    grass, radish tops
1 bunch parsley (chopped)
½ bunch green onions (chopped)
1 small green cabbage (chopped)
1 gallon water
1 pound boiled ham (diced)

1 large white onion (diced)
4 tablespoons flour
4 tablespoons shortening
2 bay leaves
2 sprigs thyme
¼ teaspoon Allspice
Salt
Pepper
Cayenne pepper
1 pint oysters

Wash greens thoroughly; remove stems and hard centers. Boil in water about 2 hours. Strain greens and reserve water. Chop greens finely. Make a brown roux of the flour and shortening in large cast iron pot. Add ham and onion, and sauté 5 minutes or until soft. Add greens and simmer 15 minutes. Add reserved cooking water, all spices and simmer 1 hour. 15 minutes before serving add oysters and any oyster water available. Adjust seasoning to taste. Serve over rice. *Yield: 6-8 servings.*

ANNE BADEAUX CONWAY

VICHYSSOISE

4 leeks, thinly sliced
4 green onions, thinly sliced
2 pounds potatoes, peeled and
    thinly sliced
½ cup butter

1 cup half and half
1 cup milk
1 teaspoon salt
1 tablespoon chopped chives
Freshly ground black pepper

Sauté leeks and green onions in butter in a deep pan. Add potatoes and enough water to barely cover them. Boil, reduce heat and simmer for about 1 hour. Press through coarse sieve. Cool and chill for 1 hour. Before serving, stir in chilled cream and milk. Sprinkle with chives and black pepper. *Serves 6.*

BEVERLY LAFAYE CLARK

CHICKEN GUMBO FILÉ I

1 large chicken, cut up
4 tablespoons cooking oil
1 large onion chopped
2 quarts chicken stock, heated
2 tablespoons parsley, minced
2 tablespoons green onion, chopped
1 clove garlic, minced

Thyme, fresh if available
Salt and pepper
1 pound smoked sausage or
    andouille
1 pint oysters
1 tablespoon filé powder

Usng a heavy bottomed pot, brown the chicken slowly in oil. Remove the chicken. Sauté the onion until soft (not brown). Return chicken and any juice that has run from it to the pot with the onions, cover and cook on low heat for about ten minutes, stirring occasionally to prevent burning. Add the heated stock, parsley, green onion and garlic. Season generously with thyme. Add salt and pepper to taste. Cook over low heat until chicken is tender. Add sausage and cook for 10 minutes. Add oysters and oyster-water and cook for 10 minutes more. Skim off excess fat. Remove from fire and immediately add the filé powder, stirring while adding. Serve over steamed rice.

MARIE L. BADEAUX

CHICKEN GUMBO FILÉ II

Salt and pepper to taste
1 3 to 4 pound hen cut-up
1 large onion, chopped
1 bell pepper
2 ribs celery
½ pound bologna, cubed

½ pound salami, cubed
½ pound ham, cubed
3 tablespoons cooking oil
3 tablespoons flour
2 dozen oysters
1 tablespoon filé

Fry hen. Sauté seasoning in fat from hen. Make a roux with flour and oil in heavy skillet. Season hen with salt and pepper and boil in water 3 to 4 inches above hen. Add seasoning and meats. Simmer to consistency of thin gravy and until chicken is very tender. Add oysters; cook until oysters curl. Add filé. Serve with white rice.

MRS. JOHN MONTALBANO

COACH HOUSE BLACK BEAN SOUP

4 cups black beans	Smoked ham bone and rind
5 quarts cold water	3 leeks, sliced thin
3 ribs celery, chopped fine	4 bay leaves
3 large onions, minced	1 tablespoon salt
8 tablespoons butter	½ teaspoon freshly ground pepper
2½ tablespoons flour	1 cup dry Madeira wine
½ cup finely chopped parsley	2 hard boiled eggs, chopped

Wash beans, cover with cold water and soak overnight. Drain. Add more cold water and cook over low heat 1½ hours.

In soup kettle, sauté celery and onions in butter until tender. Blend in flour and parsley and cook for 1 minute. Gradually stir in beans and liquid. Add ham bone and rind, leeks, bay leaves, salt and pepper. Simmer over low heat 4 hours.

Remove ham bone and rind, bay leaves and force beans through sieve. Combine puréed beans and broth with Madeira. Bring soup to a boil, remove from heat and add hard boiled eggs. Float a thin slice lemon on each serving. *Serves 8-10.*

MRS. JACK EUMONT

CLEAR MUSHROOM SOUP

1½ pounds mushrooms, chopped fine	¾ teaspoon beef extract
	Salt and pepper to taste
6 cups water	Dry Vermouth

Cook mushrooms and water in covered saucepan for 2½ to 3 hours. Strain, pressing all mushroom liquid out with the back of a wooden spoon. Reheat and stir in beef extract, salt and pepper. Stir in a little dry vermouth and serve. *Serves 6.*

MRS. OWEN BRENNAN, JR.

CORN SOUP

3 large onions, chopped	3 tablespoons cooking oil
1 ham bone from baked ham	1½ pound canned tomatoes
3 cans corn	Salt and pepper to taste
2 cans water	

Place oil in sauce pan and heat. Sauté onions until soft. Add ham bone. If baked ham bone is not available, use regular ham bone and add a pinch of sugar to the tomatoes. Add tomatoes to saucepan and simmer with onions about 5 minutes. Add corn, water, salt and pepper and simmer about 45 minutes. Serve over croutons.

TILLY FORET RIVET

WILD DUCK AND OYSTER GUMBO

1 wild duck
2 tablespoons shortening
2 tablespoons flour
1 cup onion, chopped
Salt and pepper

2 dozen oysters, with liquid
About 2 quarts hot water
¼ cup parsley, minced
¼ cup green onion tops, minced

Cut duck in 6 pieces, season with salt and pepper. Brown in shortening. Remove from pan. Make roux with shortening and flour. Add onions and cook until tender. Add duck, hot water and cook at simmering temperature until meat is very tender, about 2 hours. Add oysters, parsley and onion tops. Correct seasoning. Serve with French bread and over rice. *Serves 6-8.*

MAE O'NEIL

CRAYFISH BISQUE

Boil 6 pounds of crawfish in salted water for 20 minutes. Remove meat from tails and set aside. Pick out 2 dozen of largest heads, clean thoroughly. Prepare liquid by crushing legs and claws and boil in 2 quarts water 15 or 20 minutes. Allow to settle then strain. Prepare stuffing for heads by combining 4 sprigs parsley, 3 green onions, 1 clove garlic, 1 slice bread, 1 egg and 2 cups meat from crawfish. Fry all together in 4 tablespoons butter, pack mixture tightly into cleaned heads. Brush flour over heads and fry in hot fat until brown. Make a roux using 4 tablespoons butter, 4 tablespoons flour, 1 onion, 1 clove garlic, ½ bell pepper, 1 cup chopped celery, 1 small can tomatoes, ½ can tomato paste, salt and pepper to taste. Cook 20 minutes. Add prepared crawfish liquor to thin roux to desired consistency. Drop heads and 1 cup crawfish meat into mixture, simmer slowly until ready to eat. Serve with hot, freshly boiled rice. *Serves 4.*

MRS. GEORGE T. GUEDRY

ONION SOUP GRATINEE

4 large onions
4 tablespoons butter
1 tablespoon flour
1½ quarts consommé

6 small toasted French
    bread slices
3 ounce Gruyère cheese
3 tablespoons Parmesan cheese

Slice onions thinly and separate rings. Melt butter in large saucepan. Add onion rings and cook very slowly over a low flame, stirring with a wooden spoon until rings are soft. Blend flour well and slowly add consommé. When soup begins to boil, lower heat, cover and simmer for 20 minutes.

Place toasted bread rounds with Gruyère cheese in soup dish, sprinkle Parmesan cheese and pour soup over it. Bowl may be placed under broiler to achieve a topping of brown sizzling cheese. *Serves 6.*

JOYCE LAFAYE CREWS

OYSTER SOUP I

8 tablespoons butter
1 bunch green onions, chopped
½ cup finely chopped parsley
2 small ribs celery, chopped
3 tablespoons flour

1 cup oyster liquid
1 quart milk
3 dozen oysters, cut in thirds
Salt and pepper to taste

Sauté onions and celery in butter. Add parsley and cook 2 minutes. Blend in flour, stirring constantly. Do not allow to brown. Add oyster liquid and milk, stirring constantly. Cook slowly over very low heat for ½ hour. Before serving, add the oysters, cook for 5 minutes. Season to taste. Serve with French bread or crackers. *Serves 6.*

MRS. JOFFRE J. CROUERE

OYSTER SOUP II

4 dozen oysters
3 pints oyster-water
5 sprigs celery tops
2 bunches, green onions, minced

6 tablespoons butter
4 tablespoons parsley, minced
Salt and pepper
½ pint half and half

Simmer oyster-water and celery tops for about 20 minutes. In another pot, sauté the green onions in 4 tablespoons butter until soft. Add the oysters and cook on low heat, stirring occasionally. Strain the hot oyster-water into the oyster and green onions. Add salt and pepper to taste. Cook covered for about 20 minutes. Add parsley and the rest of the butter. Before serving, heat (do not boil) the half and half and stir into the hot soup. Serve immediately. *Serves 6-8.*

MARIE L. BADEAUX

CRAB SOUP

12 crabs
1 heaping cooking spoon flour
¼ pound butter
1 No. 2 can of tomatoes
2 ribs celery with tops, chopped
3 sprigs thyme

1 large onion, minced
4 sprigs parsley, minced
8 slices lemon
1½ teaspoons paprika
1 hard boiled egg, chopped fine
Sherry (1 tablespoon to each plate)

Clean and halve crabs. Melt butter and add flour, mixing constantly until golden brown. Add onions and let simmer for 5 minutes. Add crabs and 3 cups of hot water after putting in crabs. Simmer for 5 minutes then add tomatoes, celery, thyme and parsley and 6 cups hot water. Let boil vigorously about ½ hour. Add Sherry, lemon and hard boiled egg, salt and pepper to taste. (If soup becomes thickened add water until desired consistency is reached). *Serves 6.*

JULIA B. LAFAYE

TURTLE SOUP

2 pounds turtle meat
1 rib celery
2 green onions
1 medium white onion, minced
2 sprigs parsley
2 cloves garlic, minced
2 whole cloves garlic

12 tablespoons butter
3 tablespoons flour
8 ounces strained tomatoes
Sherry
Sliced lemon
Hard boiled eggs (2 eggs, chopped fine)

Place turtle meat in warm, salted water (enough to cover meat about 6 inches) and boil 30 minutes, skimming until clear. When clear, turn off fire and add celery, 2 green onions, parsley and 2 whole cloves garlic.

Brown flour with butter. Add onion, tomato, minced garlic. Salt and pepper to taste. Simmer about 10 minutes. Add to meat broth and cook until meat is tender or about 1 hour. Strain soup.

When serving, add to each bowl the following: 1 tablespoon Sherry, 1 slice lemon, 1 heaping teaspoon finely chopped hard boiled egg and a little turtle meat. *Serves 8 to 10.*

JULIA BERKERY LAFAYE

RED BEAN SOUP

Leftover red beans
Few pinches of thyme
Few drops Tabasco

Water
Hard French bread

Put cooked beans in blender with enough water to mix. Pour into saucepan and heat and add thyme and Tabasco. Cut slices of French bread to use as croutons and serve hot.

MRS. J. McNULTY

SPLIT PEA SOUP

1 package split peas
1 medium onion, chopped
3 cloves garlic, minced

½ pound chopped ham
4 tablespoons butter
Salt and pepper

Wash peas. Cover with 2 inches water and boil with onion and garlic, 1 hour or until soft. Strain through collander and then through fine strainer, using as much water as necessary to push purée through strainer. Add chopped ham. Simmer 45 minutes. Season to taste with salt, pepper and butter. More water can be added if soup is too thick. Heat 10 minutes and serve. *Makes 6 servings.*

MARIE L. BADEAUX

SEAFOOD GUMBO

2 medium onions	3 pounds small tender okra
2 pounds shrimp	1 bay leaf
8 crabs	1 clove garlic
1 small can of tomatoes (strained)	Salt and pepper to taste

Clean shrimp and wash thoroughly. Fry shrimp in small amount of lard on low fire for about ten minutes. Add two finely cut onions and continue frying slowly until onions melt out.

Scald 8 crabs. Clean, removing legs, and halve. Fry crabs separately, using 1 tablespoon of lard, until browned. (about 10 minutes).

Put crabs and shrimp mixture in large ALUMINUM pot and blend thoroughly. (CAUTION: do not use an iron pot. Its use will cause okra to blacken).

Slice thin 3 pounds okra. Cook separately (using aluminum ware) on slow fire until ropey substance cooks out (about 20 minutes) and okra separates. Add okra and 1 small can strained tomatoes to pot with crabs and shrimp. Add bay leaf, 1 clove garlic, salt and pepper to taste. Add two quarts of water and let boil lightly for one hour or until desired consistency is reached. *Recipe serves 12 to 14.*

JULIA B. LAFAYE

VEGETABLE SOUP

3 pounds chuck roast	1 small head cabbage
2 short ribs (optional)	1 sweet potato
1 can stewed tomatoes	2 turnips
1 can tomato paste	6 carrots
3 onions	1 can white corn
3 green onions	1 package frozen garden vegetables
1 bell pepper	1 Irish potato
½ bunch parsley	2 ears corn on cob (optional)
1 stalk celery	½ teaspoon garlic powder

Cover roast with water and boil 1 hour. Add other ingredients, all well chopped, except potatoes, corn and frozen vegetables. When meat is tender and vegetables soft, add remaining ingredients. Salt and pepper to taste. *Serves 8.*

JOYCE LAFAYE CREWS

Pirates Alley

SAUCES

There was no one in history quite like Louis XIV, the Sun King of France. Out of his intense egotism came Versailles, where he played host to the aristocracy, hundreds at a time, amid a dining splendor difficult to visualize today. During this period a master chef came to prominence who was to do much to start the classic cuisine of France on its ascendancy. In 1651 François Pierre de la Varenne published a new cookbook, *La Cuisinière Française,* which marked the departure from heavy foods and thick over-spiced sauces to a new delicacy in cooking. He taught that meats should be simmered in their own juices rather than smothered in the bread-crumb sauces of the earlier cuisine. He introduced the use of *roux* and created a series of new sauces, outstanding among them being the *sauce Bécamel,* named for Louis' Lord Steward. During the period of the French Revolution, many aristocrats came to New Orleans, exiles from their native land in search of a compatible culture. They brought with them their penchant for elegant dining, their recipes and their chefs. This infusion of pure French haute cuisine bound the food traditions of the little city on the banks of the Mississippi even more closely to that of the mother country. However, no one who has ever eaten a beef daube *à la Créole* or a chicken fricassée (New Orleans style) could ever accuse the Creoles of following derivative recipes. These are New Orleans' own, and hers too, the many sauces originated in her restaurants and served to perfection. In his own right, the Creole was a *saucier suprême.*

BARBECUE SAUCE

4 pounds onions
1 rib celery
28 ounces ketchup
20 ounces Worcestershire sauce
10 ounces steak sauce
2 tablespoons prepared mustard

¼ cup white vinegar
Juice of 2 lemons
3 cans tomato sauce (8 ounces)
1 tablespoon chili powder
4-5 pods garlic
½ gallon cooking oil

Chop onions, garlic, celery and combine with other ingredients in a large iron pot. Let simmer for several hours, stirring occasionally until all is reduced to a mash.

CHICKEN BAR-B-Q SAUCE

1 cup ketchup
1 cup water
⅓ cup bacon fat or
    cooking oil
¼ cup lemon juice
½ cup chopped celery
1 medium onion, chopped

2 tablespoons vinegar
2 tablespoons brown sugar
2 tablespoons Worcestershire sauce
2 teaspoons salt
1 teaspoon prepared mustard
½ teaspoon black pepper
½ teaspoon Tabasco sauce

Mix all ingredients together in a saucepan and cook slowly until thick. Spread over each piece of chicken as it is cooking. Continue turning chicken and spreading sauce on each piece till done.

MRS. ROBERT J. ARMBRUSTER

CREOLE SAUCE

10 soft tomatoes, chopped,
    NOT peeled
3 medium onions, chopped
3-4 ribs celery, chopped or
    the leaves from a bunch
1½-2 chopped green peppers

1 tablespoon oregano
Salt and pepper
Hot sauce to taste
1 tablespoon parsley
1 tablespoon liquid smoke flavoring

Cook onion in bacon fat until soft. Add tomatoes, one at a time, stirring over high heat (you want a sautéed flavor, not a boiled taste). Add remaining ingredients and cook 4-5 minutes.

This is great for all sorts of sandwiches and to have on hand to dress up chicken, hamburgers, leftovers. Freeze in small portions (1 cup).

MRS. MARY ELLEN NICHOLAS

HOLLANDAISE SAUCE

8 tablespoons butter
2 egg yolks, beaten

Juice of ½ lemon

Melt butter by putting in cup standing in hot water. Put egg in double boiler over very slow fire. Add lemon juice slowly and mix constantly. When egg yolks and lemon juice are thoroughly blended, remove from flame and very slowly add melted butter, stirring while adding to prevent cracking. If the sauce becomes thickened, add a little water and mix well.

JULIA BERKERY LAFAYE

INSTANT HOLLANDAISE SAUCE

1 cup butter or margarine
4 egg yolks
2 tablespoons lemon juice

¼ teaspoon salt
1 pinch cayenne pepper

Heat butter till bubbly. Meanwhile, in blender, put egg yolks, lemon juice, salt and pepper.

Cover blender and turn to high. Immediately remove cover and slowly add butter in a steady stream.

MARY ALICE McKAY

MOCK HOLLANDAISE SAUCE

2 tablespoons margarine
8 tablespoons mayonnaise

Few drops lemon juice
Freshly ground pepper to taste

Melt margarine in bowl over hot water. Mix with mayonnaise and lemon juice. Add pepper. Beat rapidly.

GEORGE ANDING

SAUCE BEARNAISE

1 cup dry white wine
4 egg yolks, beaten
2 tablespoons tarragon vinegar
1 tablespoon minced green onions
½ teaspoon chervil

1 teaspoon tarragon
1 cup melted butter
½ teaspoon salt
Freshly ground black pepper

Add 2 tablespoons of wine to egg yolks. Beat and set aside. Combine remaining wine with vinegar, green onions, ¼ teaspoon chervil, ½ teaspoon tarragon, salt and pepper and cook until reduced to two-thirds or about 15 minutes, stirring occasionally. Remove from heat. Add egg yolk mixture slowly, stirring briskly. Add butter very gradually, a few spoons at a time, beating thoroughly after each addition. Strain through a fine tea strainer. Add the remaining tarragon and chervil and stir. *Yield: About 2 cups.*

BEVERLY CLARK

NEW ORLEANS HOT PEPPER SAUCE

2 quarts whole red peppers   1 bag pickling spices
2 quarts white vinegar

Cook on high fire until bubbles form, then cook on low for 2 hours. Strain pulp and seeds out with food mill. Bottle—doesn't have to be refrigerated.

MRS JAMES G. NEEDOM

POULTRY BASTING SAUCE

12 tablespoons butter, melted
2 teaspoons paprika
1 teaspoon sugar
1 teaspoon salt
½ teaspoon pepper

¼ teaspoon dry mustard
Few grains cayenne pepper
½ cup lemon juice
½ cup hot water
Few drops hot sauce

Combine butter and seasonings. Blend in lemon juice, hot water and hot sauce. 2 tablespoons of grated onion may be added. *Yields 1½ cups.*

ANNE B. CONWAY

SAUCE FOR STEAK

6 tablespoons Dijon mustard
6 tablespoons Worcestershire sauce

10 tablespoons butter
Tabasco sauce

In small saucepan, combine mustard, Worcestershire and butter. Place over low heat, stirring constantly, until butter is melted and sauce is hot. Do not boil. Adjust seasoning with Tabasco. *Makes 1⅓ cups.*

MARCHAND DE VIN SAUCE

¾ cup butter
⅓ cup mushrooms (chopped)
⅓ cup shallots (chopped)
½ cup onions (chopped)
2 tablespoons garlic (chopped)
½ cup minced ham

2 tablespoons flour
½ teaspoon salt
⅛ teaspoon pepper
¾ cup beef stock
1 cup red wine

Melt butter sauté mushrooms, ham, shallots, onion and garlic. Add flour, salt and pepper. Brown well, blend in stock and wine. Simmer over low heat 40 minutes. *Yield: 2 cups.*

BRENNAN'S

Pittari's Restaurant

SALADS AND DRESSINGS

Salad for the Creoles, like soup, was an expected accompaniment of meals. *Salades* were served with the *petit déjeuner* and were especially favored at the hunt breakfast, when a pungent salad of green herbs, particularly chervil, complemented the menu of game and boiled grits. The green salad was the favorite, made so because of the wealth of leafy vegetables grown in the area: lettuce, romaine, escarole, chicory, endive, sorrel, water cress, roquette, spinach and chard. To add a herbaceous tang, the *cuisinière* added chives, shallots, leeks, parsley, and tarragon, and for texture contrast cabbage, radishes, cucumbers, celery and boiled okra. Special occasions brought out the artistry of the Creole cook and then were served the magnificent *Poisson à la Mayonnaise, Chevrette Rémoulade* and the like.

Being a *bonne ménagère* who understood the properties and flavors of foods, the good wife could make up into a salad a small piece of last evening's *bouilli* by mincing the meat with green onions and celery and serving it *à la vinaigrette*. She could produce a *Salade à la jardinière* out of leftover green beans, carrots, mushrooms or peas by marinating them over night with pickling spices and serving them on a bed of greens. Yesterday's red beans or simple boiled okra, when combined with thinly sliced onions and a good French dressing, were always welcome and are served to this day where old eating habits are preserved.

Tossing a salad in a wooden bowl was ritually performed at the Creole table. First the bowl itself was held sacred and was used only for this purpose, never being washed with soap and water but only wiped dry before being put away. Foreign flavors could not then find their way into the wood of the bowl and mar the flavor of the salad. A cut clove of garlic was pressed around the inside of the bowl, or bits of French bread rubbed with garlic, called *chapons*, were tossed with the salad to insinuate just the smallest hint of rich flavor, never enough to predominate or overwhelm the dressing's piquancy. Then — the supreme moment — the greens were coated with the seasoning mixture and tossed thoroughly but lightly.

The conventional French dressing was made with one part of vinegar to three parts of olive oil, and was salted and peppered to taste, allowing one tablespoon of dressing per serving. There were, however, many variants of this basic salad *assaissonement* with each Creole household having its own recipes and preferences. Some preferred wine vinegars; others added a dash of claret, lemon or lime juice, Creole mustard, horseradish, herbs or peppers. A particularly Creole condiment was made by marinating "bird's eye peppers" in olive oil or vinegar to liven up the meat or seafood salads, soups and stews. These were small peppers best described by their name and of an indescribably delicate flavor. If sufficiently marinated, one or two drops of the oil or vinegar would be all that was necessary to add a superb tang to any dish. But be careful! For this one must have *la bouche créole.*

Regardless of the recipe employed, an old Spanish saying provides the unfailing rule in making a good salad: "A miser for vinegar, a spendthrift for oil, a wise man for salt, and a mad man to mix them all together."

AVOCADO PONTCHARTRAIN WITH SHRIMP REMOULADE

¼ cup tarragon vinegar
2 tablespoons horseradish mustard
1 tablespoon ketchup
1½ teaspoons paprika
½ teaspoon salt
¼ teaspoon cayenne pepper
½ cup salad oil

¼ cup minced celery
¼ cup minced green onions
   and tops
2 pounds shrimp, cleaned and
   cooked
4 medium avocados

In a small bowl, combine tarragon vinegar, horseradish mustard, ketchup, paprika, salt and cayenne pepper. Slowly add oil, beating constantly. Stir in celery and onions. Pour sauce over shrimp; marinate in refrigerator 4 to 5 hours. Halve and peel avocados. Lift shrimp out of sauce and arrange 5 to 6 shrimp on each avocado half. Serve with cooked chilled asparagus spears, carrot strips, sliced cooked beets, and sliced hard-cooked eggs. Pass additional Remoulade Sauce or French Dressing. *Serves 8.*

MRS. JAMES L. DUNN

BEAN SALAD

1 can cut green beans
1 can cut yellow wax beans
1 can red kidney beans
¼ cup chopped green pepper
1 medium onion, sliced thin

½ cup cider vinegar
⅔ cup cooking oil
½ cup sugar
1 teaspoon salt
1 teaspoon pepper

Drain beans, rinse well and drain again. Add green pepper and sliced onion to beans. Mix other ingredients and add to bean mixture. Mix well and marinate overnight in refrigerator. *Serves 6.*

JOYCE DESHAUTREAUX

ROYAL BEETS

1—16 ounce can sliced beets
   (drained)
½ cup sugar
2 tablespoons plain flour
½ cup vinegar

½ cup orange juice
¼ cup water
2 tablespoons margarine or butter
½ teaspoon salt

Mix sugar and flour, add vinegar, orange juice and water. Cook until thick. Add salt and margarine. Mix with beets before serving. Serve on leaf lettuce. *Serves 4.*

MRS. ADA DUPLECHIN

CHICKEN GLACÉE

1 4 pound chicken	3 sprigs parsley
4 ribs celery	3 green onions
2 medium onions	2 packages gelatin

Boil chicken with celery, onion, parsley and green onion, salt and pepper. When tender, strip meat from bones. Cut in small pieces. Strain broth. There should be approximately 2 pints of broth. To each pint, add 1 package of gelatin.

Grease molds with olive oil. Half fill molds with liquid. Add minced chicken to molds and let set about 10 minutes in a cool place. Then fill molds with remaining liquid. Chill in refrigerator. Serve with mayonnaise on lettuce leaf and garnish with slice of stuffed olive. *Makes 12 individual molds.*

JULIA BERKERY LAFAYE

CHICKEN SALAD

1 4 pound hen	2 chopped hard boiled eggs
4 ribs celery	1 head lettuce, shredded
2 medium onions	2 tender ribs celery (cut small)
3 sprigs parsley	String before cutting.
4 green onions	1 pint mayonnaise

Boil chicken with a rib of celery, ½ onion, parsley and 2 green onions, salt and pepper to taste. When tender, strip chicken meat from bones. Cut in small pieces. Put cut chicken meat in mixing bowl. Add lettuce, celery, hard boiled eggs and blend with mayonnaise. *Serves 12.*

JULIA BERKERY LAFAYE

CRANBERRY MOLD

1 large can cranberry sauce	3 celery ribs
2 packages cherry jello	1½ cups pecan pieces
(regular size)	1 cup liquid (drained pineapple
1 large can crushed pineapple	juice)
1 large apple	

Drain pineapple in colander. Press out juice—yields 1 cup liquid. Add water if necessary. Mash cranberry and heat in deep pot. Boil pineapple juice. Add jello and hot cranberry to hot pineapple juice. Add crushed pineapple, apple, celery and pecans. Place in mold and chill. *Serves 6.*

MRS. HELEN WIRTH

FABULOUS CUCUMBER SALAD

Peel and slice 3 large cucumbers very thin. Mix into this a level teaspoon salt and let stand for 15-20 minutes. Then squeeze out all the juice. Optional: green onions, sliced paper-thin.

Meanwhile, prepare this dressing:

½ cup water
3 tablespoons vinegar
1 level teaspoon sugar

Paprika (sweet paprika—as much as desired for color and flavor)

Add the cucumbers and mix well. Refrigerated, this will keep for many days.

MRS. MORITZ FEKETE

ANTIPASTO
ITALIAN SALAD

1 pint salad olives
1 jar ripe Greek olives
1 3 ounce package Romano cheese
3 slices Swiss cheese

12 slices imported salami
6 ounces chopped sweet pickles
2 celery center ribs and tops
2 tablespoons olive oil

Finely chop cheese, salami and celery and combine with other ingredients. Toss well and refrigerate. Tastes best after 12 hours of marinating. *Serves 6.*

JOYCE LAFAYE CREWS

MARDI GRAS SALAD

1 can petit pois (small green peas)
1 can French style green beans
1½ cups diced celery
1 green pepper, diced
Tiny jar chopped pimento

1 small onion, diced
1 cup sugar
½ cup vegetable oil
1 tablespoon salt
¾ cup vinegar

Drain juices from beans, peas and pimento. Mix all ingredients in mixing bowl with cover (plastic is best). Let marinate in covered bowl in refrigerator. Should marinate at least 12 hours. *Serves 4.*

MRS. JACK (MARY S.) PARKMAN

POTATO SALAD

8 potatoes cooked in skin till tender, then chopped
4 hard boiled eggs, chopped fine
4 green onions, chopped fine
4 ribs celery, chopped fine
2 crispy bacon strips, chopped fine

1 large dill pickle, chopped fine
Add 1 tablespoon pickle juice
½ small green pepper, chopped fine
Salt and pepper to taste

Combine ingredients in bowl and add 4 heaping tablespoons mayonnaise or salad dressing, 1 heaping tablespoon yellow mustard. For added zip, add a little juice from bottled cocktail onions. *Serves 15 or more.*

ETHEL SEILER FITZSIMMONS

POTATO SALAD TEXAS STYLE

5 medium potatoes, boiled
   and cubed
1 medium onion, chopped
3 ounce Bleu cheese, crumbled
3 tablespoons vinegar

1 cup celery, minced
¾ cup mayonnaise
¾ cup sour cream
3 tablespoons sugar
Salt and pepper to taste

Combine above ingredients and refrigerate overnight. Garnish with pimento and olives and parsley.

MARY BRAKEHILL

RECEPTION SALAD

No. 2 can crushed pineapple
1 package lemon jello
2 3 ounce cream cheese
Small jar pimentos, drained

½ cup diced celery
⅔ cup pecans, chopped
Pinch of salt
½ pint whipping cream

Drain juice off pineapple (at least 1 cup); bring to boiling point. Add lemon jello. Cream the cheese and pimento with a fork. Mix well until it is yellow. Add cheese and pimento to cool jello.

Add: Crushed pineapple
½ cup diced celery

⅔ cup pecans, chopped
Pinch of salt

After all this is blended, whip the cream and fold into the mixture. Cover and put in refrigerator. *Serves 4.*

MRS. SIBYL K. OLSEN

MARINATED SNAP BEANS

1 pound fresh snap beans,
   cut diagonally (about 4 cups)
1 cup fresh carrots, sliced
⅓ cup fresh lemon juice
¼ cup chopped parsley
1 teaspoon salt

⅔ cup olive or salad oil
1 medium onion, thinly sliced
2 tablespoons chopped green
   pepper
⅛ teaspoon black pepper

Cover and cook green beans and carrots in a small amount of boiling water for 5 minutes. Drain and cool.

Combine ingredients in a large bowl. Add cooled vegetable mixture. Refrigerate at least 4 hours, turning occasionally. *Serves 4-6.*

MRS. JOHN MONTALBANO

POPPYSEED SALAD DRESSING

Put in blender:
  1½ cups sugar
  2 teaspoons dry mustard

  2 teaspoons salt
  ⅔ cup vinegar

Blend, then add:
  3 teaspoons onion juice
  3 teaspoons poppyseeds

  2 cups cooking oil (pour
    slowly)

Keep refrigerated. Especially good over fruit salads.

MARY ALICE McKAY

SHRIMP REMOULADE

1 pound boiled shrimp, peeled
3 green onions, minced
3 sprigs parsley, minced
2 ribs celery, minced
2 tablespoons creole mustard

4 tablespoons olive oil
1 tablespoon lemon juice
¾ teaspoon paprika
Salt and pepper to taste

Cut shrimp in 3 or 4 pieces and mix with green onion, parsley, celery (all minced) and dressing ingredients in above listed proportions. *Serves 4.*

JULIA BERKERY LAFAYE

SOUP MEAT SALAD

2 cups cooked soup meat (shredded
    and chopped)
3 green onions, chopped
Salt and pepper

1 heart of celery and tops,
    chopped
2 tablespoons parsley, chopped

Toss lightly with a sauce vinaigrette. Chill. *Serves 6.*

JULIA BERKFRY LAFAYE

SEATTLE SALAD AND DRESSING

4 ribs celery, cut Chinese
    style
1 can heart of palm

2 heads bibb lettuce
½ jar chopped Macadamia nuts

Combine ingredients and toss with dressing.

Dressing:
  ⅓ cup salad oil
  2 tablespoons lemon juice
  1 teaspoon sugar
  ½ teaspoon salt
  ½ teaspoon bitters

  ¼ teaspoon paprika
  2 tablespoons chopped green olives
  1 tablespoon chopped onions
  2 tablespoon poppy seeds

Serves 4.

PAULA PALMER

TOMATO ASPIC

5 ribs celery
4 green onions
¼ cup chopped parsley
½ cup chopped olives
2 dill pickles, chopped
¼ cup chopped parsley

46 ounces V8 juice ice
3 packages plain gelatin
Salt, pepper, Worcestershire,
  Tabasco, garlic juice,
  lemon juice
½ teaspoon sugar

Heat ½ of 46 ounces of V8 juice. Soften 3 packages plain gelatin in ½ cup water. Stir softened gelatin into warm juice until dissolved. Pour in the other ½ can of juice and stir.

Season with salt, pepper, Worcestershire sauce, few drops Tabasco, garlic juice, ½ teaspoon sugar and lemon juice. Put bowl in refrigerator to jell slightly. Finely chop: celery hearts, green onions, parsley, olives and dill pickles. Add this to the slightly set gelatin mixture. Stir. Place in a mold and set in refrigerator to jell. Serve with mayonnaise on bed of lettuce. *Serves 10.*

AIMEE VATH

WHIPPED CREAM MAYONNAISE

1 cup whipping cream
½ cup mayonnaise

¼ teaspoon salt

Whip cream. Fold in mayonnaise and salt. Delicious on plain or molded fruit salads.

AIMEE VATH

MAYONNAISE I

1 egg
1 teaspoon salt

2 tablespoons vinegar
1 cup oil

Place egg, salt and vinegar in blender or mixer. Start at high speed and *immediately* add about half of oil slowly. Continue pouring the remainder of the oil, but even slower, almost drop by drop. Turn blender or mixer off as soon as the last of the oil is added.

MARY ALICE McKAY

MAYONNAISE II

3 raw egg yolks
2 yolks hard boiled egg
2 cups chilled olive oil

Salt to taste
1½ tablespoons vinegar (or more,
  to taste)

Set blending bowl in nest of cracked ice. Mix thoroughly raw egg yolks and boiled egg yolks. Add olive oil, drop by drop, until all of the oil has been taken up by the egg. Add vinegar and salt to taste, mixing constantly until all ingredients have been well mixed. Makes about 1½ pints.

JULIA BERKERY LAFAYE

FRENCH DRESSING I

1 onion, chopped fine
2 cloves garlic, peeled but
    left whole
1 cup each: oil and vinegar
1 can tomato soup
1 teaspoon salt

1 teaspoon dry mustard
1 teaspoon paprika
1 teaspoon pepper
1 teaspoon sugar
1 tablespoon Worcestershire sauce

Mix and store in a jar for a few days to improve flavor. Keeps up to several weeks.

MRS. MARY ELLEN NICHOLAS

FRENCH DRESSING II

1 can tomato soup
½ cup sugar
½ cup vinegar
2 tablespoons yellow mustard
1 tablespoon pepper

1 tablespoon salt
1 large onion, grated
2 tablespoons Worcestershire sauce
1 clove garlic, minced
1 cup vegetable oil

Mix well and store in refrigerator. *Makes about 3 cups.*

SYLVIA GLEZEN

The Old French Market

VEGETABLES AND CEREALS

The lands are very fertile and yield several crops each year. A man here, working two days, only digging the ground and sowing it, would reap more than sufficient to support himself during all the year . . . We eat peas and wild beans and many kinds of fruits and vegetables that are strange to me. We also eat sweet potatoes, which are large roots, cooked in hot ashes as you cook chestnuts but are much sweeter, very soft and delicious . . . The Company of the Indies carries on much commerce in furs, beavers, and other wares with the savages who are persons of whom the majority are very sociable. (Excerpts from the letters of Sister Marie Madeleine Hachard, dated October 27, 1727, and April 24, 1728.)

The site of the present French Market, just inside the levee of the Mississippi River, was a trading place in the early days of the city for New Orleanian and "sociable savages." Indians living in the area of Lake Pontchartrain paddled up Bayou St. John as near as possible to the settlement and then carried their trade wares along a portage to the site of the market. The Choctaws came in from Bayou Lacombe with filé, sorrel and Life Everlasting weed, used in medicinal teas, and the Germans brought their superb vegetables all the way from the up-river section which they settled early in French Colonial history. In 1791 the Spanish administration erected a roofed structure on the site which the French called *La Halle*, and from then on the market expanded rapidly. In 1812 the market structure was destroyed by a hurricane, and when it was rebuilt in 1813 a special building, *La Halle des Boucheries*, was added as were stalls for specialties such as *daube glacée* and *boudin*. The present building is an arcaded structure with stalls on either side of a central promenade, designed for the display of fruits, vegetables and local specialties of every description. And what a display the old market could put on! First there were the beautiful leafy greens: the lettuce, watercress, escarole, parsley, cabbage and spinach; then the brilliant purples and reds and golds of eggplant, tomatoes and carrots, of pumpkins, radishes, turnips and grapes. Strings of garlic and peppers hung in festoons, and melons were heaped at the sides of stalls, some halved or plugged to show the luscious meat inside and tempt the buyer.

From the earliest days of the colony New Orleans has carried on a romance with the vegetable. Creoles bought of them heavily for their *soupe en famille* and their endless *salades*. They also stuffed them with mixtures of ham, chopped onion and bread crumbs; or again they might serve them with a *sauce veloutée* or a hollandaise. They prepared them *étouffées* with a bit of pickled pork, or combined several vegetables, or *puréed* them, or baked them with a good *fromage*, or fried them in batter or pickled them. This is so even today in New Orleans where the vegetable boiled in plain salted water is rarely served.

A perennial favorite, the mirliton, seldom heard of outside of south

Louisiana, is a vine-grown pear-shaped vegetable of the gourd family. In many of the back yards of New Orleans the mirliton vine can be seen running on fences and trellises, heavy with the weight of the beautiful pale green pears. They are usually served with a stuffing made of the pulped meat to which minced onion, garlic, shrimp, cream and bread crumbs have been added—a Creole feast!

The locally grown cereals, corn and rice, were vitally important to early New Orleanians. There is mention of two types of bread in the very early days. One was made of Indian corn meal, and the other was half flour and half rice. The early colonists also ate hominy (saccimité) which was dried corn prepared by a method taught them by the Indians. Sister Marie Madeleine wrote her father in 1727 that "The people of Louisiana find very good a food called *sagamité*, which is made of Indian corn crushed in a mortar, then boiled in water, and eaten with butter and cream." Grits is simply corn from which the yellow outer covering has been removed and which is ground to superfineness. It is served with breakfast, either buttered or with gravy, an all-time favorite being "grillades and grits." Grits can be cooled, cut in squares and fried in egg batter, or (mixed with milk and eggs and baked) as Confederate pudding. But regardless of the manner of serving, grits plays a prominent part in the city's menus today.

However, few who know the city's cuisine will deny that rice is the great New Orleans staple. It is the accepted accompaniment of all gumbos and bisques and is served with red beans to create a dish associated with New Orleans around the world. Jambalaya, a truly Creole dish in that it contains elements of both French and Spanish cookery, is a derivative of the Spanish paella. *Calas*, the delicate little rice cakes that were sold about the city streets in the by-gone days, were another specialty of the rice bowl. And there are others, all distinctive.

There was a saying among the Creoles when a young person wanted to try his luck away from New Orleans: "Tant pis pour toi! La sagamité te ramènera." (Never mind, hominy will bring you back.) Just how many ex-citizens have returned to the city for the hominy and grits is hard to say, but there is no doubt that her fragrant kitchens are remembered with joy and nostalgia by all her sons and daughters wherever they may be.

BARLEY WITH MUSHROOMS

2 cups barley
½ cup chopped mushrooms,
    canned or fresh
½ cup chopped onions

¼ cup butter
4 cups chicken stock
Salt to taste

Sauté mushrooms and onion in butter until tender. Stir in barley and chicken stock. Cover, bring to boil and reduce heat to low simmer. Cook 30 minutes or until liquid is absorbed and barley is soft. Salt to taste. Can be cooked ahead and reheated. Excellent with barbequed chicken, lamb, etc. *Serves 6 to 8.*

ANNE BADEAUX CONWAY

BAR-B-QUE BAKED BEANS

1 pound, 12 ounce can oven
    baked beans
⅓ cup sherry
2 tablespoons brown sugar
1 teaspoon instant coffee powder

1 teaspoon dry mustard
1 tablespoon lemon juice
¾ cup ketchup
2 large onions,
    minced

Combine all ingredients. Turn into casserole and bake in 300° oven about 1½ to 2 hours. *Serves 4.*

MAE O'NEIL

GREEN BEANS ALMOND

1 pound fresh green beans
¼ cup slivered blanched almonds
¼ cup butter

¼ teaspoon salt
1 to 2 teaspoons lemon
    juice

Snip ends off of green beans. Wash and cut diagonally. Cook until tender in boiling water. Drain. Meanwhile, cook almonds in butter over low heat until golden, stirring occasionally. Remove from heat and add salt and lemon juice. Pour over hot beans. *Serves 4.*

MARY MARKS

YAMS COINTREAU

4 large yams
Boiling water
¼ cup Cointreau

4 tablespoons butter
1 teaspoon salt
⅛ teaspoon pepper

Cook yams in water to cover 30 to 40 minutes, or until tender. Drain, cool and peel. Mash sweet potatoes; blend in Cointreau, butter, salt and pepper. Beat until fluffy. *Yield: 4 servings.*

YAMS TROPICANA

Peel and slice yams into ¾ inch pieces. Grease a casserole dish. Arrange layers of yams, apricot halves and sliced pineapple. (Combinations of peaches and sliced apples can also be used.) Add white raisins and pecan pieces over this. Pour juices over all. Top with brown sugar and dot with butter or margarine. Cover and bake at 325°. This is rich, but tastes heavenly.

MRS. GILMORE SNYDER
URSULINE MUSIC DEPT.

SWEET SOUR MIRLITON

6 quarts mirlitons	6 cups sugar
6 onions	½ cup mustard seeds
1 cup salt	1½ tablespoons celery seeds
1½ quarts white vinegar	¼ teaspoon cayenne pepper

Soak the mirlitons and onions that have been thinly sliced in 1 cup of salt with water to cover in stone or enamel vessel for three to five hours. Drain and taste. Rinse if too salty.

Combine vinegar, sugar, mustard and celery seeds and pepper. Bring to boil.

Simmer for 5 minutes. Add mirliton and onion mixture, bring just to simmer and hold 3 to 5 minutes.

Jar and seal while hot. *Yield: 9 to 10 pints.*

MRS. JOHN K. MAYER

STUFFED ARTICHOKES I

5 large artichokes	5 cloves garlic, finely cut
¾ pound saltine crackers	1 jar Parmesan cheese
½ cup Parmesan bread crumbs	8 ounces olive oil
½ cup parsley flakes	

Clean artichokes by snipping off pointed ends of each leaf and washing well; turn upside down and drain.

Mix all dry ingredients together on wax paper. Scoop cracker crumb mixture into artichokes, separating leaves as you do. Place in a large pot of shallow salted water. Pour olive oil lavishly over each. Boil covered about one hour. (It may be necessary to add more water.)

MRS. MOON LANDRIEU

STUFFED ARTICHOKES II

1 artichoke	½ bell pepper
1 cup seasoned bread crumbs	3 ounces shrimp, cooked
½ onion	Olive oil
1 clove garlic	⅓ cup Parmesan cheese

Cut stem and top off artichoke. Steam until tender and remove center leaves. Finely chop onions, garlic, bell pepper and shrimp. Brown in olive oil. Moisten bread crumbs and cheese with small amount of water. Add onions etc.; mix well. Stuff artichoke with mixture. Sprinkle artichoke with olive oil. Heat in 350° oven. Serve.

MARIE ELEANORA SEILER

ASPARAGUS CASSEROLE

2 cans asparagus	sliced almonds
2 cans cream of mushroom soup	American cheese, grated
4 hard boiled eggs sliced	

Place in layers, finishing with almonds and cheese. Bake at 350° for 45 minutes.

MRS. JOSEPH B. DAVID, JR.

EGGPLANT BUNDLES

1 medium eggplant, peeled	1 tablespoon green pepper, chopped
½ pound ground beef	
4 tablespoons finely chopped celery	1 tablespoon parsley, minced
1 medium onion, chopped	Salt
	Pepper

Slice eggplant lengthwise thinly. Place slices in deep dish and salt very well. Let stand 20 minutes. Rinse eggplant with cold water and drain well. Roll each slice around heaping tablespoon meat mixture, wrap in thin slice of bacon, fasten securely with toothpicks. Place side by side in baking dish. Cover with mixture of: 1 cup water; ½ cup tomato paste; 1 small can mushrooms. Bake 1½ hours uncovered at 350°, turning once.

STUFFED EGGPLANT I

2 medium eggplants	1 can peeled tomatoes (1 pound can)
1 pound bulk hot pork sausage	1 teaspoon salt
1 large onion, diced	Dash black pepper
1 clove garlic, minced	½ cup grated Parmesan cheese
½ cup celery	
½ cup sweet pepper, diced	½ cup bread crumbs
	½ teaspoon sugar

Parboil eggplants in salted water (10 minutes.) Let cool. Brown sausage quickly. Remove all but 2 tablespoons fat. Sauté onion, garlic, celery, salt and green pepper. Add eggplants, with tomatoes, sugar and cheese. Simmer 5 minutes more. Top with crumbs mixed with rest of cheese, and bake at 375° for 45 minutes.

MRS. NICK MATULICH

STUFFED EGGPLANT II

1 large eggplant, diced
2 onions
2 ribs celery
2 cloves garlic

1 pound shrimp
¾ pound crab meat
¾ cup seasoned bread crumbs
½ cup water

Sauté onion, celery and garlic in light olive oil. Add eggplant and saute until tender. Add shrimp (cut into small pieces), crab meat, bread crumbs and water. Turn into buttered casserole dish. Sprinkle with bread crumbs. Bake 1 hour or until lightly browned on top. *Serves 4-6.*

ELSA G. NADLER

STUFFED EGGPLANT III

6 medium eggplants
1 pound small shrimp
1 pound white lump crabmeat
4 bell peppers, chopped
4 medium onions, chopped

½ cup parsley
3 cloves garlic, minced
Salt and pepper to taste
½ cup chopped celery
Bread crumbs

Boil eggplants until soft; remove meat. Keep eggplant shells.

Saute bell pepper, onion, celery and garlic until limp; add eggplant meat. Smother on medium heat until most of water is cooked out; add shrimp. Cook for 20 minutes. Place in bowl and fold in crabmeat and parsley. Let cool and add enough bread crumbs to make firm enough to stuff shells. Sprinkle bread crumbs and paprika on top. Pour oil or dot with margarine. Bake at 350° until brown. *Yield: 12 stuffed eggplant halves.*

BON TON RESTAURANT

EGGPLANT SUPREME

3 large eggplants
1 large onion, chopped
¾ pound bacon, chopped
3 cloves garlic, chopped
    or ½ teaspoon garlic powder
1½ cups Italian style bread crumbs
2 tablespoons parsley flakes

¼ teaspoon rosemary leaves
¼ teaspoon ground cumin seed
⅛ teaspoon powdered thyme
¼ teaspoon Italian seasoning
½ teaspoon salt
¼ teaspoon pepper

Cut eggplants in half and place in boiling salted water. Cook until tender, about 40 minutes. Drain. When cool, scoop out the pulp and remove most of the seeds. Cook chopped bacon until brown. Drain off all but ¼ to ½ cup grease, add onions and garlic (not powdered), and cook slowly until onions are clear. Add eggplant, parsley flakes, garlic powder (if not using fresh garlic), cumin seed, thyme, Italian seasoning, salt and pepper. Cook about 5 minutes over very low fire. Add Italian style bread crumbs. Mix well and cook about 5 minutes more. Remove from heat and spoon into casserole dish. Dot with butter and sprinkle more bread crumbs over top lightly. Before serving, bake at 350° for 15 minutes or until bread crumbs are brown.

MRS. ROBERT J. ARMBRUSTER

CREOLE SNAP BEANS

2 pounds fresh green beans
¼ pound ham
3 large onions, chopped

3 cloves garlic, minced
1½ cups water, approximately
Salt and pepper

Wash, string and cut beans into small pieces. Fry ham until light brown; remove ham. Pour off drippings except for 2 tablespoons; add onions and garlic and cook until onions are soft. Return ham to skillet; add beans, ½ cup water, and salt and pepper to taste. Cover; turn heat low and cook for about 1½ hours. During cooking period occasionally add additional water. *Serves 6.*

BROCCOLI DELIGHT

1   10 ounce package frozen
        broccoli spears or
        chopped broccoli
½ teaspoon salt

⅛ teaspoon pepper
½ can cream of mushroom soup
⅓ cup evaporated milk
½ can of French fried onion rings

Prepare as package directs, cooking it only 4 minutes. Drain and put into a greased 1 quart baking dish. Sprinkle salt, pepper, and grated cheese over the broccoli. Pour over the top a mixture of cream of mushroom soup and evaporated milk. Bake at 350° for 20 minutes. Take from oven, top with ½ can of French fried onion rings. Bake 5 minutes more. *Serves 4.*

MRS. A. L. VITTER

BROCCOLI WITH HERB SAUCE

1 bunch of broccoli or
     2 packages of frozen broccoli
2 tablespoons of flour
½ cup water
½ cup sour cream
½ teaspoon horseradish

¼ teaspoon thyme
½ teaspoon marjoram
½ teaspoon lemon juice
½ teaspoon salt
Dash of pepper
2 tablespoons butter

Cook broccoli in boiling, salted water until tender. Meanwhile, melt butter in a saucepan, blend in flour. Add water and cook until thick, stirring constantly. Add all other ingredients and serve hot over cooked broccoli. *Serves 6 to 8.*

MARY MARKS

SMOTHERED CABBAGE

1 medium cabbage, cored,
 and cup-up
½ pound ham, chopped
1 medium onion, chopped

1 small sweet pepper,
 chopped
Salt and pepper
Sugar

In heavy pot, sauté ham until slightly brown. Add onion and sauté until soft. Add cabbage and sweet pepper and cook down until soft and juicy. Uncover and cook until liquid evaporates. Add salt, pepper, and sugar to taste. *Serves 6.*

MARIE L. BADEAUX

CARROTS AND WHITE GRAPES

1 (13½ ounce) can small
 whole Belgian carrots
30 seedless white grapes

4 tablespoons Cointreau
4 tablespoons butter

Drain carrots on paper towel. Wash and drain grapes. Melt butter in skillet over medium flame. When melted, add Cointreau, stir. Add grapes and carrots and cook over low flame for 4 minutes. Stir often. Serve hot with fresh mint leaves among grapes and carrots. *Serves 2.*

MRS. LEON J. REYMOND, JR.

CREAMED CORN

8 ears corn
1 cup cream

1 cup milk
1 tablespoon butter

Put butter, milk and cream in double boiler and stir constantly until blended. Add raw corn cut from cob and mix well. Cook 20 minutes. (5 to 10 minutes longer, depending on thickness desired).

JULIA BERKERY LAFAYE

CORN PUDDING

8 ears corn
2½ cups milk
5 eggs

⅓ teaspoon salt
¼ teaspoon sugar

Grate corn lightly. Mix with milk, eggs, sugar and salt until all are thoroughly blended. Grease pyrex dish with butter. Pour in corn mixture and bake for 20 minutes in moderate oven (350-400°). When baked, dot pudding with butter. Serve immediately. *Serves 12.*

JULIA BERKERY LAFAYE

EGGPLANT AND TOMATO CASSEROLE

¼ cup salad oil
1 medium onion, chopped
¾ pound mushrooms, sliced
½ medium green pepper, chopped
1 medium eggplant, cut in
    1 inch cubes, peeled
1 can (1 pound) pear shaped
    tomatoes

1 teaspoon salt
1 tablespoon chopped parsley
1 cup EACH grated Parmesan
    and shredded Mozzarella
    cheese
2 eggs, beaten

Use large fry pan, heat oil; add onions, mushrooms and green pepper. Sauté over medium heat until vegetables are limp, 5 minutes. Stir in eggplant, tomatoes, salt and parsley. Cover and simmer slowly until eggplant is tender (25 minutes), stirring often. Uncover and increase heat, if needed, to reduce liquid. Meanwhile, combine Parmesan and Mozzarella with eggs; spoon half eggplant mixture into 2½ quart casserole and top with half the cheese. Repeat layers, ending with cheese. Bake uncovered in 375° oven for 25 minutes. If prepared ahead and cold, bake 45 minutes.

PAULA PALMER

STUFFED MIRLITONS

4 mirlitons
½ cup ham, finely
    chopped
8 tablespoons butter
2 large onions, minced
1 cup cut-up shrimp,
    boiled and peeled
1 teaspoon salt

1 tablespoon parsley, minced
1 teaspoon thyme
2 bay leaves
1 teaspoon black pepper
2 cups fresh bread
    (soaked and squeezed almost
    dry)

Boil mirlitons until tender. Cut in half and scoop out the centers. Mash the centers well, then place in a pot with hot butter, heat a bit, then add chopped ham, onion, and shrimp. Add salt, parsley, thyme and bay leaves. Simmer 20 minutes. Now add soaked bread, black pepper and simmer slowly for 10 minutes, stirring almost all the time. Place in mirliton shells, or in casserole, and sprinkle with bread crumbs. Bake in 375° oven until brown and crisp.

MARY JANE WARREN

STUFFED ONIONS

10 medium white onions	½ teaspoon salt
½ pound ham seasoning, chopped	Freshly ground black pepper
1 tablespoon parsley, chopped fine	½ teaspoon celery seed
2 tablespoons shallots, chopped	¾ cup bread crumbs
	6 tablespoons butter

Peel and boil onions until tender. Remove centers and be sure to leave enough of the onion to form a cup to fill. Sauté shallots, parsley and centers (scooped from onions and chopped well) in the butter. Add ham and seasoning. Cook until all is thoroughly blended. Add ½ cup bread crumbs, mix and remove from heat. Fill onions. Top with remaining bread crumbs. Run under broiler to heat.

BEVERLY LAFAYE CLARK

ONIONS AU GRATIN

12 white onions, peeled	1 pint breakfast cream
8 tablespoons butter	Salt and pepper
½ cup flour	½ cup grated cheese

Cook onions in boiling salted water until tender. Drain. Make cream sauce with butter, flour and cream. Add salt and pepper. Pour over onions in 1½ quart casserole. Sprinkle with cheese. Bake in 350° oven until bubbly and brown about 20 to 30 minutes. *Serves 6.*

FRIED WHOLE OKRA

1 pound young okra	½ teaspoon salt
½ cup cornmeal	⅛ teaspoon pepper
Dash cayenne pepper	

Cut off stem end and tip of okra pods; wash thoroughly. Cook in boiling salted water for 8 minutes. Drain and dry completely. Roll in seasoned cornmeal. Fry in deep fat (350°) or sauté in butter until brown. Serve immediately. *Serves 6.*

SUCCOTASH

6-8 ears of corn	2 tablespoons water
1 pound fresh butter beans	¾ cup milk
2 tablespoons butter	

Boil butter beans until tender in unsalted water. Cut raw corn from cob. Place corn in double boiler with butter, water and milk. Cook steadily for 20 minutes. Add butter beans, salt and pepper to taste. Cook together about 5 minutes.

JULIA B. LAFAYE

SWEET POTATO PIE

1½ cups mashed cooked
    sweet potatoes
⅔ cup brown sugar
½ teaspoon salt
1 teaspoon allspice

2 eggs, beaten
1 tablespoon lemon juice
1 cup evaporated milk
Pecan halves
1 9-inch pie shell, unbaked

Mix all ingredients, in order, thoroughly. Pour into pie shell. Bake in 450° oven 15 minutes, reduce heat to 325° and bake 30 minutes longer. Decorate with additional pecan halves. *Yield: 6 servings.*

GLAZED SWEET POTATOES

Peel 6 to 8 cooked yams. Split lengthwise and arrange in single layer in baking dish. Pour the following glaze over the yams:

Sugar: Combine ¾ cup brown sugar, ½ cup water, ½ teaspoon salt, 2 tablespoons butter and ⅛ teaspoon cinnamon. Pour over potatoes. Bake uncovered in 350° oven 30 minutes. Baste occasionally. Turn once.

BRABANT POTATOES

3 boiled potatoes, diced
2 tablespoons shortening
1 tablespoon butter

1 tablespoon chopped parsley
Salt and pepper
1 teaspoon vinegar

Fry potatoes in shortening until lightly browned. Remove and complete browning in butter. Add remaining ingredients. *Serves 6.*

SCALLOPED POTATOES

1½ pounds raw potatoes,
    pared and sliced thin
2 tablespoons flour
3 tablespoons butter

1 teaspoon salt
⅛ teaspoon pepper
2 cups milk

Arrange half the sliced potatoes in buttered 1½ quart baking dish. Sprinkle half the flour over potatoes, dot with 1 tablespoon butter and sprinkle with half the salt and pepper. Repeat, dot top with remaining butter. Pour milk over all. Cover and bake in 375° oven 30 minutes; uncover and bake 15 minutes longer. *Serves 4.*

HASH BROWNED POTATOES

1 tablespoon bacon fat	1 tablespoon minced parsley
3 cups cubed, cooked potatoes	Salt
¼ cup milk	Pepper
1 small onion, minced	2 tablespoons butter

Heat bacon fat in electric skillet set at 365°. Combine remaining ingredients, except butter. Place in skillet and pack into large cake. Dot with butter. Turn heat to 340°; cover about 2 minutes. When butter is melted, remove cover. Cook about 6 minutes or until brown on bottom. Turn and brown, about 6 minutes. *Serves 4 to 6.*

POTATO PANCAKES

6 medium-size potatoes	¼ teaspoon baking powder
2 eggs	1¼ teaspoon salt
1½ tablespoons flour	1 thinly sliced onion

Do not peel potatoes. Cut into 1-inch cubes. Combine remaining ingredients and ¼ cup cubed potatoes in electric blender. Cover and blend. Add remaining potato cubes, ¼ cup at a time, as rapidly as possible. Lightly grease electric skillet; set at 380°. Fry pancakes until tops bubble; turn and brown. *Yield: approx. 10 pancakes.*

POTATOES AU GRATIN

2 tablespoons butter	¼ pound sharp Cheddar cheese
2 tablespoons flour	1½ pounds boiled potatoes,
½ teaspoon salt	sliced
1½ cups milk	¼ cup bread crumbs

Melt butter; blend in flour and salt. Stir until smooth. Turn heat low and slowly add milk, stirring constantly. Cook and stir until thick and smooth. Remove from heat. Add cheese and stir until cheese melts. Arrange potatoes in buttered 1½ quart casserole. Pour cheese sauce over potatoes; top with crumbs. Dot with additional butter. Bake in 350° oven 15 to 20 minutes, or until brown. *Serves 4.*

STEWED TURNIPS

1 pound pork	1 clove garlic
1 onion, chopped	1 bunch turnips
1 Irish potato	

Brown pork, take out of pan. Brown one chopped onion and 1 clove garlic. When cooked, add turnips which have been peeled, diced and soaked in water. Add an Irish potato, also diced, and cover. Cook over a low heat until the turnips are creamy. Serve with rice.

MYLDRED MASSON COSTA

STUFFED PEPPERS I

4 bell peppers
4 tablespoons butter
2 onions chopped fine
1 pound leftover roast
3 ribs celery chopped fine

¼ teaspoon garlic powder
Salt and pepper to taste
½ cup bread crumbs
1 egg

Parboil pepper halves and save liquid. Saute in butter the onions and celery. Add roast and ½ cup liquid. Then add bread crumbs, season to taste and add raw egg. Spoon mix into pepper halves. Bake 350° oven 30 minutes.

GAYLE NUNMAKER

STUFFED PEPPERS II

6 green peppers
1 large onion, chopped
1 small clove garlic,
    minced
1 pound ground meat or
    chopped seafood
1 cup canned tomatoes

3 tablespoons butter
1 teaspoon Worcestershire sauce
½ teaspoon allspice
Salt and pepper to taste
1 cup bread cubes or cooked rice
½ cup fine buttered bread crumbs

Prepare green peppers by cutting a slice off the stem end and scooping out the seeds and membranes. Parboil for 10 minutes; drain well. Saute onion, garlic, meat or seafood, and tomatoes in the butter for 10 minutes. Add seasonings and the bread cubes or rice. Stuff peppers and top with buttered bread crumbs. Place in a shallow baking dish, add 2 cups water and bake at 350° for 25 minutes. *Serves 6.*

MRS. W. E. STANLEY

BLACK EYE PEAS

1 pound black eye peas
3 quarts water
1 onion sliced
2 cloves garlic chopped
5 bay leaves

1 small ham bone
½ pound ham seasoning cubed
1 tablespoon lard
Salt and pepper

Place peas in pot and rinse several times. Add water, onion, garlic and lard. Cover and cook for one hour on medium flame. Add ham bone, ham seasoning and bay leaves. Cook covered to creamy consistency about 2 hours. Salt and pepper to taste. *Serves 8.*

GLADYS BROOKS

STUFFED TOMATOES

6 large firm tomatoes
¼ pound ham, minced
2 medium onions, minced
3 or 4 sprigs of parsley, minced

2 cloves garlic, minced
1 can of tomatoes
1 tablespoon butter
Salt and pepper

Scoop tomatoes into pot. Add 1 large can of tomatoes and stew down. Simmer minced ham and onions in a heaping tablespoon of butter. Add to tomatoes with parsley and garlic, and salt and pepper to taste. Cook until reduced but not dry. Remove from flame and add one cooking spoon of toasted bread crumbs. Fill hollowed tomato halves and bake until light brown. (Bread crumbs may be sprinkled on top of stuffed tomatoes before baking.) While hot, or before baking, dot with butter. *Makes 12 halves.*

JULIA BERKERY LAFAYE

CHINESE FRIED RICE

2 eggs, beaten
4 tablespoons cooking oil
¼ cup green onions, cut in
  ¼ inch pieces

2 tablespoons soy sauce
½ teaspoon sugar
½ cup diced cooked ham
4 cups cold cooked rice

Scramble eggs slightly (without adding milk or water) in 1 tablespoon oil. Set aside. Heat remaining oil over high heat; add green onions and stir. Add rice and stir quickly so rice will not stick and make sure rice is well coated with oil. Add soy sauce and sugar. Mix well. Add ham and scrambled eggs, mixing and breaking eggs in small pieces. Serve hot. *Serves 4 to 6.*

BLACK BEANS

1 pound black beans
10 cups water
1 large green pepper
⅔ cup olive oil
1 large onion, chopped
4 cloves garlic, chopped
4 teaspoons salt

½ teaspoon black pepper
¼ teaspoon oregano
1 bay leaf
2 tablespoons sugar
2 teaspoons vinegar
2 tablespoons dry cooking wine
2 tablespoons olive oil

Wash beans; drain. Soak beans overnight with green pepper. Using same water beans soaked in, cook beans until soft (about 45 minutes). In fry pan heat oil, sauté onion, garlic, and green pepper until tender. Add mixture to beans. Now add salt, pepper, oregano, bay leaf and sugar. Boil beans for one hour. Add vinegar and dry cooking wine. Simmer beans on low heat for 1 hour. Uncover to reduce liquid. Just before serving, add 2 tablespoons olive oil. Serve with rice. *Serves 8.*

MRS. ELVIRA PECORARO

SPANISH RICE WITH CHICKEN

2 chickens
3 cloves garlic, minced
⅓ cup oil
1 large green pepper, chopped
1 large onion, chopped
1   8 ounce can tomato sauce
½ teaspoon paprika

2 cans pimento
1 can petit pois peas
2 tablespoons salt
½ teaspoon black pepper
1 bay leaf
3½ cups beer
2 pounds rice
4½ cups water

Cut chickens; season with salt and garlic. Heat oil and brown chicken. Add onion, green pepper and sauté until soft. Add tomato sauce, salt, bay leaf, paprika, beer and water. When chicken is half cooked, add rice. Cook until rice is tender. Add peas. Decorate with pimento.

MRS. ELVIRA PECORARO

RIZ AU LAIT

1 cup rice
¾ cup sugar
½ teaspoon vanilla extract

Grated nutmeg (or cinnamon)
2 cups milk

Boil the rice until very soft, then add the milk and let it come to a good boil. Add the sugar and cook for one minute longer. Then take from the fire and add the vanilla. Place in a dish to cool. Sprinkle top with the nutmeg, and serve cold. *Serves 6.*

SISTER LOYOLA WEILBAECHER, O.S.U.

BROCCOLI WITH BROILED TOPPING

1 bunch broccoli
¼ cup mayonnaise

1 egg white
2 teaspoons lemon juice

Cook broccoli in boiling water (salted) until tender, splitting the stems lengthwise to permit uniform cooking. Drain and place in serving portions on a board or flame-proof platter.

Beat egg white until stiff. Blend mayonnaise with lemon juice. Fold mayonnaise carefully into egg white and heap on broccoli.

Place under broiler, watching carefully until puffed and golden brown. Serve immediately. *Serves four.*

BRUSSEL SPROUTS WITH CURRY SAUCE

2 10 ounce cartons brussel
   sprouts
1 clove garlic, crushed
½ teaspoon curry powder
½ cup chicken broth
¼ cup water

½ cup water
2 tablespoons butter
½ teaspoon sugar
1 tablespoon corn starch
¼ cup toasted almonds

Wash sprouts, remove loose leaves and cut an X in stem. Add to ½ cup boiling water; cover and cook 5 to 8 minutes or until tender-crisp; drain.

In saucepan, melt butter; add crushed garlic clove, curry powder and sugar. Bring to a bubble stage on low heat. Remove garlic; add chicken broth and corn starch dissolved in water. Bring liquid to a boil. Pour over cooked sprouts. Garnish with toasted almonds.

MRS. JOHN MONTALBANO

BOILED CORN AND SALT MEAT

1½ gallons water
3 pounds salt meat (salt shoulder)

1½ dozen ears fresh corn

Cut salt meat into chunks. Boil until tender about 1 hour. Drop corn in with salt meat. Boil until corn is tender. Serve chunks of meat with corn. Rub meat on corn and eat both corn and meat. It is not necessary to use butter and salt.

JOE BEAUD

RED BEANS AND RICE

2 pounds red beans
5 quarts water
2 onions sliced
2 cloves garlic chopped
5 bay leaves

1 ham bone
1 pound ham seasoning cubed
2 tablespoons lard
Salt and pepper

Place beans in large pot and rinse several times. Add water, onion, garlic and lard. Cover and cook on medium flame for 2 hours. Add ham bone, ham seasoning and bay leaves. Cook covered to a creamy consistency about 3 or 4 hours. Salt and pepper to taste. Serve over rice. *Serves 15.*

ESTHER E. SANDLIN

The Pontchartrain Hotel
Home of the Caribbean Room

CHEESE

It is said that cheese is the only food that can be served with all courses of the menu, and the Creoles evidently agreed. An early visitor to the city (1732) wrote of his amazement at the quantity of luxury items which the city of New Orleans imported, including ". . . wines and cheeses in great variety . . . which do be strange, considering that the colony is in need of commoner stuffs of daily living which it has not by nature . . ."

Today there are over five hundred different kinds of cheese, most of them native to Europe, although cream and cottage cheese originated in America. New Orleans has its own variety—Creole cream cheese—popular from early colonial days and to be found almost exclusively in the city. Today a few creameries operating outside of New Orleans produce cream cheese in a limited supply, but the product cannot be considered other than as a Creole New Orleans specialty.

The commercially produced cheese is made from skimmed milk, which is placed in a vat and heated to 75° Fahrenheit. When this temperature is reached, a bacterial culture is added of a type suited to produce the desired flavor and aroma in the cheese. Next a coagulant is added to solidify the cheese and expel moisture. It is then allowed to set at a temperature of 70° for from twelve to fourteen hours. The result is a solid mass of curd floating in whey, which is picked up in a dipper, set in perforated molds and allowed to drip at room temperature for another eight hours before being packaged for sale. Finally a dressing of cream, homogenized and stabilized, is poured over the cheese in its carton.

The cream cheese of the city's home kitchens was made by putting fresh milk out to sour. It is claimed that old milk does not make good cream cheese. Some added half a teaspoon of lemon juice to the quart of milk to hasten the process. The cheese was drained either in a muslin bag or in small perforated tin molds which can still be purchased at a few of the small hardware stores (of pleasant memory) to be found in the city.

The Creoles ate their cream cheese for breakfast with sugar and cream or with salt and pepper. It formed the basis of an especially light cream cheese cake and of a delightful ice cream known as frozen cream cheese.

It has been said that of the many styles of food preparation in the United States, New Orleans Cookery is the most fully developed, the most deserving to be called a cuisine. This is so because of the individuality of the Creoles who possessed a great disdain of imitation and a tendency toward creativity and resourcefulness. The result? Foods are served in New Orleans which can be had nowhere else in the world. High on this list of specialties are the cream cheese dishes, which as any Creole would tell you are entitled to a preferred place.

EGGS

Americans generally associate the egg with breakfast. But for French New Orleans, breakfast was not such an institution as we know it today. The first cup of *café noir* was had early and was followed at a later hour by *Le Petit Déjeuner* of the sort that Madame Begue was to make famous. At her little restaurant at the corner of Madison and Decatur back in 1863, Madame served the butchers of *Les Halles* a "breakfast" from eleven to three o'clock. These were hard-working men whose day began at five and who, by eleven, were ready to do justice to Madame's offerings. The meal started with a heavy soup, and included fish from local waters or perhaps a shrimp or crawfish dish, followed by a rack of lamb Creole or liver (her specialty!) with a crisp salad. Then there was a dessert and a good brûlot. To be served such foods could not long remain the prerogative of the city's butchers alone, and before long all of New Orleans had found its way to Madame Begue's door.

But actually, the richness of such foods and the number of courses served at breakfast were not unusual, for in Creole households of the time breakfast was a considerable affair. A cook book popular in the late 1800's offered the following list of suggestions to the housewife.

BREAKFAST

Hors d'Oeuvres for Breakfast: Celery, olives, radishes, cress, pickles canapes, sliced cucumbers, raw tomatoes sliced, lettuce, raw oysters (when in season).

Cereals for Breakfast: Grits, Hominy, Oatmeal, cracked Wheat, Cornmeal Mush, Farina. All of these may be served with cream, milk, milk and sugar, or gravy.

Vegetables for Breakfast: Potatoes in any form, Stewed Tomatoes, Fried Sweet Potatoes, and any vegetable not included in the hors d'Oeuvres.

Warm Breakfast Dishes: Broiled Tenderloin Sirloin, Broiled Chops, Chicken, Ham, Small Fancy Game, Quail on Toast, Snipe, Woodcock, Liver and Bacon, Fried Pork, Fried Pigs Feet, Grillades, Fried Soft Shell Crabs, Breaded Veal Cutlets, Sausage, Stewed Tripe, Stewed Kidneys, all kinds of hash, all kinds of meat, fowl or fish croquettes, codfish balls, creamed codfish, and eggs in every variety of cooking (boiled, fried, scrambled, poached, or in omelet.)

Breakfast Breads and Cakes: Bakers Bread, rolls such as **Grenouilles** Biscuits, Muffins, Corn Cakes, Griddle Cakes, Batter Cakes, Corn Bread, Muffin Bread, Sweet Potato Bread, Fritters, Beignets, etc.

Breakfast Beverages: Café, Cocoa, Tea, and any light white wine. Claret may be substituted if highly preferred.

However, despite the richness of the morning bill-of-fare, the lowly egg did find its way to the Creole breakfast table, but when it did, it ceased to be lowly. Omelets were made with cheese, asparagus points, or mushrooms, and the *omelette à la Créole* with its flavorsome tomato filling was a traditional dish of the Easter Sunday breakfast. Omelets were given a filling of preserves *(aux confitures)* or they were flambéd *(omelette au rhum)*, but then they were served as sweet *entremets* or desserts. A soufflé, within Creole cuisine, was a gourmet dish of ceremonial preparations, and arguments of much heat were generated over such points as whether or not to butter the inside of the baking dish. Some held that a buttered vessel retards rising, and that a soufflé wants something to cling to as it pushes and puffs itself into that crown of golden goodness. And so the argument goes, back and forth, to this day.

Et vous, mon ami, que dites-vous?

CHEESE STRATA

12 slices day-old bread
½ pound sliced Cheddar cheese
4 eggs
2½ cups milk

½ teaspoon prepared mustard
1 tablespoon chopped onion
1½ teaspoon salt
Dash of pepper

Arrange 6 slices of bread (crust trimmed) in 12x7x2 inch baking dish. Cover with cheese, then remaining bread. Beat eggs, add milk, mustard, onion, salt and pepper; pour over bread. Let stand 1 hour. Bake at 325° for 1 hour. *Serves 4.*

CHEESE SOUFFLÉ

2 tablespoons butter
2 tablespoons flour
¾ cup milk
4 egg yolks

1 cup cheese
5 egg whites
Salt
Cayenne pepper

Melt butter in top of double boiler. Stir in flour and when blended add milk and seasonings to taste. Remove from heat and beat in egg yolks, one at a time, alternating with cheese. Put pan over hot water and stir until cheese has melted. Remove from hot water and cool. Fold in stiffly beaten whites and pour batter into a well buttered soufflé dish. Bake at 375° for 30 minutes.

JOYCE LAFAYE CREWS

CHEESE RAREBIT

1 pound American or Cheddar cheese
1 tablespoon butter
1 cup beer or ale

½ teaspoon paprika
½ teaspoon dry mustard

Cut into pieces 1 pound cheese. Melt butter in top of double boiler. Add cheese, and as it melts gradually add ale or beer, stirring constantly with wooden spoon. Season with paprika and mustard. Stir mixture constantly until cheese is melted. Serve on toast. *Serves 6.*

MARY ANN BENDERNAGEL

SWISS CHEESE FONDUE

1 clove garlic, halved
1½ tablespoons corn starch
⅓ cup Kirsch
1½ cups dry white wine

1½ pounds natural Swiss
   cheese, grated
¼ teaspoon baking soda
Dash of white pepper, paprika,
   and nutmeg

Rub inside of electric fondue pot with garlic, then discard. Mix corn starch and Kirsch; set aside. Put wine in electric fondue pot with control set at No. 4½ until bubbles start to rise to the surface. Add cheese by thirds, stirring constantly until all the cheese is melted. When mixture starts to bubble, quickly add cornstarch mixture, stirring constantly until thickened. Reduce heat to No. 4, add baking soda and spices, mixing well. Stir occasionally. Serve with French bread cubes.

EGGS BENEDICT

6 slices toast or
   Holland Rusk
6 slices broiled ham

¾ cups hollandaise sauce
6 eggs
Paprika

Place ham on toast and top with poached egg. Cover with hollandaise and sprinkle with dash of paprika. *Serves six.*

OEUFS SARDOU

8 artichokes
16 anchovy fillets
8 poached eggs
½ cup chopped cooked ham

1 tablespoon glacé de viande
   or meat glaze
4 slices truffle
1 cup Antoine's Hollandaise Sauce

Cook artichokes in boiling salted water until tender. Remove petals and choke; reserve bottoms. Place bottoms on baking pan; place two anchovy fillets on each. Run under low broiler flame to keep warm. Have poached eggs ready and warm on the side. Have a hollandaise at hand, this luke-warm. Now assemble the dish; on each artichoke, over the anchovy fillets, place poached egg. Cover egg and artichoke with hollandaise. Sprinkle chopped ham over, and add a few drops glacé de viande over ham and sauce. Place one slice of truffle on the very top. Serve immediately. *Yield: 4 portions.*

ANTOINE'S RESTAURANT

EGGS HUSSARDE

2 large thin ham slices, grilled
2 Holland Rusks
¼ cup marchand de vin sauce
2 slices grilled tomato

2 soft poached eggs
¼ cup hollandaise sauce
Paprika

Lay a slice of ham across each Holland Rusk and cover with marchand de vin sauce. Lay slices of tomato on the sauce and place poached eggs on tomato slices. Top with hollandaise sauce and garnish with a sprinkling of paprika. *Serves 1.*

BRENNAN'S

CREOLE EGGS

½ cup finely chopped onion
½ cup finely chopped green pepper
½ cup finely diced celery
2 tablespoons butter, margarine
    or pure vegetable oil
1 can (1 pound, 4 ounces) tomatoes
1 teaspoon salt

Dash of pepper
1 teaspoon Worcestershire sauce
½ teaspoon basil
8 eggs
⅓ cup grated cheddar cheese
    (optional)

Sauté onion, green pepper and celery in butter, margarine or oil until tender. Add tomatoes; break tomatoes up with fork. Stir in salt, pepper, sugar, Worcestershire and basil. Simmer, uncovered, for 15 minutes. Pour ¼ cup sauce into each of 8 shirred-egg dishes or small custard cups. Carefully break an egg into each dish; sprinkle with cheese. Bake at 350° for about 12 minutes or until eggs are just set. *Serves 8.*

MARY MARKS

SPANISH OMELET

1 No. 2 can tomatoes
3 tablespoons butter
1 teaspoon salt
Few grains pepper
Few grains cayenne
1 sprig thyme
1 tablespoon minced parsley
1 bay leaf
2 cloves garlic, minced
1 tablespoon flour

6 chopped shallots, or
    ½ cup minced onion
5 tablespoons chopped
    green pepper
½ cup white wine
½ cup canned button
    mushrooms
½ cup cooked peas
4 eggs
1 tablespoon olive oil

Combine tomatoes and one tablespoon butter, simmer 10 minutes, stirring occasionally. Add salt, pepper and cayenne; cook 10 minutes. Add thyme, parsley, bay leaf, and garlic. Cook 15 minutes, or until sauce is thick. Melt one tablespoon butter, blend in flour; cook until brown. Add shallots, green pepper; brown slightly. Add wine, stirring constantly until slightly thickened. Add mushrooms and peas. Beat eggs until well blended; add tomato mixture. Heat remaining butter and olive oil in skillet, pour in egg mixture. Shake skillet until eggs begin to set, lifting edges of omelette to allow uncooked mixture to flow under omelette. When cooked, fold over. If desired, garnish with chopped parsley. *Yield: 4 portions.* ANTOINE'S RESTAURANT

QUICHE LORRAINE

1   9 inch pie shell
½ pound bacon
12 slices of Swiss cheese
4 eggs
1 tablespoon flour

½ teaspoon salt
⅛ teaspoon cayenne pepper
⅛ teaspoon nutmeg
1 pint half and half cream
1½ tablespoons butter

Lightly bake pie shell and when cool, line pie shell with fried bacon and cheese. Make a custard of beaten eggs, flour, salt, cayenne, nutmeg, cream and melted butter. Pour custard over bacon and cheese and bake at 375° for 45 minutes or until custard is set and nicely browned. *Serves 6.*

Cooked crabmeat and shrimp may be substituted for bacon and cheese.

JOYCE LAFAYE CREWS

OMELETTE AU RHUM

4 eggs
3 tablespoons butter
Pinch of salt

2 tablespoons granulated sugar
½ cup rum

Make a regular omelet cooked in butter. Keep it soft and add pinch of salt and 1 tablespoon of sugar. Turn omelet onto a hot plate and sprinkle the top with remaining tablespoons of sugar. Pass under broiler to caramelize sugar.

Heat the rum, pour it over omelet and ignite. Spoon burning rum over omelet and when fire goes out, serve immediately. *Serves 2.*

ANTOINE'S

CREOLE MACARONI AND CHEESE

8 tablespoons butter
1   7 ounce package of elbow
     macaroni
½ cup chopped onion
½ cup chopped green pepper
1 teaspoon salt
¼ teaspoon pepper
¼ teaspoon oregano

¼ teaspoon dry mustard
2 cups water
1 tablespoon flour
1 large can evaporated milk
2 tablespoons chopped pimento
½ pound shredded sharp cheddar
     cheese

Melt butter at simmer temperature in electric fry pan. Add macaroni, onion, green pepper, salt, pepper, oregano and dry mustard. Cook, stirring occasionally, at 260° for 7 minutes, or until onions become transparent. Add water and bring to a boil. Cover and simmer at 212° for 20 minutes or until macaroni is tender. Sprinkle flour over mixture and blend well. Stir in evaporated milk, pimento and shredded cheese. Cook 5 minutes longer at simmer until cheese has completely melted, stirring occasionally. Serve immediately. *Serves six to eight.*

MARY MARKS

MEXICAN MACARONI

8 tablespoons butter
2 heaping tablespoons flour
1 cup milk
1 cup cream
1 6 ounce jalopeños cheese
4 ounces Swiss cheese
1 10 ounce package frozen spinach

1 small can green chili peppers,
  chopped fine
1 package elbow macaroni
Chopped parsley
Bread crumbs
Dash Worcestershire sauce
Salt and pepper to taste

Melt butter, add flour, then cream to make cream sauce. Melt cheeses in sauce, stirring occasionally. Add well-drained cooked spinach, parsley, chili peppers, Worcestershire sauce, salt and pepper. Combine with cooked macaroni, top with bread crumbs and bake until browned on top, approximately 25 minutes at 350°. *Serves eight.*

MARY EASON

EGGPLANT FLORENTINE WITH BEEF

1 medium size eggplant
4 tablespoons butter
1 pound ground beef
1 tablespoon instant minced onion
1 teaspoon salt
⅛ teaspoon black pepper

1 teaspoon sugar
¼ teaspoon basil leaves
¼ teaspoon ground oregano
1 can (8 ounces) tomato sauce
¼ cup grated Parmesan cheese
½ pound Mozzarella cheese, sliced

Wash eggplant, peel if desired; cut into ½ inch slices. Melt butter; add eggplant and brown lightly on both sides, adding extra butter if needed. Place in shallow 2 quart baking dish. To drippings in skillet, add ground beef, onion, salt, pepper, sugar, basil leaves and oregano; mix well and cook until meat is lightly browned. Spoon meat mixture over eggplant; add tomato sauce and Parmesan cheese. Bake uncovered in 350° oven for 20 minutes. Place remaining cheese over top of casserole. Bake 10 minutes longer or until cheese is melted. *Serves 6.*

Chapel of the Second Ursuline Convent
Destroyed by the River in 1912

BREAD

Because wheat could not readily be grown in the vicinity of New Orleans, there was always a shortage of white flour in the early days of the city's history. The only source of supply was France, whose vessels, loaded with food stuffs for the little colony, would arrive in port every two or three months, barring storms, pirates and navigational disasters. The precious flour, never in sufficient quantities, would be stored in the city's warehouses, to be doled out when and to whom the government officials pleased. So the daily bread of the early citizens of New Orleans often was Indian corn meal cake, a poor substitute for the crisp, fragrant loaves of their native France. One of the groups of women sent to become wives to the men of the colony, not only refused to eat the crude ash cakes, but locked themselves in their houses until wheat flour was distributed to them from the colony's storehouse. But the bread picture was not long in changing. Soon rice bread began to appear on these early tables and the amount of flour imported increased so that by 1720 the city could boast of its first bakery. As the years went on, French tastes predominated and *pain français* became the city's undisputed Creole favorite.

Bread was baked in oval clay ovens out of doors until the 1800's when dwellings were improved to include kitchens with the large brick ovens that were used with such success for so long. The *pain français* was eaten traditionally in the city of New Orleans itself, whereas the folk in the red hills to the north preferred corn pone, cracklin bread, Johnny Cake and the like with their greens and "pot likker." Baker's breads *(pain du boulanger)* were and still are baked in an assortment of shapes and sizes, including the original flute loaf, the *pistolette*, the *gigot*, or soup stick, and the *pain tresse* or twist loaf. The term *pistolette* is said to have been applied to these crusty rolls by the city's young hotbloods who would pause for a cup of strong *café noir* and a hot buttered roll before taking to the dueling field. For them the little rolls were symbolic of the shoot-out, and so the name "little pistols."

One famous use of the baker's loaf brought it a whimsical title,— *La Médiatrice*, as it was known in the Vieux Carré. Here was something that every Creole man knew could effectively plead for forgiveness from his wife after he had spent a night carousing in the saloons of the town. The top surface of a hot pan loaf was sliced off horizontally and the soft center of the bread scooped out. This hollowed-out cavity was then well buttered, filled with crisp fried oysters and slices of dill pickle, sprinkled with ketchup and the toasted top replaced. A man could buy his "mediator" in the French Market just before going home, certain of a happy reception regardless of the sin.

Fifty to seventy-five years ago, horse drawn wagons clattered through the city streets with the still warm French loaves, and carts drawn by goats and driven by women brought bread to the "up-town" sections. In those days the bread was delivered unwrapped and left on the porch, to be simply dusted off by the housewife before serving. The loose cylinders of paper in which the loaves are encased today are the best type of wrappers for French bread because they allow the loaves to "breathe." The delicate texture of the bread makes it highly absorbent, and moisture condensing within a tightly sealed and waxed wrapper would result in wilting and softening the crust.

This French bread so dear to the hearts of New Orleanians has an incredibly light and tender interior and a crisp, flaky crust. Other breads, whether Italian, Jewish or even the loaves of the mother land of France, are heavier since they are made with greater amounts of rich ingredients. The square "American" loaf is perfectly suited to the sandwich eating-generation of today, but as long as there can be found in the city that small aristocracy, Creoles at heart, who choose the better things of life, *pain français* will be part of the city's good eating.

BISCUITS

¼ cup shortening
2 cups sifted flour
1 teaspoon salt

4 teaspoons baking powder
¾ to 1 cup milk

Cut shortening into sifted dry ingredients. Add milk gradually to form soft dough. Knead ½ minute on lightly floured board. Roll out to ½ inch thickness. Cut with floured biscuit cutter. Place on greased cookie sheet. Bake at 450° for 12 to 15 minutes. *Yield: 12 biscuits.*

MRS. EDWARD C. HENDERSON

MOCK BEIGNETS

2 cans refrigerated biscuits (plain)

Hot grease
Sifted powdered sugar

Cut biscuits in half and roll flat with a rolling pin. Drop in hot grease, a few at a time. Turn once. Watch carefully as they brown quickly. Drain on absorbent paper. Sprinkle with powdered sugar. *Yield: 40 doughnuts.*

MRS. ROBERT J. ARMBRUSTER

POPOVERS

3 eggs
1 cup milk
1 cup sifted regular all purpose flour

½ teaspoon salt
pinch sugar
2 tablespoons melted butter

In a bowl, beat eggs slightly. Add ⅓ cup milk. Blend in flour, salt and sugar. Add remaining milk and butter. Beat only until free of lumps. Pour into buttered muffin tins filling cups half full. Bake 45-50 minutes or until golden brown in preheated 375° oven. Five minutes before end of baking time, prick each popover four times with toothpick to allow steam to escape. Serve immediately.

LIGHT CORN BREAD

1 teaspoon soda
1 teaspoon salt
¼ teaspoon baking powder
2 cups cornmeal

½ cup sugar
4 tablespoons shortening
½ cup flour
2 cups buttermilk

Put sugar, salt, soda and baking powder in a bowl; add buttermilk. Stir well. Add cornmeal and flour alternately. Melt shortening in loaf pan and add to mixture. Sprinkle a little cornmeal in loaf pan. Heat pan. Pour mixture into hot pan. Bake at 350° for 45 to 60 minutes. *Yield: 16 squares.*

PAIN PERDU (LOST BREAD)

2 tablespoons sugar
½ cup milk
⅛ teaspoon salt
¼ teaspoon brandy or vanilla
2 eggs, beaten

6 slices stale bread
2 tablespoons shortening
1 tablespoon butter or bacon
    drippings
Confectioners sugar, honey or
    syrup

Combine sugar, milk, salt, flavoring and eggs. Soak bread in mixture. Cook in hot shortening and butter until well browned on both sides. Sprinkle with confectioners sugar and serve hot, with syrup or honey. *Yield: 8 servings.*

LES BRIOCHES DE TANTE TINIA

1 yeast cake
½ cup tepid water
5 eggs
1½ cups sugar
Butter

½ cup milk
½ teaspoon salt
Flour
Anise seeds

Levain: To make levain (baking powder), dissolve yeast cake in ½ cup tepid water and add enough flour to make a soft batter. Set aside and let rise for 2 hours.

Dough: Beat well 5 eggs and add sugar. When thoroughly creamed, add one tablespoon butter, then the milk. Pour in levain and mix well. Sift flour twice with salt and fold in enough to make a soft dough. Set aside in warm place to rise for about 4 hours. When well risen, roll dough very thin on a slightly floured board. Spread butter generously over ½ of rolled dough and fold in two. Roll again, butter as before, and fold over. Roll very thin again, butter, and cut into strips 1½ in. wide. Roll as for jelly roll and place on greased or buttered tins. Set aside in warm place to rise about 4 hours. Sprinkle sparingly with anise seeds (or simply season with vanilla). Bake in moderately hot oven. Serve hot with café au lait.

SISTER LOYOLA WEILBAECHER, O.S.U.

PUMPKIN SPICE BREAD

1¾ cups flour
1½ cups sugar
1 teaspoon soda
1 teaspoon cinnamon
½ teaspoon salt
½ teaspoon nutmeg

⅛ teaspoon ground cloves
½ cup margarine, melted
1 cup pumpkin
1 egg, beaten
⅓ cup water

Sift dry ingredients together; make a well in center. Add margarine, pumpkin, egg and water. Mix until dry ingredients are moistened. Pour into greased and floured 9x5 inch loaf pan. Bake at 350° for 1 hour and 10 minutes or until done.

PAULA PALMER

HOT YEAST ROLL DOUGH

This dough is so easy you can serve your family hot rolls any time. The real joy of this recipe is that you knead it only once and then let it rise for 6 hours in the refrigerator. The dough will keep fresh for 7 days in the refrigerator.

5 pounds all purpose flour
1 quart milk less ¼ cup
1 cup sugar
2 packages yeast
¼ cup warm water

1 teaspoon salt
2 teaspoons baking powder
1 teaspoon baking soda
1 cup vegetable shortening
8 quart enamel pot

In an enamel pot, combine milk, sugar, vegetable shortening and salt. Let come to a slow boil. As soon as the milk begins to rise, take off the heat and set aside. Cool for 1½ hours. When cool, add baking soda and powder. Dissolve yeast in ¼ cup warm water and add to milk. Mix well. Add enough flour (about 5 cups) to make thin dough. Let rise 15 minutes. After it has risen, add enough flour to make dough thick (about 5-7 cups). Mix well. Dough will be sticky. Turn out on a well floured (2 cups) board and knead for 5 minutes. Add more flour if needed while kneading. Put dough back into the enamel pot. Spread vegetable shortening on top of dough. Cover pot with wax paper and the lid. Let rise for 6 hours in the refrigerator. Keep lid on the pot at all times during the rising period.

After rising time is over, pinch off small pieces of dough and shape into any shape rolls you desire—cloverleaf, crescent, Parker house, etc. Let rise 1 hour. Bake at 350° until brown.

FRIED FRUIT PIES

Use hot yeast roll dough
from above

Stewed fruit or preserves

Pinch off small wad of dough. Flatten out with your fingers. Fill with 1 teaspoon stewed fruit or preserves. Turn over and seal. Let rise 1 hour. Fry in hot bacon fat.

CINNAMON ROLLS

Use hot yeast roll dough
from above

2 tablespoons cinnamon
3 cups sugar

With floured rolling pin, roll dough out to a 10x13 inch rectangle ⅛ inch thick. Mix cinnamon and sugar together. Spread evenly over dough. Roll on the length of dough and seal the edge. Cut into ½ inch rings. Place on a cookie sheet and let rise 1 hour. Bake at 375° until brown. *Yield: 20 rolls.*

DRIZZLE TOPPING (OPTIONAL)

2 cups powdered sugar
1 tablespoon margarine or butter

¼ cup milk

In a small saucepan, warm milk just enough to melt margarine. Do not boil. Add enough of this mixture—a few drops at a time—to the sifted powdered sugar to make the topping easy to spread on top of each roll.

MRS. ROBERT J. ARMBRUSTER

BANANA FRITTERS

1¼ cups flour
1½ teaspoons baking powder
2 heaping tablespoons sugar

½ cup milk
2 eggs
¼ teaspoon salt

Sift flour, then measure and add baking powder, salt, sugar. Sift three times and add milk and eggs. Cut bananas in quarters and dip into batter. Drop into hot, hot grease. Dust with powdered or granulated sugar.

Bananas may be diced through the batter and dropped by tablespoon or from ¼ or ½ cup into hot grease.

MARY ALICE McKAY

BANANA NUT BREAD

1 cup sugar
½ cup butter, margarine or
    shortening
2 eggs
2 cups flour
1 teaspoon baking powder

1 level teaspoon soda
    (in few drops water)
1 pinch salt
1 cup pecans, chopped (optional)
2 or 3 bananas (very ripe and
    mashed with a fork)

Cream butter and sugar; add eggs and cream together. Add bananas and salt, then add baking powder to flour and pour gradually into mix. If you use nuts they should be added next and lastly soda. Mix well and divide into 2 loaves. Bake in greased loaf pans or dishes at 325° for 40 to 50 minutes —test with a straw. Garnish with slices of bananas, cherries or glazed fruit.

MARY ALICE McKAY

SPOON BREAD

2 cups whole milk
2 tablespoons sugar
¾ cup cornmeal

1 teaspoon salt
6 eggs, separated
½ teaspoon baking powder

Put salt in milk and bring to a boil. Add cornmeal and stir until cooked (almost 2 minutes). Beat egg whites like meringue and add to it the yolks (also whipped) and baking powder. Add this mixture to the first, beat and pour in greased baking dish. Bake at 375° for 30 minutes.

MARY ALICE TOSO McKAY

HUSH PUPPIES

½ cup sifted flour
1 cup cornmeal
1 onion, minced
1½ teaspoon baking powder

1 egg
1 teaspoon salt
1 teaspoon sugar
½ cup milk, approximately

Combine all ingredients with just enough milk to moisten to rather stiff dough. Drop from spoon into deep hot shortening (350°) until brown, about 3 to 4 minutes. *Yield: 24 hush puppies.*

YORKSHIRE PUDDING

1 cup flour
½ cup water
½ cup milk

½ teaspoon salt
2 eggs
4 tablespoons fat drippings

Mix together thoroughly and chill. Heat fat in round baking pan in 450° oven. Pour pudding into pan and bake 15 minutes or until risen. Reduce heat to 350° until pudding is well browned. To make popovers, use muffin tins. *Yield: 4-6 servings.*

MRS. ALFRED CHAPMAN
YORKSHIRE, ENGLAND

BANANA BREAD

2 cups flour
1 teaspoon baking soda
1 teaspoon salt
½ cup shortening

¾ cup sugar
2 eggs
3 tablespoons buttermilk or
   sour cream
1 cup mashed bananas

Sift and measure flour. Resift with soda and salt. Cream butter and sugar until light. Add eggs beaten, buttermilk and bananas to creamed mixture. Add flour mixture, beating thoroughly. Pour into well-greased loaf pan and bake at 350° about 1 hour.

PAULA PALMER

CINNAMON COFFEE CAKE

1 package white cake mix	1 teaspoon cinnamon
½ cup sugar	¼ cup sugar
½ pint sour cream	¼ cup chopped pecans
¾ cup salad oil	1 cup powdered sugar
4 eggs	Juice of 1 lemon

Blend cake mix, sugar, sour cream, oil and eggs to form batter. Set aside.

Mix cinnamon, sugar, and pecans. Place ¼ of mixture on bottom of a tube pan. Add ½ cake batter. Sprinkle ¼ nut mixture on top of cake batter, then pour in the rest of the batter. Top with remaining nut mixture and bake at 325°, for 1 hour.

Glaze while warm with a mixture of powdered sugar and lemon juice.

MRS. GEORGE W. BEELER
LAMARQUE, TEXAS

COUSH-COUSH

2 cups cornmeal	2 teaspoons baking powder
½ teaspoon salt	3 eggs, beaten
1½ cups boiling water	1 teaspoon shortening

Stir meal and salt into water. Cool and add baking powder and eggs. Preheat skillet with shortening and pour in mixture. Cook over medium heat 5 minutes. *Yield: 8 servings.*

FRENCH MARKET BEIGNETS

1 cup homogenized milk, scalded	1 teaspoon nutmeg
2 tablespoons margarine or	1 fresh egg
vegetable shortening	1 teaspoon salt
1 tablespoon brown sugar	1 package granulated yeast
1 tablespoon granulated sugar	Oil for deep frying
3 cups enriched plain flour	

Heat milk in saucepan to scalding stage. Do not let it scorch. Stir often. Place shortening in a mixing bowl and add sugar. Pour in the scalded milk and stir until ingredients are melted. Cool to lukewarm stage. Add yeast. Stir until yeast is dissolved. Sift dry ingredients—salt, nutmeg and flour. Gradually add approximately ½ of flour mixture to milk mixture to form batter. Add whole egg. Beat thoroughly. Stir in remaining flour mixture. Cover. Set aside to allow to double in bulk (approximately 1 hour). Knead gently. Roll out on floured board to ¼ inch thickness. Cut in diamond shapes. Cover. Let rise in warm place from ½ to 1 hour.

Fry in hot oil (385°), turning only once. Drain and dust with confectioners sugar. Serve warm.

MRS. JACK (MARY S.) PARKMAN
MONTICELLO, MISS.

Brennan's Restaurant

DESSERTS

The desserts of New Orleans invite wistful reminiscences of busy kitchens, deliciously fragrant with the odors of apples roasting and cakes baking. For in the early Creole days the making of desserts was the province of the housewife, not the professional baker. This good wife knew the art of making a *pâté feuilletée* (the secret is ice water), and her *blanc mange* manifested the light touch of the artist. Her ingenuity produced *ambroisie* and *riz à la neige* which were local dessert innovations. But probably her greatest triumph was in the serving of elegant, truly imaginative little cakes planned around native fruits—figs, pears, oranges and berries—and requiring a baking expertise seldom found among non-professionals. These were the *méringues,* the *mêlées* and the *bouchées,* which could be turned out to perfection by even the humblest kitchen. Given a hint of spices and a sprinkling of nuts, she could create totally new confections, and today even their names intrigue: *croquignoles, massepains, Madeleines.* It is New Orleans loss that such an art is disappearing.

But among the Creole desserts that are with us still is the *Gâteau des Rois* or "King's Cake," which is inseparably connected with the Mardi Gras and with the development of the city's now-famous carnival balls. The whole complex evolved out of the Creole custom of choosing a king and queen on Twelfth Night, January 6, called *Le Jour des Rois.* This feast day commemorates the visit of the three Wise Men of the East to the Christ Child in Bethlehem. It was much stressed by the Spanish and even today is considered the Spanish Christmas, at which time gifts are presented to family and friends recalling the gifts of the Wise Kings. With the Creoles the day became *Le Petit Noël,* or Little Christmas, and following the Spanish custom there were always grand balls. A King and a Queen were chosen for the occasion, and a new royal pair every week thereafter until Mardi Gras. Ever since those early days the period between January 6 and Mardi Gras Day has been the accepted carnival season, with the calendar of activities becoming more and more crowded as each year rolls around.

The method of choosing the first king was by cutting the King's Cake. This famous *Gâteau des Rois* was made of brioche batter, shaped into an enormous ring and decorated with bon bons, dragées and colored sugars. Generally some grand mansion was chosen for the ball. At the stroke of midnight the guests were invited to be seated around the spacious dining room table, and each was served a piece of the cake with a glass of champagne. Hidden cleverly within the cake was a bean or a pecan. Excitement would be at high pitch until the bean was found, embedded within the slice of cake by one of the guests. If the finder were a lady, she chose her king by presenting him with a bunch of violets provided along with the cake. If the finder were a gentleman, he would choose his queen by offering her the flower in his lapel and would then escort her around the parlor in *le tour de salon.* At the end of the promenade the king would raise his hand to stop the march and would announce: *"Mes sujets, voici votre reine! Recevez ses commandements!"* Then followed an ovation of smiles, applause and compliments, as though the lady were indeed a queen succeeding to her born rights, and the honors of that night clung to her and were remembered long years afterward.

The prettiest old-time courtesies were connected with the round of balls that followed. These balls were always given at the home of the queen. The king, whether he found the bean or was simply chosen by the lady who had found it, was expected to bear the entire expense of the ball of which he was king and to provide the next king's cake. He was also expected, before the end of the week, to present the queen with a gift, usually of some type of jewelry. These gifts of jewels from the king were the only ones that the Creole mother ever allowed her daughters to accept from any gentlemen. To this custom of presenting the queen of the week with jewels may be traced the present custom of our Carnival kings of giving elaborate gifts to their consorts.

And so week after week, the festivities went on: a king's cake was cut, a new king and queen chosen, and the round continued until the grand culminating ball of Mardi Gras night. It was considered a piece of wonderful good fortune to find the bean and it was for this reason that the bean was cut in two, half to be held by the king, and the other half by the queen. The lucky bean was faithfully preserved as a good luck piece, and in many old Creole families the little shriveled prize still rests on its velvet bed in jewel box or curio case.

BREAD PUDDING WITH WHISKEY SAUCE

1 loaf stale French Bread
1 quart milk
3 eggs
2 cups sugar

2 tablespoons vanilla
3 tablespoons margarine
1 cup raisins

Soak stale bread in milk. Crush with hands until well mixed. Add eggs, sugar, vanilla and raisins; stir well. Pour margarine in bottom of thick pan and bake until very firm. Let cool; cube pudding and put in individual dessert dishes. When ready to serve, add sauce; heat under broiler.

WHISKEY SAUCE

8 tablespoons butter or margarine
1 cup sugar

1 egg
Whiskey to taste

Cream butter and sugar. Cook in double boiler until very hot and sugar is well dissolved. Add well beaten egg and whip really fast so egg doesn't curdle. Let cool and add whiskey to taste.

ALZINA PIERCE

CRÊPES SUZETTE

1⅛ cups sifted flour
4 tablespoons sugar
Salt (pinch)
3 eggs
1½ cups milk
1 tablespoon melted butter
1 tablespoon cognac

1 teaspoon butter
½ cup butter
½ cup powdered sugar
1 teaspoon orange rind, grated
  juice of 1 orange
¼ cup Grand Marnier or Cointreau
¼ cup brandy

Sift together sifted flour, sugar and salt. Combine eggs (beaten) and milk. Stir into dry ingredients until smooth. Stir in butter and cognac. Let stand for 2 hours.

In a frying pan, heat sweet butter. Pour in 1 tablespoon of batter to cover bottom of pan with a thin layer. Rotate pan to spread batter evenly. Cook one minute on each side. Stack crêpes one on top of the other, separated by wax paper.

Cream butter and powdered sugar and orange rind. Add orange juice and ¼ cup Grand Marnier or Cointreau. Spread on crêpes and fold or roll them up. Arrange on hot serving dish. Sprinkle with sugar and ¼ cup warmed brandy. Ignite and serve flaming. *Serves 6.*

JOYCE LAFAYE CREWS

CHOCOLATE SOUFFLÉ

3 tablespoons butter
2 tablespoons flour
1 cup milk
¼ teaspoon salt

½ cup sugar
2 squares baking chocolate
4 egg yolks
5 egg whites

Melt butter in saucepan and blend in flour. Slowly add milk, salt, sugar and chocolate. Stir until chocolate is melted and sauce well blended. Add egg yolks and beat well. Fold in egg whites stiffly beaten.

Butter a soufflé dish and sprinkle with sugar. Pour in batter and set dish in a pan of hot water. Bake at 400° for 15 minutes. Reduce heat to 375° and continue to bake for 25 minutes. Serve with favorite sauce. *Serves 6.*

STRAWBERRY SOUFFLÉ

3 tablespoons butter
2 tablespoons flour
½ cup milk
5 egg yolks

1 cup chopped strawberries
4½ tablespoons sugar
Brandy
6 egg whites

Melt butter in saucepan; add flour and cook until golden. Add hot milk and cook stirring constantly for 5 minutes. Add egg yolks, lightly beaten with 2 tablespoons sugar. Add chopped strawberries mixed with 2 tablespoons sugar and sprinkle with brandy or Cointreau. Beat egg whites until stiff, adding ½ tablespoon sugar and fold into mixture. Pour batter into buttered and sugared baking dish and place a few whole berries on top. Bake at 350° for 40 minutes. Serve with strawberry sauce. *Serves 6.*

BAKED BANANAS

4 firm bananas
1 teaspoon cinnamon
2 tablespoons sugar

1 teaspoon nutmeg
½ cup honey
8 tablespoons butter

Peel bananas and cut them in half and then cut each half lengthwise. Arrange pieces in a casserole and sprinkle them with cinnamon, sugar and nutmeg. Pour honey generously over the top and dot with small pieces of butter. Bake in oven at 300° for about 20 minutes. *Serves 6.*

MRS. JOHN J. McGOEY

BAKED FRUIT

2 large cans of fruits for salad
  (remove cherries and add 1 can
  Bing cherries)
3 bananas
1 package coconut macaroons,
  crumbled

¼ cup Triple Sec. Cointreau,
  Cherry Brandy, Grand Marnier,
  Gold Liqueur or any other
  liqueur you prefer

Grease pyrex dish and spread alternate layers of cookie crumbs, fruit and bananas. Dot with butter and cover with aluminum foil. Bake at 300° for 40 minutes. Just before serving, pour liqueur over baked fruit. *Serves 6-8.*

MARY ALICE McKAY

QUICK FRUIT COBBLER

1 cup flour
1 cup sugar
1 cup milk
¼ teaspoon salt

2 teaspoons baking powder
¾ stick butter
1 can fruit of choice—
  if cherries are selected, add one
  cup sugar and one tablespoon
  corn starch

Combine and mix like batter: flour, sugar, milk, salt, baking powder and butter. Melt 6 tablespoons of butter in a large baking dish. The fruit and juice must be heated and very hot. Pour cake batter over the melted butter and add the hot fruit and juice. Bake at 500° for 15 to 20 minutes. *Serves 4-6.*

MRS. OWEN BRENNAN, JR.

BREAD PUDDING

4 cups bread crumbs (made from
  stale French bread grated in
  blender)
1 cup sugar
3 cups milk

2 cups seedless raisins
1 cup coarsely chopped pecans
1 tablespoon lemon extract
3 tablespoons vanilla
½ teaspoon cinnamon

Combine and pour into greased 2 quart square baking dish. Bake uncovered at 350° for one hour and fifteen minutes. Serve hot or cold. *Serves 8-10.*

HARD SAUCE FOR BREAD PUDDING

4 tablespoons butter
1 cup powdered sugar

1½ ounces Bourbon or rum

Combine and cream with a fork. Pour hard sauce over bread pudding. Slice into squares and top with cherries.

MRS. THOMAS M. TOOKER

POTS DE CREME

1 small package semi-sweet
chocolate bits
3½ teaspoons dripped coffee

1 egg
2¾ teaspoons sugar
2 teaspoons brandy or
crème de menthe

Place in blender or electric mixer and blend ingredients until chocolate bits are fine. Add 1 cup Half & Half cream which has been heated to boiling point. Blend ingredients again until chocolate bits are dissolved. Pour into small dessert cups and chill. Take from refrigerator and let set at room temperature approximately 10 minutes before serving. *Serves 6.*

ADELE SMITH

GRAPE FRUIT FLAMBÉ

4 large grapefruits
½ cup Kirsch or rum

2 tablespoons honey

Peel 4 large grapefruits and remove all of the thick white pulp. Carefully separate the fruit into sections over a bowl to catch all of the juice. Put the juice and 2 tablespoons honey in the blazer of a chafing dish, bring to a boil, and add the grapefruit sections. Spoon the liquid over them until they are heated through. Pour in ½ cup warm Kirsch or rum and ignite the spirit. *Serves 4.*

MRS. OWEN BRENNAN, JR.

ALMOND TORTE

8 tablespoons margarine
1 cup light brown sugar
½ teaspoon almond extract
1 egg

5 tablespoons flour
½ cup chopped pecans
½ cup chopped almonds
1 cup heavy cream, whipped

Blend butter and sugar, add almond extract, egg and flour. When well blended, add nuts. Mold into roll with hands and wrap in aluminum foil. Place in freezer. When ready to serve, allow 30 minutes thawing time. Slice 1 inch thick and top with whipped cream. Roll may be decorated with slivered almonds. *Serves 6-8.*

PAT RYAN LAFAYE

CHERRIES JUBILEE

1 pound can Bing cherries
1 tablespoon corn starch
1 tablespoon sugar

¼ cup cognac
1 quart firm vanilla ice cream

Drain cherry liquid into saucepan. Mix cornstarch and sugar with a little cherry liquid and then mix with all of the liquid in the saucepan. Heat until mixture thickens. Add cherries and reheat. Heat cognac in a small pot. Pour over hot cherries and ignite. When flame dies down, ladle cherries over very firm vanilla ice cream. *Serves 4.*

ANNE BADEAUX CONWAY

PERSIMMON PUDDING

1½ cups persimmon pulp
1 cup sugar
2 eggs
½ cup sour milk

½ teaspoon soda
1 cup flour
¼ cup melted butter
Pecans or other nutmeats

Combine and pour into a greased baking pan. Bake at 350° for 30 minutes. Remove and add the following sauce by making small dents in the pudding to let the sauce soak into the pudding.

½ cup sugar
½ cup water

1 tablespoon melted butter

Bake another half hour at 350°. May be served warm or cool topped with whipped cream. *Serves 6-8.*   SANDRA FRANZ MARTIN

POACHED ORANGES

6 navel oranges
3 tablespoons slivers of orange peel
1½ cups sugar

¾ cup water
2 tablespoons orange-flavored liqueur

Peel the rind and the white membranes from 6 navel oranges. Slice enough of the orange rind to make about 3 tablespoons slivers and combine them with 1½ cups of sugar and ¾ cup of water. Cook the syrup over moderate heat, without stirring, for about 8 minutes or until it thickens slightly. Put the oranges in the syrup and cook them over very low heat, basting constantly, for about 5 minutes, or until they are warm but still firm. Remove them from the heat and add 2 tablespoons of orange-flavored liqueur. Chill the oranges, basting them occasionally with the syrup. Serve them very cold. *Serves 6.*   BARBARA CONNICK

APPLE CRISP

8 apples sliced (1 quart)
1 teaspoon cinnamon
½ cup flour

½ cup water
¾ cup sugar
½ cup butter (¼ pound)

Peel and slice apples thin. Fill a casserole with sliced apples, water and cinnamon. Blend remaining ingredients until crumbly in texture. Spread mixture over top of apples and bake uncovered in hot oven 425° for 50 minutes. *Serves 6-8.*   MRS. ALDEN BAEHR

NEW ORLEANS RICE PUDDING

1 cup uncooked rice
1 quart milk
8 tablespoons butter
¾ cup sugar

1 teaspoon vanilla extract
½ cup raisins
5 eggs (beaten)
1 teaspoon cinnamon

Combine rice and milk. Bring to a boil, cover and cook over low heat until rice is tender and has absorbed most of the milk. Add butter, sugar, vanilla, raisins and eggs. Turn into a buttered 2 quart casserole. Sprinkle with cinnamon. Bake at 350° for 25 minutes. *Serves 6-8.*   MRS. JAMES NEEDOM

ORANGE BRANDY SOUFFLÉ

4 tablespoons flour
4 tablespoons butter
1 cup milk
½ cup sugar
1 tablespoon vanilla extract
1 teaspoon orange extract

2 tablespoons grated orange peel
¼ cup brandy
4 egg yolks
6 egg whites
Pinch of cream of tartar

Butter a 1½ quart soufflé dish on the bottom, and partially up the sides. Sprinkle with granulated sugar; shake out the excess. Use eggs that are at room temperature. Melt the butter in a saucepan slowly over a medium heat. Add the flour and mix well. Slowly add the milk, stirring constantly until very thick and bubbly. Add the vanilla extract, orange extract, brandy and grated orange peel. Mix well and remove from heat.

Slowly stir in the egg yolks and mix well. At this point the mixture should be rather thick. If it is too thin, heat it slightly after the egg yolks have been added.

In a separate bowl beat the egg whites and cream of tartar until fluffy and form soft peaks. Add about 1 cup of the beeaten egg whites mixture to the cooked base mixture—gently fold into mixture. Pour the base mixture into the bowl of beaten egg whites—gently fold together. Pour this mixture into the prepared soufflé dish. Bake for 25-30 minutes at 425°, or until puffy and golden. *Serves 6.*

GERALDINE P. VOCKE

MILE HIGH ICE CREAM PIE

Crust:

1½ cups sifted flour
½ cup shortening

½ teaspoon salt
4-5 tablespoons cold water

Pie:

1 pint vanilla ice cream
1 pint chocolate ice cream
4 egg whites

½ teaspoon vanilla
¼ teaspoon cream of tartar
½ cup sugar

To make crust: Sift together flour and salt. Cut in shortening until pieces are the size of small peas. Sprinkle 1 tablespoon cold water over flour mixture and gently toss with fork. Repeat until all is moistened. Form into a ball with fingers and roll out to ⅛ inch thickness on lightly floured surface. Fit loosely into a 9 inch pie pan, pricking well. Bake 10-12 minutes at 450°. Cool.

Layer ice cream in pie shell. Beat egg whites with vanilla and cream of tartar until soft peaks form. Gradually add sugar, beating until stiff and glossy and sugar is dissolved. Spread meringue over ice cream to edges of pastry. Broil 30 seconds to 1 minute to brown meringue. Freeze at least several hours. Drizzle chocolate sauce over each serving. *Serves 8-12.*

CARIBBEAN ROOM
PONTCHARTRAIN HOTEL

BANANAS FLAMBÉES

This old recipe, as good today as years ago, was brought to Louisiana by a distant relative of Empress Josephine, at whose table Bananas Flambées was often served.

3 bananas
3 tablespoons butter

1 cup sugar
2 ounces rum

Peel bananas, splitting lengthwise and cutting in halves. Place bananas in a buttered, shallow, oven-proof baking dish and dot with butter. Sprinkle sugar over bananas. Bake uncovered at 325° for about 35 minutes. Set dish on stove, being careful to keep warm. Pour rum in a long-handled spoon, which has been warmed by dipping in boiling water. Set a match to the rum and as it flames pour over bananas. As it runs down in the dish, ladle it up and over the bananas until the flaming ceases. The secret of this dessert is to have all ingredients warm, otherwise it will not flame well. *Serves 4.*

MRS. REGINALD C. WATSON

BANANA PUDDING

½ cup flour
1 cup sugar
2 tablespoons corn starch
2½ tablespoons margarine
1 box vanilla wafers

2 cups milk
2 egg yolks
1 teaspoon vanilla extract
3 bananas

Mix flour, sugar, corn starch. Stir in enough milk to make a paste. Stir in egg yolks. Add rest of milk. Cook over medium heat until thick, stirring constantly. Remove from heat. Stir in vanilla and butter. Cool slightly. Cover the bottom of a bowl with some of the vanilla wafers, then add a layer of sliced bananas. Pour part of the partially cooled pudding over the wafers and bananas, then add another layer of the wafers and bananas and more pudding, finishing with wafers and bananas on top. Meringue topping is optional.

Meringue:
3 egg whites
½ teaspoon vanilla

¼ teaspoon cream of tartar
6 tablespoons sugar

Beat egg whites with vanilla and cream of tartar till soft peaks form. Gradually add sugar, beating till stiff and glossy peaks form and sugar is dissolved. Spread on pudding and bake at 350° for 12 to 15 minutes, or till meringue is golden. *Serves 6-8.*

MARY JANE DAVID

BANANAS FOSTER

1 tablespoon butter
2 tablespoons brown sugar
1 ripe banana, peeled and
  sliced lengthwise

Dash cinnamon
½ ounce banana liqueur
1 ounce white rum

Melt butter in a chafing dish. Add brown sugar and blend well. Add banana and sauté. Sprinkle with cinnamon. Pour over banana liqueur and rum and ignite, basting banana with flaming liquid. Serve when flame dies out. *Serves 1.*

BRENNAN'S

SABAYON

6 eggs, separated
¾ cup sugar
¾ cup cream sherry

¾ cup heavy cream, whipped
1 tablespoon vanilla

Beat egg yolks with sugar until creamy. Add sherry and cook in a double boiler until thick. Cool in a bowl 10-15 minutes. Add whipped cream and vanilla. Fold in stiffly beaten egg whites. Divide into 4 small ramekins and chill 2-3 hours. *Serves 4.*

MASSON'S

PRALINE PECAN PIE

1 prepared pie shell
1 pint Plantation praline pecan
  ice cream

½ pint whipping cream
½ teaspoon vanilla
1 tablespoon granulated sugar

Bake pie shell in 350° oven for 15 minutes. Cool and fill with softened ice cream. Freeze. Top with cream that has been whipped with the vanilla and sugar.

Return to freezer until a few minutes before serving.

Garnish with a small piece of the praline candy.

BEVERLY CLARK

CHOCOLATE MINT PARFAIT

6 ounce package semi-sweet
  chocolate pieces
Pinch salt
1 egg

1 teaspoon vanilla extract
¾ cup hot milk
Crème de menthe
Whipped cream

Combine in blender chocolate, salt, egg, vanilla extract and milk. Blend at high speed for one minute. Pour into parfait glasses and chill until firm, about three hours. Top with 1 tablespoon creme de menthe, whipped cream and a cherry.

MRS. THOMAS M. TOOKER

FLOATING ISLE

3 egg yolks
¾ cup sugar
1 large can evaporated milk
1 can water
Pinch of salt

2 teaspoons vanilla extract
3 tablespoons corn starch
3 egg whites
1 tablespoon sugar

Combine egg yolks and ¾ cup of sugar. Add milk, water, salt, vanilla extract and corn starch and cook until the mixture begins to thicken. Beat egg whites and one tablespoon of sugar until stiff. Pour custard mixture over egg whites mixture and gently streak it through. Cool before serving. *Serves 4-6.*

MARY ALICE McKAY

LEMON FLUFF

1 package plus 1 teaspoon
    unflavored gelatin
½ cup water
8 eggs—separated
1¼ cups sugar
3 lemons, juice of 3 and rind of 2

10 marshmallows
½ pint whipped cream
1 package lady fingers

Dissolve gelatin in water. Cream egg yolks, gradually adding ¾ cup of sugar. Combine both mixtures in a double boiler, adding lemon juice, lemon rind and marshmallows. Cook until mixture is thickened, about 20 to 25 minutes, stirring frequently. Cool custard. Whip egg whites and gradually add remaining sugar, about one-half cup. Fold custard into egg whites.

Line sides of a spring pan with lady fingers (cut off rounded bottoms) and pour mixture into it. Refrigerate overnight and top with whipped cream before serving.

LOUISE MIOTON TOUPS

MAMMA'S OLD-FASHIONED EGG CUSTARD

2½ cups milk
2 eggs

4½ heaping tablespoons sugar
1 teaspoon vanilla extract

Scald milk. Mix well the eggs and sugar. To this mixture pour the scalded milk slowly, stirring constantly. Add the vanilla. Fil 6 greased custard cups three-quarters ful. Bake at 350° in a pan of wateer 1 inch deep for about 1 hour. Custard is done when the blade of an inserted knife withdraws clean.

Caramel topping:
    2 tablespoons sugar

1 cup water

Mix the sugar and water and cook over medium heat until mixture darkens and thickens, stirring constantly until mixture has the consistency of dark syrup. Pour over the cooked custard. *Serves 6.*

MRS. A. L. VITTER

COFFEE JELLY

2 packages unflavored gelatin
½ cup coffee liqueur
3 cups hot coffee

¾ cup sugar
Pinch of salt
1 pint whipped cream

Sprinkle gelatin over coffee liqueur to soften. Add coffee, sugar and salt. Stir the mixture until clear. Fill 8 individual molds and chill until firm. Shortly before serving, unmold and place on a bed of lightly sweetened whipped cream, piped from pastry bag. Add a touch of whipped cream on top of each jelly. *Serves 8.*

BARBARA CONNICK

CHOCOLATE FONDUE

1 large (8 ounce) bar milk chocolate
⅓-½ cup light cream
Juice of ½ orange

½-¾ cup quartered almonds
Cointreau
Fresh strawberries

Melt the chocolate over hot water. Stir in enough light cream until the mixture is of a smooth, creamy consistency. Add the orange juice, almonds, and Cointreau to taste. Stir well to blend. Spear whole or sliced strawberries with a fondue fork and dip into mixture. Other firm fresh fruit, such as peaches, can also be used.

PAULA BADEAUX RAULT

RUM DE LA CREME

4 egg yolks
4 tablespoons sugar
3 egg whites, beaten stiff

1½ cups whipped cream
½ cup rum

Beat egg yolks and sugar until thickened. Fold in egg whites and cream. Stir in the rum and freeze for about 8 hours. *Serves 10.*

MRS. CARL W. HALL

FRENCH MINT

1 cup butter
2 cups powdered sugar
4 squares semi-sweet chocolate
Vanilla wafers

4 eggs
1 teaspoon peppermint flavoring
2 teaspoons vanilla extract

Beat butter and eggs until fluffy. Add chocolate, eggs and flavoring; beat 10 minutes. Pour mixture into a 9 x 9 pan that has been covered on the bottom with crushed vanilla wafers, and freeze. *Serves 12.*

PAULA PALMER

VERY GOOD DESSERT

2 eggs
2 cups brown sugar
¾ cup flour
1 teaspoon vanilla

1 teaspoon baking soda
1 cup chopped nuts
1 pint whipped cream

Beat eggs. Add sugar, flour, vanilla, soda and nuts. Bake in pre-heated oven (350°) exactly 25 minutes, in a greased 9"x9" or 7"x11" pan. It will not be thoroughly cooked and will fall when removed from oven. When cooled, crumble the cake and fold into whipped cream. Freeze. *Serves 6.*

MARY ALICE McKAY

FROZEN CREAM CHEESE

4 pints Creole cream cheese
1 quart milk
1 quart whipping cream

3 cups sugar
3 or 4 teaspoons vanilla extract

Mix milk, cream, and sugar in container of ice cream freezer. Mash cream cheese through a colander to prevent lumping. Add to milk mixture. Add vanilla. Mix thoroughly and freeze.

JULIA BERKERY LAFAYE

ANGEL RING WITH CHOCOLATE MOUSSE

1-10 inch angel food cake,
    bought or made
½ cup cold water
2 envelopes unflavored gelatin
½ cup coffee (boiling)
6 tablespoons cocoa

3 squares bitter chocolate, melted
6 eggs, separated
⅔ cup sugar
Pinch salt
2 teaspoons vanilla

Dissolve gelatin in cold water 5 minutes. Add coffee, then cocoa and chocolate. Beat well. Beat egg whites and yolks separately, then blend together and add sugar and salt. Fold into chocolate mixture and add vanilla.

Scoop out center of angel food cake, reserving some cake to pad bottom of angel ring. Fill with chocolate mousse and let set at least an hour.

Frost with Mocha-fluff:
    1 cup whipping cream
    ½ cup sifted confectioner's sugar

1 tablespoon instant coffee
½ cup cocoa

Mix together in chilled bowl. Beat with chilled beater until stiff enough to hold a point. Frost cake and decorate with chocolate curls made by warming a square of bitter chocolate to room temperature and "peeling" with vegetable peeler.

DOROTHY KERR COHEN

APPLE CAKE

2 cups sugar
½ cup salad oil
2 eggs
2 teaspoons cinnamon
4 cups diced peeled apples

2 cups self rising flour
2 teaspoons baking soda
1 teaspoon vanilla
Pinch salt
1 cup chopped pecans

In mixer, combine sugar, oil, eggs and cinnamon. Gradually add sifted flour and soda. Batter will be hard. At low speed add apples and vanilla. Fold in pecans. Bake in 9x13" greased pan at 350° for 45 minutes.

Icing:
1½ cups powdered sugar
6 ounces Philadelphia cream cheese
3 tablespoons butter

1 teaspoon vanilla
Salt (pinch)

Let cheese and butter soften, mix all ingredients together in electric mixer until smooth. This is a "pan cake", spread icing on top after cake has cooled. Sprinkle crushed pecans on top.

MRS. LEON J. REYMOND, JR.

CHEESE CAKE

Crust:
8 tablespoons butter
½ cup sugar

1 cup graham cracker crumbs

Line an 11x7 pyrex dish with crust; bake at 375° for 8 minutes; take crust from oven; cool.

Cheese cake:
3 eggs
1 cup sugar

1 teaspoon vanilla
1 pound Philadelphia cream cheese

Cream sugar and eggs, add cream cheese and vanilla; beat well until fluffy. Put into pie crust and bake in 350° oven for 25 minutes; cool.

Topping:
1 pint sour cream
1½ teaspoon sugar

A little vanilla

Mix well. Put topping on cake and return to oven for 7 minutes and no longer; cool; refrigerate overnight.

MRS. HAROLD FUSELIER

STRAWBERRY CHEESECAKE

20-24 graham crackers
8 tablespoons butter
1-3 ounce package Philadelphia
   cream cheese
1 cup granulated sugar
3 eggs

1 carton sour creeam
1 package strawberry jello
1 large package frozen sliceed
   strawberries
1 cup water

Crust: Crush 20-24 graham crackers with rolling pin or glass. Add melted butter and mix until graham crackers are all moistened. Press into 9"x9" square cake pan (or equivalent) bringing crust about 1 inch up sides.

1st Layer: Cream sugar and Philadelphia cream cheese. Add 3 well beaten eggs and mix by hand. Pour into crust and bake at 350° for 30 minutes.

2nd Layer: Stir sour cream in carton until smooth and pour over 1st layer. Bake 20 minutes at 350°. Set aside until *cold*.

3rd Layer: Dissolve Jello in 1 cup boiling water. Add defrosted strawberries and liquid and gently pour over 2nd layer. Cover with foil and refrigerate at least 6 hours, or overnight.

Yield: Sixteen 2" squares.

MRS. OWEN BRENNAN, JR.

CHERRY DUMP CAKE

1 can pie cherries
1 can pie apples
1 small package yellow cake mix

½ cup pecan pieces
8 tablespoons butter or margarine

Dump cherries and apples in dish greased with butter. Sprinkle cake mix on top. Pour melted butter and pecans over this. Bake at 350° for 1 hour. Allow to sit in oven on "off" for 15 minutes.

MRS. HELEN WIRTH

COCOA CAKE

2 cups sugar
1 cup butter or margarine
4 eggs
¼ cup hot water
1 teaspoon soda

1 cup buttermilk
3 tablespoons cocoa
1 teaspoon vanilla
2½ cups flour sifted

Cream butter, add sugar gradually and cream until light. Add eggs one at a time; beat well. Sift cocoa and flour together. Add alternately with buttermilk. Dissolve soda in hot water and add last. Makes three 9-inch layers. Grease and flour pans. Bake at 350° for 35 minutes.

Icing:

4 tablespoons butter
1 box powdered sugar
1 egg

2 tablespoons rum or
1 teaspoon rum extract
3 tablespoons cocoa

Mix together; if too stiff add cream. Spread on cake.

MRS. LAWRENCE R. SMITH
TEXAS CITY, TEXAS

COCONUT FEATHER CAKE

3 cups flour
4 teaspoons baking powder
¼ teaspoon salt
8 tablespoons butter

2 cups sugar
4 eggs
1 cup milk
1 teaspoon vanilla

Mix the baking powder and salt with the sifted flour. Cream the butter and add the sugar gradually creaming while adding. Beat the eggs without separating the whites and yolks. Add to the well creamed butter and sugar. Sift in the flour mixture a little at a time, alternating with the milk. Add the flavoring and beat long enough to mix thoroughly. Pour into well greased pans and bake.

Yield: 2 - 9 inch layers or
3 - 8 inch layers or
24 - cup cakes

Temperature for layers—375°. Time 30-35 minutes.
Temperature for cup cakes—375°. Time 18-20 minutes.

FILLING FOR COCONUT CAKE

½ cup sugar
¼ cup flour
½ cup water
1 tablespoon corn starch

½ cup coconut milk
1 tablespoon butter
Coconut

In the top of a double boiler mix sugar, flour, water and corn starch. Cook this mixture over hot water until it thickens, stirring constantly. Let it cook for 15 minutes more stirring constantly. Then add the coconut milk and butter, cook 3 minutes. Remove the top part of the double boiler from the lower part, set aside to cool. Spread on cake and sprinkle coconut thickly over it.

MRS. NICK MATULICH

DATE CAKE

1 pound pitted dates
1 pound walnuts or pecans
1 cup flour
2 teaspoons baking powder

½ teaspoon salt
1 cup sugar
4 eggs
1 teaspoon vanilla

Sift flour and baking powder together twice; then sift with the sugar again. Sift flour, baking powder and sugar over the dates, walnuts or pecans. Beat the yellow of the eggs and add to the first mixture. Beat whites last and mix altogether. Put in pan that has been greased, then lined with brown paper and greased again. Mixture will be stiff. Bake at 325° for 1 hour.

MRS. EDWARD H. SEILER

HEAVENLY HASH CAKE

2 eggs
1 cup sugar
¾ cups self-rising flour
1 cup pecans, chopped

8 tablespoons margarine
1½ cups miniature marshmallows
1 teaspoon vanilla
3 tablespoons cocoa

Cream sugar and margarine. Add eggs and other ingredients except marshmallows. Bake in buttered 9"x9" by 2 inch pan, 350° for 30 to 35 minutes. Test with toothpick. While cake bakes make icing.

Icing:
2 tablespoons cocoa
2 tablespoons margarine
½ box powdered sugar

2 to 4 tablespoons evaporated milk
icing will be thin

Remove cake from oven and while cake is hot pour marshmallows over cake to cover. When completely cooled put icing on cake in pan. Cut in 36 squares (1½ inches each).   MARION HENNINGS

LEMON DOBERGE CAKE

Batter for 8 thin layers:
1 cup butter
2 cups sugar
4 large eggs, separated
2¾ cups regular flour, sifted
    before measuring
(All at room temperature)

3 teaspoons baking powder
¼ teaspoon salt
1 cup sweet milk
1 teaspoon vanilla

Cream butter and sugar until light and fluffy. Add beaten egg yolks. Blend until smooth. Sift together flour, baking powder and salt four times. Add alternately with milk to creamed mixture. Mix on lowest speed only until blended. Add vanilla. Fold in stiffly beaten egg whites. Grease 9 inch cake pans and line with waxed paper rounds to yield 8 thin layers. Pour ¾ cup batter into each pan, spreading evenly over bottom of pan. This takes some doing. Use rubber spatula.

Bake in 375° oven 12 to 15 minutes or until very lightly browned. Remove to cake racks and repeat baking process until batter is entirely used. When cool, put lemon jelly filling between layers and frost top and sides with same lemon jelly filling. (Make lemon jelly filling first so that it will be cool by the time the cake is ready.)

Lemon Jelly Filling for Doberge Cake:
Juice and grated rind of 6 lemons
3 cups sugar
3 eggs

1 cup water
3 rounded tablespoons butter
3 rounded tablespoons flour

Mix flour and sugar, stir in whole eggs, add the water, lemon rind, and juice. Drop the butter on top. Cook over boiling water, stirring until mixture thickens. Cool.

It takes a little while to cook. When ready, it should have a jelly-like consistency—thick   enough to hold shape. If it is cooked too much, it gets "gummy".

SANDI NEWMAN BURK

PINEAPPLE PUDDING CAKE
(A quick "company's coming" cake)

Topping:
2	#2 cans crushed pineapple	1 cup water
2	3 ounce packages vanilla pudding	

Cake:
  1 package white or yellow cake mix, follow package directions.

Combine crushed pineapple, vanilla pudding and water in a saucepan. Bring to a boil. Boil for about 3 minutes, stirring constantly. Pour pineapple mixture into a 10"x13" pan, and chill until firm.

Prepare cake mix according to directions. Pour cake mix over chilled pineapple pudding. Bake in a pre-heated oven at 350° for 30 minutes. Cool on a wire rack for 15 minutes before inverting on a large tray or platter.

MRS. ETHEL HERZOG

POUND CAKE

8 tablespoons butter or margarine	1 tablespoon vanilla
1 cup vegetable shortening	1 tablespoon lemon juice
2 cups sugar	1 tablespoon orange juice
6 eggs	2 cups flour

Cream sugar, butter or margarine, and shortening well. Add eggs, one at a time, mixing well after each. Add flavorings and flour. Mix well. Bake in greased tube pan at 325° for 50-60 minutes.

MARY ALICE McKAY

SUPREME POUND CAKE

1 package yellow or lemon cake mix	½ cup cooking oil
1 package instant lemon, banana or French vanilla pudding mix (4 serving size)	1 cup water
	4 eggs

Blend all ingredients in a large bowl, then beat at medium speed for 2 minutes. Bake in a greased and floured 10-inch tube at 350°, for about 44-55 minutes, until center springs back when touched lightly. Cool right side up for about 25 minutes, then remove from pan. Glaze if desired: blend 1 cup confectioners sugar with either 2 tablespoons milk or 2 tablespoons lemon juice or banana flavor, or sprinkle lightly with confectioners sugar.

MRS. WALTER J. CROOK, JR.

SOUR CREAM POUND CAKE

1 cup butter
6 eggs
3 cups all-purpose flour
1 tablespoon almond extract

3 cups sugar
½ pint sour cream
¼ teaspoon baking soda

In large bowl of an electric mixer, cream butter and sugar. Add eggs, one at a time. Beat well after each egg is added. Blend in sour cream. Add flour with soda mixed in. Mix well, add extract. Bake in 10″ tube pan that has been greased and dusted with flour. Bake at 325° for 1¼ hours. Cool for 15 to 20 minutes before removing.

MRS. LOUIS CASSO

SUNSHINE CAKE

5 eggs
⅓ cup water
1¼ cup sugar
1 teaspoon vanilla

1 teaspoon almond extract
1 cup flour
½ teaspoon creme of tartar

Beat egg whites stiff, then add water, sugar and almond. Pour egg yolks, whipped and with vanilla added, over the egg white mixture.

Slowly sift in flour with creme of tartar added. Fold gently and pour in greased tube pan. Bake at 325° 35 to 40 minutes. Test with a straw.

"SCHWARTZ" CAKE

½ cup boiled and cooled milk
1½ cups sugar
½ cup butter
3 eggs, separated and
    3 egg yolks
12 tablespoons cocoa

¼ teaspoon salt
½ cup cold milk
1 teaspoon baking soda
1 teaspoon vanilla
2 cups flour
1½ teaspoons baking powder

Batter:
Scald ½ cup milk and cool. Cream together sugar and butter. Add the 6 yolks of eggs one at a time, beating after each until well mixed. Dissolve the baking soda in ½ cup of cold milk and add to the sugar and butter mixture and beat.

Sift together the flour, baking powder and cocoa. Beat 3 egg whites (the other three egg whites will be used for the frosting) until stiff with the ¼ teaspoon salt. Add the flour mixture, alternately with the egg whites, to the sugar and butter mixture. Add vanilla. Beat in the scalded milk last.

Bake in layer cake pans (preferably 9″), which have been buttered and floured, in 350° oven for 45-50 minutes. Cool in pan 5 minutes. Remove to wire racks to cool.

Chocolate Filling:
While the cake is baking, make the Chocolate Filling: Boil together until quite thick, beating and stirring constantly, and spread between layers of cake.

1 egg
¼ cup milk
½ cup sugar

1 teaspoon corn starch
3 tablespoons cocoa
Coconut

Beat the egg in the milk, then add to the other ingredients and boil for just a few minutes. Frost the cake with Three Minute Frosting.

Frosting:
Beat until blended, then place in double boiler over boiling water.

3 unbeaten eggs
⅛ teaspoon salt

½ cup sugar
2 tablespoons cold water

Beat these ingredients for 3 minutes or until stiff. Remove from fire and add 1 teaspoon vanilla or almond extract. Beat the frosting well. Spread all over cake and top with shredded coconut.

MRS. J. RUSSELL WALSH

UPSIDE DOWN CAKE

8 tablespoons butter or margarine
1½ cups sugar
1 tablespoon vanilla
1 cup milk
2½ cups flour

3 teaspoons baking powder
2 eggs, beaten
6 tablespoons butter or margarine
1 cup sugar
1 small can pineapple slices

Cream butter, sugar and vanilla. Add alternately milk and flour, sifted with baking powder. Add eggs.

In heavy skillet, melt butter or margarine. Sprinkle 1 cup sugar over butter and cook until slightly brown. Place pineapple slices in pan. Pour batter over all. Bake at 350° for 30 to 40 minutes.

MARY ALICE McKAY

GATEAU ROLLA

4 egg whites
1½ cups sugar
½ cup finely ground almonds
2 egg whites

½ cup sugar
2 tablespoons cocoa
1 cup softened butter
¼ pound German chocolate, melted

Whip egg whites until stiff and add gradually the sugar and the almonds. Cut out four rounds of brown paper about 8 inches in diameter. Spread each round of paper with meringue and bake on a baking sheet in a slow oven (250°) for about 15 minutes or until the meringue is dry. Turn the layers over and continue to dry for about 5 minutes.

In top of double boiler, over hot but not boiling water, beat egg whites until foamy. Beat other ingredients in gradually. Beat well and remove from heat. When the filling is cool and firm, spread it on three of the meringue layers and put them together, the fourth layer on top. This cake should ripen for 24 hours. Will keep for days in the refrigerator and indefinitely in freezer.

EMILY WILSON

CREOLE WHITE FRUITCAKE

1½ pounds citron, cut fine
1½ pounds golden raisins
1½ pounds blanched almonds,
   cut fine
1½ pounds candied pineapple,
   cut fine
1½ pounds grated or flaked coconut
1 pound butter

1 pound flour
1 pound sugar
2 grated nutmegs
   (do not use pre-ground)
1 teaspoon almond extract
1 tablespoon vanilla extract
½ pint sherry
6 eggs

Cream butter and sugar well. Add eggs one at a time, beating well after each. Sift flour with freshly grated nutmegs. Put half of the flour over fruits and nuts and blend the other half into the butter mixture, adding alternately with the sherry. Add flavoring, then fold in the floured fruits and nuts.

Line the bottom and sides of a tube pan with paper (2 layers of oiled brown paper, 1 layer of waxed paper—the waxed paper will be next to the batter). Fill pan with batter. Cover the top of the cake pan by tying down over the top several thicknesses of waxed paper or use one sheet of aluminum foil. Place the cake pan in a pan of water so that the water comes up about 3 inches on the sides of the pan. Steam in a 275° oven for about 3½ hours. Remove the cover and the pan of water and bake for another half hour at 325°.

MRS. RAYMOND R. FITZGERALD

RED VELVET CAKE

½ cup vegetable shortening
1½ cups sugar
2 eggs
2 cups flour
1 tablespoon cocoa
1 cup buttermilk

1 teaspoon vanilla
2 ounces red food color
1 teaspoon soda
1 teaspoon vinegar
½ teaspoon salt

Cream shortening and sugar, add eggs. In separate bowl sift flour and cocoa and salt. Beat flour mixture into creamed mixture alternately with buttermilk. Add vanilla and color, beat after each addition. Add soda and beat, add vinegar and beat. Bake 350° for 30 minutes. Use two 8″ buttered pans.

Icing:

1 cup milk
⅓ cup flour
1 dash salt
8 tablespoons butter

½ cup vegetable shortening
1 cup sugar
1 teaspoon vanilla

Mix milk, flour and salt in top of double boiler. Get all lumps out. Heat stirring until mixture forms pudding. In separate bowl cream shortening and butter. Add sugar and vanilla. When pudding mixture is cooled beat both mixtures together. Ice cake when cooled.

MARION HENNINGS

KING'S CAKE

1 package yeast
¼ cup warm water
6 tablespoons milk, scalded
    and cooled
4 cups flour

1 cup (2 sticks) butter
¾ cup sugar
¼ teaspoon salt
4 eggs
Melted butter

In a bowl, dissolve yeast in warm water. Add milk and enough flour, about ½ cup, to make a soft dough. In another bowl, combine butter, sugar, salt and eggs with the electric mixer. Remove from mixer and add soft ball of yeast dough. Mix thoroughly. Gradually add 2½ cups flour to make a medium dough that is neither too soft nor too stiff. Place in a greased bowl and brush top of dough with butter. Cover with a damp cloth and set aside to rise until doubled in bulk, about 3 hours. Use remaining 1 cup flour to knead dough and to roll with hands into a "rope" shape. Place on a 14x17-inch greased cookie sheet and form "rope" of dough into an oval shape. The center should be about 7x12 inches. Connect ends of dough by dampening with water. Cover with a damp cloth and let rise until doubled in bulk, about 1 hour. (A bean may be placed in cake if desired.) Bake in 325°F. oven for 35 to 45 minutes, or until lightly browned. Decorate by brushing top of cake with corn syrup and alternating 3-inch bands of purple, green and gold colored granulated sugar. (To color sugar, add a few drops of food coloring to sugar, and shake in tightly covered jar until desired color is achieved.)

PIE CRUST

2 cups sifted enriched flour
1 teaspoon salt

⅔ cup shortening
4 to 6 tablespoons ice water

Sift flour and salt together. Cut in the shortening with a pastry blender or two knives until pieces are the size of small peas. Sprinkle water, a tablespoon at a time, over a part of mixture. Gently mix with a fork and push to one side of bowl. Sprinkle next tablespoon of water over another small part of mixture and follow the same procedure. Repeat until all is moistened, but be sparing with water because too much makes pastry tough. Use just enough water to make it possible to gather dough together with the fingers so that it cleans the bowl. If possible, chill the dough for about ½ hour before rolling it out on a lightly floured board. Always roll dough lightly but evenly from center to edges, and thinly.

To make pastry extra tender and flaky, divide shortening in half. Cut in first half until mixture looks like corn meal. Then cut in second half until pieces are the size of peas. Then proceed with the water as directed. Makes pastry for one 8 inch double crust pie.

MRS. JAMES TUCKER

BLACK BOTTOM PIE

½ cup sugar
1 tablespoon corn starch
2 cups milk, scalded
4 egg yolks, beaten
1 package (6 ounces) semi-sweet
  chocolate pieces
1 teaspoon vanilla
1 9 inch pie shell, baked and
  cooled

1 envelope unflavored gelatin
¼ cup cold water
4 egg whites
½ cup sugar
1 cup whipping cream, whipped
Chocolate decorettes

Combine sugar and corn starch. Slowly add milk to yolks. Stir in sugar mixture. Cook over very low heat until custard coats spoon. To 1 cup custard, add chocolate pieces. Stir until chocolate is melted. Add vanilla. Pour into bottom of pie shell. Chill. Soften gelatin in water, add to remaining hot custard. Stir until dissolved. Chill until slightly thick. Beat whites, adding sugar gradually, until stiff. Fold into custard-gelatin mixture. Pour over chocolate layer and chill until set. Garnish with whipped cream and decorettes.

BRANDY ALEXANDER PIE

1 envelope unflavored gelatin
½ cup cold water
⅔ cup sugar
⅛ teaspoon salt
3 eggs, separated

¼ cup cognac
¼ cup crême de cacao
2 cups whipped cream
1-9 inch graham cracker crust*
Chocolate curls for garnish

Sprinkle gelatin over the cold water in a saucepan. Add ⅓ cup of the sugar, salt and egg yolks. Heat over low temperature until gelatin dissolves and mixture thickens. Do not boil. Remove from heat.

Stir in liqueurs and chill until mixture mounds slightly. Beat egg whites until stiff. Gradually beat in remaining sugar and fold this into the thickened gelatin mixture. Fold in 1 cup of the whipped cream. Turn into crust and chill several hours. Garnish with remaining whipped cream and chocolate curls. *Serves 6-8.*   * A pastry crust is equally suitable.

ANNE BADEAUX CONWAY

BAKED ALASKA

½ gallon vanilla ice cream
  (rectangle shape)
1 pound cake
8 egg whites
1 cup sugar

Optional:
  5 ounces Grand Marnier
    (Orange Brandy) or Cointreau

Place ice cream on china baking dish. Cover sides and top with thinly sliced pound cake. Beat egg whites until peaks form. Add sugar and beat again until peaks form. Cover completely with meringue. Bake at 550° for 5 minutes or until slightly browned. If desired, pour ½ ounce Grand Marnier (orange brandy) or Cointreau over each serving. *Serves 10.*

JOYCE LAFAYE CREWS

TOASTED COCONUT PIE

1 baked 9 inch pie shell
1 (3½ ounce) can angel flake
    coconut
1⅛ cups sugar
4 eggs

4 tablespoons flour
2 cups milk
1 teaspoon vanilla
4 tablespoons butter
⅛ teaspoon salt

Toast coconut in oven until golden brown. Mix sugar, salt and flour in sauce-pan. Beat eggs until whites and yolks are thoroughly beaten. Add eggs slowly to sugar mixture to avoid lumping. Stir in milk. Cook over low heat stirring constantly until mixture bubbles. Remove from heat. Mix in butter, vanilla and all but 4 tablespoons of coconut. Pour in baked shell and cool to room temperature. Refrigerate until thoroughly chilled. Top with whipped cream, garnish with remaining coconut. This pie should be refrigerated 3 or 4 hours before serving.

AMANDA MARTIN

LEMON CREAM PIE FILLING

3 egg yolks
1½ cups sugar
2 cups milk
2 tablespoons flour
4 tablespoons corn starch

1 teaspoon salt
3 tablespoons butter or margarine
¼ cup lemon juice
1½ teaspoon grated lemon rind

Beat the egg yolks until thick and add the sugar to them. Mix a little of the milk with flour, corn starch and salt to make a thin, smooth paste. Scald the remainder of the milk and add a little of it to each of the two above mixtures. Slowly stir them into the scalded milk. Cook over hot water, stirring constantly until custard is thickened. Remove from heat and add butter, lemon juice and grated rind. Pour into baked pastry shell, and cover with a meringue.

MRS. RUBY ARMBRUSTER

LEMON MERINGUE PIE

7 tablespoons corn starch
1½ cups sugar
¼ teaspoon salt
1½ cups hot water
3 egg yolks, beaten

2 tablespoons grated lemon rind
½ cup lemon juice
3 tablespoons butter
1-9 inch baked pie shell

Cook corn starch, sugar, salt, water over medium heat, stirring constantly for 6 minutes, or until mixture is thick and translucent. Remove from heat and add yolks. Return to low heat and cook, stirring constantly for 6 minutes. Add juice, rind and butter; stir until well blended. Pour into baked pie shell, and top with meringue.

Meringue:

3 egg whites

¼ teaspoon cream of tartar

6 tablespoons sugar

Beat whites and cream of tartar until frothy. Sprinkle sugar gradually over and beat at high speed until glossy and meringue stands in firm peaks. Spread over warm or hot filling, being careful to seal to edges of crust. Make decorative swirls on top. Bake at 350° for 12 to 15 minutes or until golden brown. Cool several hours before cutting.

MRS. EDWARD C. HENDERSON

LEMON REFRIGERATOR PIE

1 can condensed milk

3 eggs, separated

Juice of 3 lemons

6 tablespoons sugar

1   8 inch crumb pie shell

Combine milk and yolks; blend in juice. Pour into pie shell. Beat egg whites until frothy. Add sugar gradually continuing to beat until stiff. Spoon meringue over pie and bake at 350° for 12 to 15 minutes.

MINCEMEAT PIE

2½ cups prepared mincemeat

¼ cup apple cider

1½ cups finely chopped tart apples

1 plain pastry shell

Combine mincemeat, cider and apples. Pour into pie shell. Cover filling with strips of pastry. Bake at 400° for 30 to 40 minutes.

PECAN PIE

Narrow strips of pastry

4 tablespoons butter

½ cup sugar

3 eggs

1 cup white corn syrup

1 teaspoon vanilla

1 cup chopped pecans

1   9 inch plain pastry shell

Cream together butter and sugar. Beat in 3 eggs one at a time. Add 1 cup white corn syrup. Beat together well; add 1 teaspoon vanilla and 1 cup chopped pecans. Pour into pie shell and bake at 300° until center is firm, about 1 hour.

MARY ANN VALENTINO

PECAN AND RAISIN PIE

1 cup sugar
2 eggs, separated
½ cup pecans
½ cup raisins
½ teaspoon vinegar

1 teaspoon allspice
1 teaspoon cloves
1 teaspoon cinnamon
2 tablespoons butter
1   9 inch plain pastry shell

Cream butter and sugar. Add egg yolks, then spices and vinegar. Add whipped egg whites. Pour into pie shell and bake at 350° for 30 minutes.

MRS. ELVE LOUISE IRELAND

PINEAPPLE CHESS PIE

3 eggs
1 cup sugar
4 tablespoons melted butter
3 tablespoons flour

1 small can crushed pineapple
¼ teaspoon salt
1   9 inch   pastry shell

Beat eggs by hand until frothy. Mix together sugar, salt and flour and add to eggs. Add pineapple with juice. Pour in melted butter. Pour into pie shell and bake for 30 to 40 minutes or until "set" at 325°.

MRS. NINA DeSAUTEL

PINEAPPLE "PHILLY" PIE

⅓ cup sugar
1 tablespoon corn starch
1 cup crushed pineapple,
     not drained
1   8 ounce package cream cheese
½ cup sugar

½ teaspoon salt
2 eggs
½ cup milk
½ teaspoon vanilla
1   9 inch plain pastry shell
¼ cup chopped pecans

Blend the ⅓ cup of sugar with the corn starch and add the pineapple. Cook, stirring constantly until the mixture is thick and clear. Cool.

Combine the cream cheese with the ½ cup sugar and salt, and stir until smooth and well blended. Add the eggs, one at a time, stirring well after each egg is added. Blend in the milk and vanilla.

Spread the cooled pineapple mixture over the bottom of the pastry shell. Pour in the cream cheese mixture and sprinkle with the chopped pecans. Bake at 400° for 10 minutes, then reduce the heat to 325°, and bake for an additional 50 minutes. Cool before serving.

ELOIS L. WEBER

PRIZE PUMPKIN PIE

Filling:

1½ cups steamed and strained
    pumpkin
⅔ cup brown sugar
1 teaspoon cinnamon
½ teaspoon ginger

½ teaspoon salt
2 eggs
1½ cups milk
½ cup thick cream

Patsry:

1   9 inch plain pastry shell

Topping:

Cream cheese

Mix the ingredients together for filling; pour into pie shell and bake at 300° for 1 hour. Cool.

Top pumpkin pie with cream cheese thinned to spreading consistency with cream.

MRS. GEORGE T. GUEDRY

RUM PIE

Crust:

2 small boxes chocolate snaps
½ ounce unsweetened chocolate,
    grated

6 tablespoons butter or margarine,
    melted

Crumble chocolate snaps in blender or with rolling pin. Mix melted butter with crumbs and chocolate. Press into 9 inch pie pan and place in freezer to set while making the filling.

Filling:

1 package unflavored gelatin
3 eggs
¾ cup sugar

¼ cup water
¾ cup whipping cream
3 tablespoons rum

Dissolve gelatin in water. Combine gelatin, egg yolks and ½ cup sugar in top of double boiler. Beat with egg beater while cooking over boiling water for 3 to 5 minutes or until slightly thickened. Cool.

Beat egg whites; add remainder of sugar. Whip cream. Fold egg whites into filling, and then fold in whipped cream. Fold in rum.

Pour into crust and grate unsweetened chocolate on top for decoration. Let set in refrigerator at least 3 hours before serving.

NINA DeSAUTEL

RHUBARB PIE

3 cups cut rhubarb
1 cup sugar
½ teaspoon grated orange rind
3 tablespoons flour

½ teaspoon salt
2 tablespoons butter
1 plain pastry for 9 inch double crust

Combine rhubarb and sugar, orange rind, flour and salt. Fill 9 inch pastry-lined pie pan; dot with butter and adjust top crust. Bake at 450° for 10 minutes; reduce heat to 350° and continue to bake for about 30 minutes.

URSULINE NUNS

TARTE A. BOUILLIE
(French Custard Pie)

Sweet Dough Crust:
    1½ cups flour
    ½ cup sugar
    1 egg
    ⅓ cup shortening

1 teaspoon baking powder
¾ teaspoon nutmeg
1 pinch of salt

Cream sugar and shortening. Add beaten eggs, flour, nutmeg and salt. Knead slightly. Roll out to the size of a pie plate. Crust will be thick. Pour custard in crust and bake at 400° until brown.

Custard Filling:
    ⅔ cup milk
    ⅓ cup milk
    2 eggs, beaten
    3 tablespoons flour

½ cup sugar
⅛ teaspoon salt
1 teaspoon vanilla

Bring ⅔ cup milk to a boil. To the ⅓ cup cold milk, add beaten eggs, flour, sugar and salt. Carefully combine all ingredients to boiling milk and cook until thick. Remove from heat and add vanilla.

MRS. CLARA McCANN

Galatoire's Restaurant

CREOLE "SUCRERIES" AND SPECIALTIES

Lafcadio Hearn in 1880 bemoaned the fact that the "good old Creole lore" was fast disappearing. And we, almost a hundred years later, with the forces of time working inexorably around us, can join him in his lament. The Vieux Carré, petite and architecturally charming, still sits like a quaint, old-fashioned jewel in the midst of modern garishness. And to see her clinging to the simplicity of her early days—her courtyards fragrant with sweet olive of a warm summer afternoon and second-story galleries valentine-like with pink geranium and lacy grill—this is enough to make one nostalgic.

Time has robbed us of the charm of the *pralinières* in starched white apron and tignon, who went about the streets of the old town vending *Pralines aux Pacanes, La Colle* and *Candi Tiré à la Nélasse* for a "picayune." A picayune was a coin in circulation in Colonial Louisiana worth approximately five cents. In the early days a picayune could buy a bit of heaven, for the Negresses of the city, who had learned their skills in the old French ancestral homes, were experts in the concocting of these Creole delicacies. Each morning they hawked their *sucreries créoles* along Royal and Bourbon Streets or in Jackson Square. In fact, so much a part of the daily life were these sweets that the Creole children sang of them in their *banquette* games:

Soeur Rosalie au retour de matines
Plus d'une fois lui porta des pralines.

The *cala* woman was the daily vendor of sweet rice cakes which the inhabitants of the Vieux Carré customarily ate with the cup of *café au lait*. She went her rounds in bandana and guinea blue dress, carrying on her head a covered bowl of hot cakes. Her cry of *"Belle Calas Tout Chaud, Madame,"* would send the Creole cooks hurrying into the street to buy the first fresh hot calas for the master and mistress of the house.

Gone are such days and their charming customs, but the recipes, at lease, are with us still. Anyone can serve a hot *cala* with a good cup of Creole coffee or make up a batch of *Maïs Tac Tac* or *Pralines Roses de Coco*. Lest we forget, here are the recipes:

MAÏS "TAC-TAC"

1 pint Louisiana molasses ¾ pound Indian corn (parched)

Boil molasses and when it comes to a boil add corn. Stir well and pour into paper cases about 5 or 6 inches long, 3 inches wide and ½ inch deep. Let it cool.

PRALINES ROSE DE COCO
(Pink Pralines)

1 pound granulated sugar 4 tablespoons water
1 freshly grated small coconut 1 tablespoon cochineal

Put sugar and water in saucepan. When it begins to form a syrup remove from fire and stir in coconut. Return to fire, stirring constantly until it begins to bubble. Add cochineal and remove from fire. Spoon mixture on to a marble slab or buttered dish, forming neat round cakes ¼ inch thick. Let them dry and raise them gently with a knife from the slab.

GRALÉ

1 cup pecans 3 drops violet perfume
⅓ cup sugar

Put sugar in pan and add just a little water to melt it (about 3 teaspoons). Boil until you see little bubbles all over. Turn off heat. Add violet perfume and then nuts (work quickly). Stir to coat all nuts. When you see them turn sugary, turn out on dry dish and separate nuts.

MRS. ELVE LOUISE IRELAND

GRAPEFRUIT GLACÉ

The skin of 1 grapefruit Cold water
Granulated sugar

Quarter the skin and then cut in thin strips. Add just enough water to cover and boil 7 times. Each time the water boils, pour it off and add fresh water and boil again for 7 times.

In the seventh water, add one cup of sugar for each cup of water and boil until it forms a syrup (234°). Remove with a fork and place on absorbent paper. Roll each piece in granulated sugar.

MRS. ELVE LOUISE IRELAND

KISSES

3 egg whites, beaten until stiff 2 tablespoons minced pecans
6 tablespoons granulated sugar

To stiffly beaten egg whites, gradually add sugar, whipping after each addition. Beat until mixture stands up stiffly on back of spoon. Mix in pecans.

Drop a tablespoon of mixture on baking paper 1½ inches apart. Dry out in very slow oven (200°), until firm. *Yield: 24 candies.*

COCONUT PRALINES

3 cups granulated sugar
2½ cups coconut meat (grated)
1 tablespoon butter

1 cup coconut milk (if coconut does not contain cup of liquid, milk may be added to make cup)

In deep saucepan, combine sugar, coconut and milk; mix well with wooden spoon. Bring to boil over medium heat stirring occasionally until it forms a soft ball when tested in cold water (240° on a candy thermometer). Remove from fire, add butter and beat until the mixture begins to sugar. Drop by spoonfuls on wax paper. *Yield: 3 dozen pralines.*

PAT GIGLIO UNDERDAHL

PIGS' EARS
Oreilles de Cochon

5 egg yolks
1 whole egg
8 tablespoons butter
1 cup sour cream
1½ ounces rum

5 cups flour
1 tablespoon sugar
3 teaspoons baking powder
Vegetable oil

Mix ingredients in a large bowl in the above order. Sift the flour, sugar and baking powder together before adding to other ingredients. Knead for about 30 minutes. Pound with a rolling pin for a few minutes. Roll out thin; cut 4-6 inches diamond shaped pieces. Make a slit in the middle of each piece and pull one tip through slit. Fry in a deep fat. *Yield: 80.*

FLORENCE TUCKER

CREOLE MERINGUES
Kisses

6 tablespoons granulated sugar
3 egg whites

1 teaspoon vanilla extract

Beat egg whites until they form peaks. Add sugar gradually, then vanilla. Beat until very stiff. Spoon on to brown paper. Dry out in oven of 250° for approximately 2 hours and 15 minutes. Allow to cool before removing from brown paper. *Yield: 1 dozen Kisses to each egg white.*

BEVERLY LAFAYE CLARK

DIXIE DIVINITY

4 cups granulated sugar
1 cup white corn syrup
¼ teaspoon salt
1 cup water

3 stiffly-beaten egg whites
2 teaspoons vanilla
1 cup pecans

In heavy saucepan combine sugar, corn syrup, water and salt. Cook, stirring constantly over low heat until sugar is dissolved; and mixture comes to boil. Then cook quickly to hard-ball stage (250°) without stirring. Remove from heat.

Pour hot syrup in a thin stream over beaten egg whites, beating constantly. If using electric beater use high speed. When all the syrup has been added, place the bowl of candy over hot water. Continue beating until mixture forms soft peaks and loses its gloss. Remove from the hot water. Stir in vanilla and broken nutmeats.

Drop by spoonfuls on waxed paper; swirl each candy to a peak. If divinity becomes too stiff for twirling, add a few drops of hot water, or place bowl over the hot water until all the mixture has been dropped. If you prefer the divinity cut in squares, spread the candy upon an oiled platter and cut. *Yield: 2 dozen candies.*

MRS. DON A. GIGLIO

DATE LOAF

3 cups granulated sugar
1 cup evaporated milk
½ pound dates

1 tablespoon butter
2 cups pecans

Bring sugar and milk to boil, add butter, then dates. Cook until a soft ball is formed when dropped in cold water. Remove from fire, beat and add pecans.

Pour into cold wet towel which has been wrung out and shape into a long loaf. *Slice into 24 candies.*

MRS. STEPHEN C. HARUN

NEW ORLEANS BABA

2 eggs
½ cup sugar
1 cup flour, sifted

1½ cups water
1 cup sugar
2 ounces rum

Beat eggs and sugar until light and frothy. Mix well with flour. Pour into buttered molds or paper cups. Bake at 350°, 15 to 20 minutes.

Make syrup of sugar and water and bring to boil. Add rum to syrup and pour over cakes until they are thoroughly soaked. Decorate with whipped cream. *Yields 6 to 8 babas.*

MYLDRED COSTA

PEANUT BRITTLE

2 cups raw peanuts
1 cup sugar

½ cup water
½ cup corn syrup

Mix and cook until peanuts pop. Add 1 tablespoon soda and 1 teaspoon vanilla. Beat well and pour into buttered pans.

MYLDRED MASSON COSTA

PECAN PRALINES

1 cup brown sugar
1 cup white sugar
1 cup pecan meats

½ cup cream
2 tablespoons butter

Dissolve sugar in cream and bring to a boil, stirring occasionally. Add the butter or margarine and pecans and cook until the syrup reaches the soft ball stage (238°). Cool without disturbing, beat until somewhat thickened but not until it loses its gloss and drop by tablespoons onto a well greased flat surface or on a waxed paper-lined surface. The candy will flatten out into large cakes. *Yield: 20 pralines.*

URSULINE NUNS

SHERRY ORLEANS PRALINES

1 cup brown sugar, firmly packed
1 cup granulated sugar
½ cup evaporated milk

1 tablespoon sherry (or vanilla flavoring)
2 cups pecan halves or pecan chunks

Mix ingredients (except Sherry) in a heavy saucepan. Cook over medium heat to soft-ball stage (236°), stirring constantly.

Remove from heat and when mixture stops bubbling, stir in sherry. Cool slightly, then beat mixture until it thickens slightly.

Drop candy from a tablespoon onto waxed paper to form patties. If candy becomes too stiff, drop in a few drops of hot water. *Yield: approximately 20 creamy pralines.*

MRS. JACK (MARY S.) PARKMAN

PRALINE PARFAIT SAUCE

⅓ cup boiling water
⅓ cup brown sugar

1 cup white corn syrup
1 cup chopped pecans

Bring water to a boil. Add sugar, then add the corn syrup. Cook slowly until the mixture comes to a boil. Add the pecans. When cool, pour into a jar or similar container and refrigerate. Mixture will thicken when cool. Pour over ice cream.

MRS. LAWRENCE DERBES

HEDGEHOGS

2 cups walnuts or pecans
2 eggs
1 cup brown sugar

8 ounces pitted dates (1 cup)
1 cup shredded coconut

Blend nuts until fine and set aside. Blend eggs, sugar and dates until fine and mix with nuts and coconut. Shape into rolls 1 inch long and ½ inch thick.

Roll each cookie in bowl with remaining coconut. Bake on greased cookie sheet at 350° for 15 minutes. *Yield: 1 dozen.*

MRS. CHESTER WILLIAMS

ICE BOX COOKIES

8 tablespoons butter
1 egg
⅓ cup brown sugar
⅓ cup white sugar
2 cups flour

⅓ teaspoon soda
⅓ teaspoon cinnamon
⅓ teaspoon nutmeg
⅙ teaspoon salt
⅓ cup pecans

Cream butter and sugar and add eggs. Add dry ingredients, lastly pecans. If dough is not firm enough to hold shape, add more flour than called for above. Wrap in wax paper and put in refrigerator for several hours, or freeze for future use. When ready to bake, slice cookies ¼ inch thick and bake at 350° for 15 minutes. *Yield: 2 dozen.*

MRS. NICK MATULICH

SNICKERDOODLES

1 cup soft shortening; part butter
1½ cups sugar
2 eggs
2¾ cups sifted flour
2 teaspoons cream of tartar

1 teaspoon soda
¼ teaspoon salt
Sugar
Cinnamon

Mix shortening, sugar, and eggs together thoroughly. Sift together and stir in flour, cream of tartar, soda, and salt. Roll into balls the size of small walnuts. Roll balls in mixture of 2 tablespoons sugar and 2 teaspoons cinnamon. Place balls 2 inches apart on ungreased baking sheet. Bake until lightly brown but soft. They puff up at first and then flatten out. Bake at 400° 8 to 10 minutes. *Yield: 5 dozen 2".*

LINDA CROOK

FIG PRESERVES

3 cups sugar
3 quarts figs

1½ cups water
1 slice lemon

Figs should be scalded and drained before cooking.

Combine sugar and water in large pot, bring to boiling point. Add figs and lemon and cook slowly about 2 hours. Seal in sterilized jars.

MRS. JAMES NEEDOM

FUDGE

3 cups sugar
3 tablespoons cocoa
1 small can evaporated milk

½ cup white corn syrup
3 tablespoons butter
1 cup chopped pecans

Mix sugar, cocoa, corn syrup and milk together. Cook over low heat (for best results use candy thermometer) until soft-ball stage, stirring only 2 or 3 times during cooking process.

After candy reaches soft-ball stage, remove from heat, add butter and let set until pot is cool enough to touch the bottom. Add pecans and beat by hand a few times and pour into buttered pan. *Yield: 24 candies.*

MRS. NINA DeSAUTEL

ITALIAN CUCCIDATI
(Fig Cookies)

6 cups flour
4½ teaspoons baking powder
½ teaspoon salt
1¾ cups sugar (granulated)

¾ cup shortening
4 eggs
⅓ cup milk
1 teaspoon vanilla

Sift together flour, baking powder. Mix sugar and shortening together. Beat together eggs, milk and vanilla and add to creamed mixture. Knead dough until very smooth (about 15 minutes). Cut dough into 10 pieces. Roll each piece out to ¼ inch thick. Cut into stripes about 4 inches wide. Fill with fig filling. Roll up and then cut into any design desired. Bake 10 to 15 minutes in moderate (300° to 325°) oven. They will turn light brown. Spread on icing (if desired). *Yield: 6 dozen or more.*

FIG FILLING

3 pounds dried figs
2 pounds dates
¾ pound raisins

1 pound pecans
1 jar (1 pound) peach preserves
4 ounces pineapple slices (glazed)

Grind all together and mix well.

ICING
(If Desired)

Combine 2 cups powdered sugar, and add enough milk to make spreadable.

MRS. GASPAR CAMARDA

MACAROONS

1 pound almond or macaroon paste
1 pound granulated sugar

6½ fluid ounces of egg whites

To the sugar add 3 ounces of egg whites and mix well. Cut the paste into small pieces and add it to the mixture. Mix well, gradually adding the other 3½ ounces of egg whites. Mix to a smooth batter, free from lumps. Small batches may be mixed by hand using a flexible spatula or by mixer. Drop the macaroons on brown paper lined pans and bake at 320° for 10 to 12 minutes. Leave the oven door slightly open until the macaroons rise and crack (about 5 to 8 minutes). Then close the door and continue baking about 12 to 15 minutes or until light brown. After baking, the macaroons should be allowed to cool for at least 10 minutes. They are easily removed from the paper by turning upside down and thoroughly moistening the back of the paper. In a few minutes the macaroons may be readily taken off. *Yield: 8 dozen.*

MARY ALICE TOSO McKAY

OATMEAL DROPS

1 cup margarine
2 cups sugar
2 teaspoons vanilla
2 eggs
1 cup chopped raisins

½ cup chopped nuts
2½ cups flour
1 teaspoon salt
1 teaspoon baking soda
2 cups oatmeal

Cream margarine, sugar and vanilla until light and fluffy. Add 2 eggs, one at a time, and beat thoroughly. Add raisins and nuts and mix well. Sift flour, salt and soda and add to mixture. Mix again. Add oatmeal and mix thoroughly. Drop in small mounds on ungreased cookie sheet and bake at 400° for 10 minutes. *Yield: 9 dozen.*

SYLVIA GLEZEN

ORANGE DROP COOKIES

¾ cup shortening
¼ cup butter
1½ cups brown sugar
2 beaten eggs
¼ cup orange juice
1 tablespoon grated orange rind
1 teaspoon vanilla

1 cup sour milk
3½ cups flour
¼ teaspoon salt
2 teaspoons baking powder
1 teaspoon soda
1 cup chopped dates or nutmeats

Cream shortening and sugar; add eggs, orange juice, rind, vanilla and sour milk; mix well. Add sifted dry ingredients. Add dates or nutmeats. Drop from teaspoon onto greased cookie sheet. Bake in moderate oven (350°) for 15 minutes. *Yield: 5 dozen.*

URSULINE NUNS

PECAN COCOONS

1 cup butter
4 tablespoons powdered sugar
2¾ cups flour

4 teaspoons vanilla
1 cup finely chopped pecans
1 tablespoon ice water

Mix all ingredients together. Work dough well with the hands until it can be handled like pie pastry. Break into small pieces and roll between the hands into cocoons. Place on ungreased cookie sheet 1 inch apart. Bake at 350° until very delicate brown. Remove from oven and roll in powdered sugar while still hot. When cool, roll in powdered sugar again.

Yield: approximately 3 dozen.

MRS. ROBERT J. ARMBRUSTER

ANISE COOKIES

2 teaspoons anise seed
8 tablespoons butter
¾ cup sugar
2 large eggs

2 cups sifted all-purpose flour
½ teaspoon double-acting baking powder
¼ teaspoon salt

Crush anise seed and mix with shortening. Gradually blend in sugar. Beat in eggs. Sift flour with baking powder and salt. Gradually stir into the first mixture. Mix dough until ingredients are well blended and smooth. Shape into 1 inch balls. Place on a lightly greased cookie sheet, 2 inches apart.

Bake at 350° for 10 minutes or until light brown. Cool on wire cooling rack, store air tight. *Yield: 2-3 dozen cookies.*

MRS. NICK MATULICH

ALMOND TOFFEE

12 tablespoons butter
1 cup sugar
4 tablespoons corn syrup
3 tablespoons hot water

1 cup chopped and toasted
   slivered almonds
4 squares semi-sweet chocolate

Melt butter, add sugar, stirring constantly, add water and corn syrup mixed together. Cook until brittle when dropped into cold water (hard crack). Add almonds and pour on aluminum foil in a thin layer.

Melt 4 squares semi-sweet chocolate over boiling water and spread on top, sprinkle with finely chopped almonds.

MRS. KENT SATTERLEE, JR.

BROWNIES

1 cup butter (melted)
2 cups sugar
4 heaping tablespoons cocoa
1½ cups flour

4 eggs
2 teaspoons vanilla
Salt to taste
2 cups pecans

Mix all ingredients. Bake at 325° for 30 minutes in 15½"x10½" pan. *Yield: 2 dozen.*

ICING

4 tablespoons butter
¾ box powdered sugar
1 egg

2 tablespoons rum
2 tablespoons cocoa

Mix and spread on brownies.

MRS. KENT SATTERLEE, JR.

DATE AND PECAN SQUARES

1 pound dates
2½ cups dark brown sugar
½ cup milk
½ cup water
2 cups pecan pieces

2½ cups flour
2½ teaspoons baking powder
4 eggs
1 teaspoon vanilla

Combine dates, brown sugar, milk and water and cook until dates melt. To this add the 2½ cups of flour, the baking powder, the 4 eggs, one at a time, and the vanilla. To this mixture, add the nuts. Batter will be stiff— add a little milk, if necessary. Pour in buttered pan and cook in 350° oven for about 25 minutes. *Yield: approximately 2½ dozen squares.*

MARY ANN VALENTINO

BOURBON BALLS

2½ cups vanilla wafer crumbs
1 cup pecans, finely chopped
⅔ cup Bourbon

1 cup confectioners sugar
3 tablespoons cocoa
2 tablespoons white corn syrup

Break vanilla wafers into container, ¾ cup at a time; cover, blend to crumbs. Blend pecans ½ cup at a time. Put in bowl, mix well. Put remaining ingredients in container; cover, blend thoroughly 10 seconds. Pour liquids over dry ingredients and mix well. Roll into balls 1 inch in diameter; then roll balls in more confectioners sugar.
    Store in airtight container. Age 18 to 24 hours before using.
Yield: 40 to 48 balls.
Note: Blender was used for blending, but ingredients may be blended
    in bowl just as well.

HARRIET STERN

FUDGE ICING

3 tablespoons cocoa
8 tablespoons margarine
½ cup evaporated milk

2 cups sugar
¼ cup corn syrup
1 teaspoon vanilla

Bring all ingredients, except vanilla, to soft-ball stage, cool and add vanilla, beat and spread on cake.

MRS. THOMAS GILES
HOUSTON, TEXAS

HOT FUDGE SAUCE

5 squares semi-sweet chocolate
8 tablespoons butter or margarine
1 large can evaporated milk

3 cups powdered sugar, unsifted
1½ teaspoons vanilla

Melt chocolate and butter in double boiler. Remove from heat and add alternately milk and sugar. Bring to a boil over medium heat and cook about 8 minutes or until thick and creamy, stirring constantly. Remove from heat and add vanilla. *Yield: 3 cups.*

MARY ALICE McKAY

LEMON ICING

1 cup butter
4 cups confectioners sugar (1 pound)
4 tablespoons lemon juice

3 tablespoons lemon rind
Dash of salt
⅓ cup milk

Cream butter and lemon juice and rind. Sift sugar; add sugar and milk alternately. After icing cake, refrigerate.

BEVERLY KLUNDT

GRANDMOTHER BEAUFORD'S CARAMEL ICING

1 15-ounce can condensed milk   1 cup sugar
   8 tablespoons butter

Combine ingredients, cook over slow fire or in double boiler, stir constantly, scrape sides often to prevent burning. Test a drop or two in a cup of water for firmness. Remove from heat, place pot in cold water container and beat icing until cool and firm but still spreadable. Put between layers and all around top and sides. Add whole shelled pecans on top and/or cherries.

MISS GERTRUDE M. BEAUFORD

CALAS (Recipe dictated by Pouponne D'Antilly — 1809-87 — to her mistress Blanche Livaudais)

1½ cups cooked rice, soft   ½ teaspoon salt
3 eggs, beaten   Nutmeg to taste
1½ cups self-rising flour (originally   ¼ cup warm milk with 1
    regular and yeast was added)   teaspoon vanilla added
½ cup sugar

Place soft rice in a bowl; add eggs, flour, sugar, salt and nutmeg. Beat until smooth. Drop by tablespoon in deep hot fat and fry golden brown. Serve sprinkled with powdered sugar. *Yield: 8 servings.*

MYLDRED MASSON COSTA

WANT TO BE A CREOLE COOK,
A HOSTESS WITH A FLAIR?

The hostess of today, although she has at her fingertips the finest of ingredients, all manner of electrical appliances, and every kitchen gadget imaginable, finds her greatest challenge in serving the unusual. Exotic dishes have made their way to the humblest table and only the most remote areas find specialty ingredients hard to come by. The result is that American at-home dining is quite frequently a gourmet affair, and being the "hostess with the mostest" is no longer an easy matter. If this sounds like you, why not go "Creole" and glamorize your menus. For truly spectacular results take your pick from among the following:

1. Decorate your table *à la Créole* with a shrimp or a crayfish bush. Simply decorate a styrofoam cone with curly parsley and attach shrimp or crayfish with toothpicks.
2. Surprise your guests with Creole hors d'oeuvres such as stuffed cherry tomatoes and chicken or duck patties.
3. Cook a good thick gumbo.
4. Impress your friends with a New Orleans specialty as an entrée. May we suggest *bouillabaisse* or *chicken a la Creole*?
5. Serve a stuffed vegetable: mirliton or eggplant become exotic with the Creole touch.
6. Try a dessert of Creole or French origin. Frozen cream cheese or crêpes Suzette are really fun foods.
7. Top off a meal with a *petit brule*.
8. Try the kind of "French frying" that produces *beignets, calas* or *pain perdu*.
9. Salt your own pecans and almonds.
10. Give Creole cakes and candies at Christmas. For a gift your friends will not soon forget, give a tray arrayed with Creole meringues and pecan pralines.

GLOSSARY

A la Créole — Dishes cooked in the Creole style, usually with tomatoes, green peppers and onions as characteristic ingredients

Agneau — Lamb

Andouille — Hard smoked Acadian sausage

Asperge — White asparagus served au gratin, Hollandaise or cold with vinaigrette sauce

Aspic — Any jellied dish or jellied glaze

Au gratin — Sprinkled with crumbs and/or cheese and baked brown

Au jus — Served with natural juice or gravy

Au lait — With milk

Au naturel — Plainly cooked

Aux champignons — Cooked with mushrooms

Baba — Cake made of leavened dough steeped in a liqueur syrup

Boeuf — Beef

Boucherie — Butcher shop that specializes in sausage and other meat delicacies

Boudin — Acadian pork blood sausage, highly seasoned and containing rice. The proportion of blood to rice produces "white" or "red" boudin.

Bouilli — Boiled

Braise — Braised, food well browned in a little hot fat, then simmered in a little liquid, covered until tender

Brioche — A sweet yeast bread usually shaped like a fat muffin with a little cap on top, most often served at breakfast

Café au lait — Half hot black coffee and half hot milk

Café noir — Black coffee

Canard — Duck

Céleri — Celery

Cepes — Large strongly flavored mushrooms, to be sautéed in butter with garlic and parsley

Chapon — Crust of bread rubbed with garlic and tossed in a bowl with green salad

Chaurice — Hot sausage

Chervenil — Deer or venison

Chicory — Endive. The root of the chicory is used as a substitute or adulterant in coffee. Dried and ground the addition produces chicory coffee

Chou-fleur — Cauliflower

Choux de Bruxelles — Brussel sprouts

Coeurs de Céleri — Hearts of Celery

Coq — Rooster

Coq au vin — Rooster cooked in a red wine sauce

Coquilles St. Jacques — Scallops prepared in butter and served with parsley or cream sauce in a scallop shell

Courtbouillon — Liquid in which fish has been cooked. The Creole courtbouillion is a fish stew

Couscous — A semolina preparation very popular in African and Near Eastern Cuisine. The Acadians make a variation similar to cornmeal mush

Créole Cuisine — A mixture of French and Spanish cooking with influences from Negro and Indian culture

Crevettes — Shrimp

Crêpe — Light thin pancakes

Croissant — Crescent-shaped breakfast roll made from puff pastry

Croquettes — Mixtures of meat, fish, vegetables, etc. finely chopped, bound with a sauce, formed into various shapes and fried

Croûtons — Slices or cubes of bread toasted and browned in melted butter or just toasted

Croustade — Hollowed-out toast case or pastry shell issued as a container for fillings

Daube — A round roast, usually beef, braised in stock with various seasonings and vegetables

Daube Glacé — A roast braised with various seasonings with the addition of geletinous substances, then refrigerated in the stock to form a cold jellied meat

Diable — Deviled

Écrevisse — Crayfish

En brochette — Broiled or served on a skewer

En Coquille — Served in the shell or on a shell

En gelée — In jelly

En papillote — Baked in an oiled paper bag

Épice — Spice

Escargots — Snails

Etouffée — Smothered

Faisan — Pheasant

Farci — Stuffed

Filé — Powdered leaves of the sassafras tree, sprinkled sparingly over gumbo as a flavoring and thickening agent

Fines Herbs — A mixture of minced herbs like chives, parsley, tarragon or thyme

Flambé — Ignited and served with spirits poured over

Foie — Liver

Foie gras — Literally fat liver, usually refers to goose liver

Fond — Bottom

Fonds d'Artichauts — Artichoke bottoms

Fondue au fromage — A melted cheese dish

Fraises — Strawberries

Frappé — Iced drink

Fricassée — Braised poultry or meat

Frit — Fried

Froid — Cold

Fumé — Smoked

Garni — Garnished

Gâteau — Cake

Glace — Ice, ice cream

Glacé — Iced

Grenadine — A syrup made from pomegranates

Grillé — Grilled

Grillades — Beef or veal round steak, browned and then simmered until tender in a brown tomato sauce

Haché — Finely chopped

Haricots Rouges — Red beans

Haricots Verts — Whole green string beans

Herb Bouquet — A bunch of aromatic herbs used to flavor soups, stews, etc.; also called Bouquet Garni

Homard — Lobster

Huile — Oil

Huîtres — Oysters

Jambalaya — A dish in which raw rice is simmered in a seasoned liquid with cooked meat, shrimp, sausage until the liquid is absorbed. Variations are endless.

Jambon — Ham

Julienne — Match-like strips of meat, vegetables or cheese

Langoustine — Spiny African Lobster

Légumes — Vegetables

Lyonnaise — Cooked with onions

Life — Everlasting Weed - Sedum. Formerly used as a medicinal herb, now as a fried flower

Maïs — Corn

Marinate — Allow to stand in liquid, usually oil and acid mixture to improve flavor

Mirliton — Also known as mango squash, vegetable pear or chayote

Mousse — A light, airy cold dish containing beaten egg whites and whipped cream

Oeufs — Eggs

Oie — Goose

Pain — Bread

Pâté — Pie or pastry with a filling of meat, fish, vegetables or fruit

Pâté de foie gras or Bloc de foie gras — Rouleau de foie gras — Paré de foie gras — Rôlade de foie gras — Mousse de foie gras — Goose liver paste containing at least 75% goose liver and up to 25% other meat, salt and spices

Patty shell — Vol-au-vent pastry cup used to hold creamy hot dishes

Petits Pois — Tiny sweet French green peas

Pièce de résistance — The main dish

Poisson — Fish

Pommes de terre — Potatoes

Porc — Pork

Potages — Soups
Poule — Hen
Poulet — Chicken
Purée — Mashed
Pousse Café — After-dinner drink of several liquers layered according to weight to produce a rainbow effect
Quenelles — Finger-shaped seasoned dumplings made of various farcemeats, cooked in fish stock on tomato sauce
Rôti — Roast
Roux — A mixture of flour and fat used for thickening sauces and soups
Sagamité — Dried corn, hominy
Salmis — Game sautéed until brown and then cooked until tender in a seasoned liquid usually including red wine
Sauté — Fry lightly in a little fat
Shallot — Green onion , used in its entirety in Creole cooking
Sirop — Syrup
Soufflé — A baked fluffy main dish or dessert containing beaten egg whites
Terrine — Earthenware crock (usually made for foie gras)
Truffles — A black edible fungus of the wild mushroom family
Veau — Veal
Vichyssoise — A cold creamed leek and potato soup
Vinaigre — Vinegar
Vinaigrette — A marinade or salad dressing of oil, vinegar, pepper and herbs
Volaille — Poultry
Vol au vent — Small pastry cup made from puff pastry

Copyright 1971

OVEN CHART

	Temperature	Time in Minutes
BISCUITS, baking powder	125	12 - 15
BREADS		
White (yeast) bread	350 - 400	45 - 60
Whole wheat bread	400	30 - 40
Rye bread	375	30 - 40
Corn bread	425	20 - 25
CAKES		
Angel food cake	350	40 - 45
Cup cakes	375	20 - 25
Layer cake	350 - 375	25 - 35
Loaf cake	300 - 350	50 - 80
Sponge cake	350 - 375	12 - 40
COOKIES		
Drop cookies	375	8 - 12
Ginger cookies	375	10 - 12
Rolled cookies	375 - 400	6 - 12
CUSTARDS		
Individual	325	10
Large	325	75
Custard pie	425	30 - 35
MUFFINS	425	15 - 20
PASTRIES		
Pastry shell	450	10 - 12
Double crust pies:		
cooked filling	400 - 450	30 - 45
uncooked filling	400	40 - 60
CASSEROLES (uncooked foods)	350	60 - 120
FISH (baked)		
Fillets	400	20
Steaks	400	30
Whole fish	400	10 per lb.
ROASTS		
Beef, rib - rare	325	20 - 25 per lb.
medium	325	25 - 30 per lb.
well done	325	30 - 35 per lb.
Ham	325	25 - 30 per lb.
Lamb, leg	300	30 - 35 per lb.
Pork, loin	350	30 - 40 per lb.
Veal	325	30 - 35 per lb.
Chicken	300	30 - 45 per lb.
Duck	325	20 - 30 per lb.
Turkey, 8 - 12 lb.	300	20 - 25 per lb.
12 - 20 lb.	300	15 - 20 per lb.
BROILING		
Steak, 1 in. thick, 3 in. from heat	500	12 - 15
2 in. thick, 4 in. from heat	500	25 - 35
Lamb chop, ¾ in.	500	10 - 12
Ham slice, 1 in.	450	20 - 25

WEIGHTS and MEASURES

Dash = less than ⅛ teaspoon
3 Teaspoons = 1 Tablespoon
2 Tablespoons = 1 Liquid Ounce
4 Tablespoons = ¼ Cup
8 Tablespoons = ½ Cup
16 Tablespoons = 1 Cup
2 Cups = 1 Pint
2 Pints = 1 Quart
4 Quarts = 1 Gallon
16 Ounces = 1 Pound
2 Cups, Liquid = 1 Pound
2 Cups Butter = 1 Pound
2 Cups Granulated Sugar = 1 Pound
4 Cups Flour = 1 Pound
¼ Pound Print Butter = ½ Cup
Chocolate, 1 square bitter = 1 Ounce
Cheese, 4 cups grated = 1 Pound
Egg Whites, 8 = 1 Cup, approx.
Egg Yolks, 16 = 1 Cup, approx.
Lemon, juice of 1 = 2 to 3 Tablespoons
Marcaroni, 1 Cup raw = 2 Cups Cooked
Rice, 1 Cup raw = 3 to 4 Cups Cooked

CONTENTS of STANDARD CANS

Picnic - 1¼ Cups   No. 2 - 2½ Cups
No. 300 - 1¾ Cups   No. 2½ - 3½ Cups
No. 1 Tall - 2 Cups   No. 3 - 4 Cups
No. 303 - 2 Cups   No. 5 - 7⅓ Cups
No. 10 - 13 Cups

SUBSTITUTES THAT ARE SAFE

IF RECIPE CALLS FOR	USE
1 cup sifted all purpose flour	1 cup + 2 tablespoons sifted white cake flour
1 cup sifted all purpose flour	1 cup self rising flour and omit salt, baking powder and/or soda called for in recipe
1 teaspoon baking powder	¼ teaspoon soda + ½ teaspoon cream of tarter
1 whole egg (in cookies)	2 egg yolks + 1 teaspoon water
1 whole egg (in custards)	2 egg yolks
1 cup homogenized or pastuerized milk	1 tablespoon powdered milk + 1 cup water
1 cup homogenized milk	½ cup evaporated milk + ½ cup water
1 cup homogenized milk	½ cup condensed milk plus ½ cup water
1 cup honey	¾ cup sugar + ¼ cup liquid called for in the recipe

OVEN TEMPERATURES

250 - 300 = Slow
325 = Slow-Moderate
350 = Moderate
375 = Quick-Moderate
400 = Moderately Hot
425 - 450 = Hot
475 - 500 = Very Hot

INDEX

NOTES: